Growing Happy Clients

Our processes and experiences for growing fortune 500 corporates & the fastest growing startups

Daphne Tideman

Ward van Gasteren

Copyright © 2020 Daphne Tideman and Ward van Gasteren
All rights reserved.
ISBN: 9798550262993

Table of Contents

Introduction	1
What makes being a growth consultant unique?	1
Who are we?	4
The structure of this book	6
The Five Principles	8
Confidence is key	9
Five Core Principles of Exceptional Growth Consultants	11
Principle-based way of working	11
1. Be Them	13
2. Be Real	15
3. Be Open	16
4. Be Bold	19
5. Be Focused	21
Which of the five principles are most relevant for you?	23
PRE-CONTACT	27
Why Do Companies Hire A Growth Hacker?	29
1.1 The changing perception of growth hacking	29
1.2 Internal culture or internal resistance?	32
1.3 Why did they specifically hire a growth hacker?	34
Your Contact Person's ABC	37
2.1 The ABC Model	37
2.2 The Awful	39
2.3 The Barriers	40
2.4 The Cravings	41
2.5 Practising your ABCs	42
Different Types of Personalities of Clients	47
3.1 The Insights Discovery Personality test	47
3.2 Identify your client's colour	51
3.3 How to deal with the colours	53
3.4 Red: Goal-Oriented Clients	54

3.5 Yellow: Visionary Clients 56
3.6 Green: Process-Oriented Clients 59
3.7 Blue: Researcher Clients 61
3.8 The Client Colour Cheatsheet 63

Watching Out for Risks and Pitfalls 65
4.1 Let's keep it realistic 65
4.2 Orange traffic lights to slow down for 66
4.3 Red traffic lights to stop for 68
4.4 Finding the real underlying reasons 71
4.5 How do you deal with orange and red traffic lights? 75
4.6 Should you end the collaboration? 77

STARTING OFF 81

The First Contact With Your Client 83
5.1 A new client! 83
5.2 Setting the scene 84
5.3 Understand their growth 85
5.4 Getting them ready to go 87

The Kickoff 93
6.1 Why is the kickoff crucial? 93
6.2 Agenda for the kickoff 94
6.3 The secret to a successful kickoff 101

North Star Metric 103
7.1 Navigating with a map 103
7.2 The North Star Metric 106
7.3 Setting the NSM 108

The Crucial Basics to Get Into Place 113
8.1 Why do we need to get the basics in place? 113
8.2 Which basics are essential for (almost) every client? 114

One Metric That Matters 123
9.1 OMTM 123
9.2 Why is it essential to set a OMTM? 124
9.3 How to handle conflicting KPIs? 124
9.4 Can you have multiple OMTMs? 126
9.5 Setting the OMTM 128

How to set the Right Expectations and Priorities   131
    10.1 The importance of managing expectations   131
    10.2 How to manage expectations   132
    10.3 Start with the deliverables and the definition of 'done'   133
    10.4 Relate it to your client's ABCs   135
    10.5 Let the data talk   136
    10.6 Calculating the potential impact   138
    10.7 Always look for alternatives rather than saying no   142

Bottlenecks   145
    11.1 Beer? A story about Daphne   145
    11.2 Where are the bottlenecks?   146
    11.3 Bottlenecks in the organisation   147
    11.4 Will the bottleneck stay the same?   148
    11.5 Long-term vs short-term focus   148

Planning and Preparing the Working Process   155
    12.1 Sprint-based approach   156
    12.2 Deadline-based approach   160

To Experiment or Not to Experiment?   163
    13.1 When not to experiment   164
    13.2 When to experiment   166

THE REAL HUSTLE   171

Ideation - How to get new, great ideas and get involved   173
    14.1 The challenges With ideation   173
    14.2 Taking the time to brainstorm   174
    14.3 Documenting ideas   176
    14.4 How do you know if you have enough ideas?   177

Prioritising - More or Better Tests   181
    15.1 A growth strategy without prioritisation   181
    15.2 How to prioritise   182
    15.3 More or better tests?   185

Structured - Tracking Experiment Progress   189
    16.1 Risks of not documenting   190
    16.2 How best to document   191
    16.3 How to leverage your documentation   193

Presenting the Results — 195
- 17.1 The basic storyline — 196
- 17.2 How to tell your story — 198

ABEing - Always Be Evaluating — 205
- 18.1 Failing to get feedback — 205
- 18.2 Why is feedback crucial in consulting? — 206
- 18.3 Plan in retrospectives — 207

Quarterly Zoom Out — 211
- 19.1 Caught up in the day-to-day — 211
- 19.2 What does a quarterly zoom out look like? — 212
- 19.3 When to have a quarterly zoom out at another time — 216

Internal Fans — 219
- 20.1 Goodbye my friend — 219
- 20.2 What are internal fans? — 221
- 20.3 How to create internal fans — 222
- 20.4 Internal fans are not a magical solution — 223

Getting the Board on Board — 225
- 21.1 Why is it your job to get the board on board? — 225
- 21.2 Step-by-step: how to get the board on board — 227

Brand - Policing or Protecting? — 231
- 22.1 Branding vs conversions — 231
- 22.2 The big brand versus growth fight — 232
- 22.3 The best of both worlds — 233
- 22.4 Growing without a strong brand — 235

Development - Your Fleeting Friend — 239
- 23.1 IT & growth hacking together — 239
- 23.2 How to work around having no development resources. — 240
- 23.3 Getting to know the developers — 241
- 23.4 Improving the collaboration with development — 243
- 23.5 Inviting development to growth meetings — 244

Sales: Commission and Data — 247
- 24.1 What drives sales? — 247
- 24.2 The win-win of sales and growth — 249

Customer Support - The Fuel You Need — 253
- 25.1 The role of Customer Support — 253
- 25.2 How to gain their insights in a frequent and systematic manner — 254
- 25.3 Should customer support be a part of the growth meetings? — 256

Legal - Your Essential Ally — 259
- 26.1 Where Legal can block growth and why — 259
- 26.2 How to prevent them from impacting your speed or blocking your growth endeavours — 260
- 26.3 Cookie policy — 261
- 26.4 Inviting Legal to growth meetings — 262
- 26.4 Cheatsheet for Creating Internal Fans — 262

Breaking Down Silos — 267
- 27.1 Silos are still around — 267
- 27.2 Breaking down Silos — 268

THE UPS AND DOWNS — 271

Fixed Mindsets Alert! — 273
- 28.1 Spotting a fixed mindset — 273
- 28.2 Dealing with a fixed mindset — 274
- 28.3 When you start seeing bears — 276

Too Many Focus Points, Too Much Choice — 279
- 29.1 The risks of scattered focus — 280
- 29.2 Dealing with multiple focus points — 281

Too Many Stakeholders, Too Many Opinions — 287
- 30.1 Trying to get a browser notification live — 287
- 30.2 Techniques to reduce stakeholder overload — 289

Experiments are on the Side — 295
- 31.1 Causes of experiments becoming a side track — 295
- 31.2 Moving growth back from a side track to THE project — 296

Any Slower and We'd Be Going Backwards — 301
- 32.1 Six months and 1,260 coffees later… — 301
- 32.2 Time to start moving forward, fast — 302

The Needle Isn't Moving — 307
   33.1 Is it a blip? — 307
   33.2 What should you do when growth slows down? — 308
   33.3 Turning it around — 309

WHAT COMES NEXT? — 313

Should You Continue? — 315
   34.1 Let's keep working together — 316
   34.2 Time to say goodbye — 317

How to Upsell and Cross-sell — 321
   35.1 Don't worry about it — 321
   35.2 Value adding opportunities — 323
   35.3 How to upsell and cross-sell — 325

Dealing With a Downscale — 329
   36.1 Downscales happen — 329
   36.2 Dealing with a downscale — 331

Project Reflection — 335
   37.1 What is project reflection? — 335
   37.2 What to cover — 336

Where to go from here — 339
   Action drives results — 339
   A final farewell to that lack of confidence — 340

Acknowledgements — 343
About the Authors — 346

Growing Happy Clients

Introduction

It all started with questions, as it often does. We both noticed that emerging growth consultants have a lot of questions about how to help their clients best. Heck, we were filled with endless questions in the beginning too. Yet, there are no resources that provide the answers to these questions for you. No place that shows you the reality of being in growth and a consultant which often differs so much from the theory.

The theory has told you how to run a growth program but not what to do when it doesn't go as planned when you struggle to move the needle or get overwhelmed with too many focus points. We wanted to write out the answers we learned along the way, in the hope of helping others, to give you the playbook that was missing in our growth journey. We wanted to help fellow growth consultants grow in confidence and learn how to drive lasting results, especially as we feel that being a growth consultant is so different from being a specialist or a management consultant.

What makes being a growth consultant unique?

Growth (hacking) consultants are different from specialist consultants (e.g. SEO, Social) or even generalist high-level consultants (e.g. management, branding). As a growth hacking consultant, you come in to solve the bigger picture. The challenges come in various forms, but it always comes down to the same goal:

Growth. Growth that is not happening, or at least, not fast enough.

Maybe the company is struggling to understand why growth isn't happening. Perhaps they feel like they have tried everything, but nothing is working. Now is your chance as a consultant to change that, but what makes being a growth hacking consultant so different then?

Unlike a SEA or SEO consultant, you don't come in as a specialist for one area and create growth just through that one area. Specialists often have the freedom to make the changes they want within their area of expertise. Generalists also have that same freedom, and for both, it drives change. They often work for one of the Big Four and come in at a management level. The upper management has paid big bucks for them to make things happen as a consultant.

You come in to fix the whole package of growth. Even though growth is an obvious problem, the cause of this problem differs for every company. It is unlikely to be one area. That's because there are so many variables. Maybe the company struggles with building a strong brand, has an activation issue or, even a more formidable challenge, the product isn't wanted by the market: there is no Product-Market Fit. As a growth hacker, you are looking at everything that influences growth: the product, the funnel, the brand, the strategy and everything that surrounds it. From there, it is about determining what drives impact and knowing how to bring focus to the project, which we will help you with.

Unfortunately, you rarely get hired by upper management. Instead, it's the marketing manager which limits your span of control to the marketing side. Companies often believe that growth is a marketing problem and expect you to only look at it through that lens. Whilst the marketing manager is enthusiastic about creating results; their impact is limited. How can you drive real growth if you can't impact the whole business? Often the most significant wins are on the product or technology side. Yet, if the development roadmap is planned for the coming six months and your client expects results, how do you manage that?

We don't say this to be pessimists or doomsayers. Instead, we want to highlight the sweet challenge of your position as a growth hacking consultant. If you are to be successful as a growth consultant, this challenge should excite you. You know that it will be tricky, but that makes it rewarding - it's the thrill of the chase.

There are still ways to influence a product even if you come in via marketing. There are ways to grow your influence within the organisation; it comes down to those consultancy skills again from knowing how to best work with various stakeholders and influence them to create focus throughout the project. All of which, and more, we will show you how to do in this book.

In short, you differ from a specialist because you don't focus on one area, but you have a far better big picture view. At the same time, you also differ from a management consultant because you usually don't come in at the highest level. Still, you as growth consultant know how to execute strategy and not just deliver endless reports. You can use these other positions to describe the scope of a growth consultant, but not to capture them entirely, as it is the unique combination of all these specialisations. It is that combination and your skills to see both the big picture and ensure action is taken that will drive growth.

By demonstrating that growth is so much more than marketing and actively expanding your influence within an organisation, you will ensure a lasting impact for your efforts. It requires starting the project right, dealing with the risks and various stakeholders, and learning how to drive action. Sounds tough but don't worry, we will break it down into small pieces. Through the lessons of this book, we will show that you can create a more substantial and lasting impact for your clients. This will allow you to generate far more sustainable growth than you ever could with a single Google Ads campaign. What we want to show you is that it's about far more than what you do or know in terms of hands-on skills. You have the hard skills, so now it is time to sharpen those consultancy skills, and that is what we are here for. It's about how you approach what you do. That is what we have learnt from our 10+ years of combined experience in growth hacking, and by the end of this book, you'll be better prepared for your future in growth hacking too.

Who are we?

We are Daphne Tideman and Ward van Gasteren. Combined, we have over ten years of experience consulting with companies and helping them with growth hacking. During this time, we have been consultants to hundreds of companies. We have taught companies how to grow, we have spoken at events about growth hacking, and we have coached fellow growth hacking consultants along the way. You could say that we eat, sleep and breathe growth hacking, and we're not going to deny it. We've been obsessed with it, and through that, we have gathered everything we need to help you to fuel a similar obsession.

Daphne Tideman was the former Head of Growth Consultancy at RockBoost. Daphne joined RockBoost as their very first employee. From there, she grew RockBoost to an organisation of twenty-five individuals and worked for large clients such as Cisco, Fox Network Group, ING and Parkmobile along the way. She ran the three consultancy teams at RockBoost as well as the operations. After RockBoost Daphne joined Heights as their Head of Growth, an innovative venture-backed startup focused on brain care.

Ward van Gasteren has been active as a freelance growth hacking consultant for fast-growing startups (e.g. Catawiki, TikTok, Planto), Fortune 500 corporates (e.g. KPMG, Rabobank, NN), and innovation & growth agencies (e.g. StartupBootcamp,

Aimforthemoon, Spark Optimus). Ward has an entrepreneurial background and was one of the first twenty certified growth hackers in Europe through Growth Tribe's first class. Next to that, he has a blog on growth hacking and gives talks about growth hacking to share the knowledge.

In 2019, RockBoost brought in Ward to strengthen their consultancy team. He and Daphne collaborated for over a year while he worked with multiple growth agencies in that time. Out of shared enthusiasm and one too many debates fuelled by beers, this book was born.

We have both been the consultant, advised other team members and had the less enjoyable position of hearing why a client wasn't happy (as well as the fun moments when they were delighted!). We realised that we both did the same: we couldn't help but study our growth hacking clients. We wanted to understand them, how to become better partners and how to help them grow. This book collects all of those learnings into one source.

As a result of the countless debates along the way, we genuinely believe that we have been able to bring the content of this book to the next level showing what works and the best approach. This book reflects our own beliefs and approach to being a growth hacking consultant. It does not reflect those of any of the growth hacking agencies we've worked with in the past.

We have also enlisted some of our favourite growth consultants to share their advice too. That allows you to get a far broader perspective than just two people could offer. We received contributions by the amazing Abi Hough, Arnout Hellemans, Chris Out, Craig Sullivan, Els Aerts and Ethan Garr (when we write it like that it looks like we didn't make it past E on our alphabetised list, guess we will have to ask F-J for the next book!).

The structure of this book

Just like you probably are, we're tired of those books with endless chapters that say the same thing in five different ways. You know the ones, they take basic advice and package it with an oddly specific example and cookie-cutter enthusiasm. We don't believe in a book that stays in the vague theoretical realm, unable to reflect reality. We're not going to put you through that as we know that you, our lovely readers, are too smart and quick for that kind of nonsense.

So instead, we promise the following in terms of our chapters:

- They will be short and to the point.
- They will be focused on practicality and filled with examples.
- They will be filled with our templates and cheat sheets to help you implement information. We will link several times to growinghappyclients.com/resources, where you can find all the extra resources that accompany this book.
- They will be actionable. You will get action points regularly for you to apply and test. Do these, and it will ensure that you get your money's worth from this book.
- They will be honest and truthful, not painting a picture of how it *should* be, but rather how it *is* in reality. This is our job, what we do daily and what you can similarly expect, so we will always give you the full truth, no exaggerations.
- Each chapter will have the key takeaway summarised at the end.

During the book, we walk through the full process of being a growth consultant from the kickoff to saying goodbye to a client. We guide you through each step of the way. Therefore, we have broken this book down into sections that cover each part of that journey:

1. **Pre-Contact.** From the very beginning, we'll focus on how to truly understand your client and the questions you must be asking to do so. We mention some potential risks to be on the lookout for, which we cover in more in-depth later in the book.
2. **Starting Off (Month 0).** When collaborating the start phase is crucial. Here we talk about those first contact moments and the kickoff, as well as setting (realistic) expectations and priorities. We look at what basics you need to get in place, including the North Star Metric and the One Metric that Matters. From there, we show you the importance of identifying critical bottlenecks for their growth and how to structure your project.
3. **The Real Hustle (Month 1 - 3).** Here we talk about each aspect of the growth hacking loop: ideation, prioritisation, testing and presenting results, as well as consistently evaluating the progress and zooming out. We discuss how to work together with the various stakeholders from across the company: from Brand Managers to Developers, Board Members to Salespeople.
4. **The Ups and Downs (Month 3 - 12).** Now that the honeymoon phase is over, you've most likely tackled the quick wins and showed your best tricks, so the real hard work begins. Discover the most prominent issues a consultant faces during these months and various strategies to deal with them. How do you handle too many focus points? What do you do if the tempo is too slow? We look at how you can solve these challenges and many more.
5. **What Comes Next?** Should you continue working together? Should you try to upsell your client? How do you best deal with a downscale? These are only a few of the questions we answer in the final section. Find out the best way to reflect on a completed project.

The Five Principles

We are not going to pretend clients are perfect, but neither are we as consultants. We want to trigger you to think of what you can change: focus on what's within your control, rather than continually focusing on what your client could do better. Our goal is that at the end of this book, you are a better and more confident consultant, one that can handle the toughest of clients.

You'll become a growth hacking consultant who understands your clients, knows what they need and, as a result, can drive more impact. We believe it all comes down to:

Empathetic communication that drives your client into action

That is why, before we dive into the previously mentioned sections, we will detour first to explain our five core principles of being an exceptional growth consultant. These principles will teach you how to do the above. As we guide you from the start to the finish line, everything will centre around these five principles:

1. Be Them
2. Be Real
3. Be Open
4. Be Bold
5. Be Focused

We will cover what these principles mean in the following chapter, but you'll also notice that they have an essential role to play throughout your learning journey in this book. Whenever it feels overwhelming, or you aren't sure what to do, keep these in mind. We will give you a ton of practical tools and techniques that will help you to use these five principles.

Confidence is key

Before we move on to those principles, there is still the elephant in the room that we must address. See you can follow our step by step process, complete every single action point and breath the five principles through and through. But you may still struggle. You may even have that nagging voice in the back of your head that tells you that you can't do it. That you aren't good enough that you have no idea what you are doing. That you are a fraud... that voice sucks, doesn't it?

Confidence can get in the way of your journey as a consultant. The Dunning-Kruger Effect highlights this perfectly, our confidence is sky-high in the beginning but drops with the more we know:

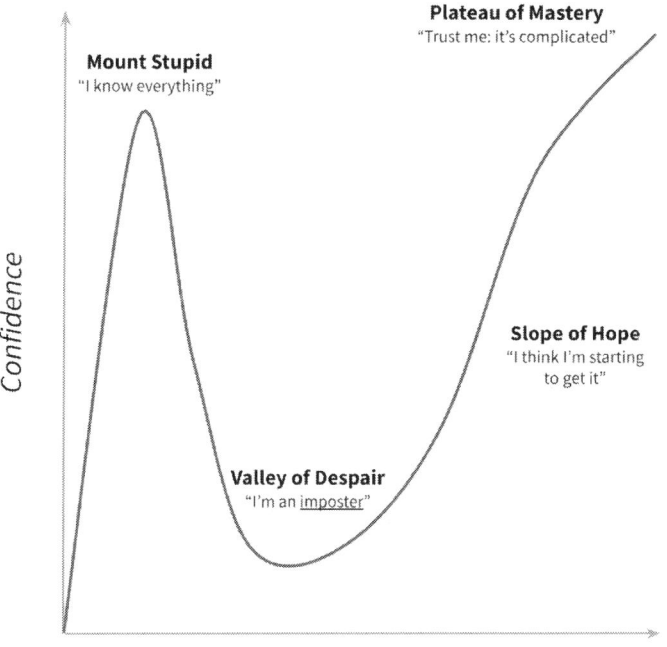

The Dunning-Kruger Effect

When you start as a consultant, it can feel like you've got a feel for how to be a Growth Hacker and are strolling along. Then the more you learn from reality, the less you feel like you know. That is when that lovely voice in your head starts to put you down.

In the middle is where you are probably now, where you have experience (but still have a lot to learn), your confidence is low. Way lower than what it was when you had no experience. That confidence killer impacts how you handle your client. If you don't believe in what you are suggesting, how can they?

If you struggle with this, that's okay. It often stems from a desire to be perfect or from comparing yourself to others. We both had it at the beginning, and it sometimes still hits these days. When writing a book about being a growth hacking consultant, the temptation to feel like you must be a perfect consultant is high, that we can never make a mistake again. Yet, do we need to be perfect to teach you some of the lessons we've learned?

This book is not about how to be a perfect consultant because we aren't perfect (nobody is). Instead, it is about how to do your best to drive results, help your client take action, and get better each day. That is what matters. There is no golden standard to live up to, just principles and techniques to help you along the way, become your very own growth hacking project. But also be kind to yourself and remember, perfect doesn't exist.

We hope this book gives you the confidence you need to be a better growth hacker.

Five Core Principles of Exceptional Growth Consultants

Principle-based way of working

Tools and techniques are great for helping you to take action, but they are just ways to implement underlying principles. Using tactics without first understanding how those underlying principles work would be like walking the streets with your eyes glued to Google Maps. You see nothing of what you pass by or understand the best route to take for next time. Yes, Google Maps will help you figure out where to go and how to get there. But watch out! Because the minute your phone dies, the roads change, or you go to an unplotted territory, you'll end up lost.

Knowing the principles is like being able to navigate, no matter where you are. You do not blindly follow the map, but instead, choose the best route for your needs. With tools and techniques in your belt, you can then look critically at whether they are suitable. We believe it all comes down to the five core principles, with the first, Be Them, at the centre of it all.

Five Core Principles of Exceptional Growth Consultants

Be Real

Be Open

Be Them

Be Bold

Be Focused

We will take you through each principle and refer back to them continuously, as they are your core values as a growth hacker. The goal of these five principles and the book in its entirety is relatively simple; we want to teach you the following skill:

Empathetic communication that drives your client to take action.

That is the secret, and by learning how to do this, you'll be able to drive action, because, at the end of the day, the action taken is what drives results. The first principle Be Them revolves around empathy for your client; it is about putting yourself in their shoes, but even more than that, it is about putting them in the spotlight rather than yourself. From there learning how to Be Real and Be

Open is all about your communication style. Finally, Be Bold and Be Focused are the principles that will teach you how to drive the right type of action.

Now let's walk through them.

1. Be Them

At the centre of it all is thinking from your client's perspective rather than from your own. It's about getting in their head:

- What are they looking to achieve?
- What do they find valuable?
- What are their frustrations?

As a growth consultant, you know the importance of customer research; everything revolves around measuring and understanding what drives the end consumer. In this case, your client is your customer, so you want to be continually communicating from their perspective and placing yourself in their shoes. This is far more effective as it helps you think a few steps ahead in terms of what could become potential challenges and how to prevent them.

Whenever you face issues with your clients, try to zoom out on the situation and ask yourself the following question:

Why is it logical for my client to act this way?

Full credit goes to Chris Out (co-founder of RockBoost, now an international speaker and growth consultant) for this question. It was the first question he asked at RockBoost every time a client issue came up. He would not allow you to get frustrated with the situation (we all have those moments) but instead, he would first encourage you to answer the question: why is it logical for my client to act this way? Suddenly, your client is no longer an irrational individual that you don't understand. You see the person behind the situation, one who's struggling too. Yes, they blocked you from focusing on SEO even though you know this will have a considerable impact, but:

- Is it because they don't know how to convince other team members of the value of SEO?
- Did they spend a year trying to improve the organic rankings and never manage to?
- Maybe your contact person worked at a company where SEO never brought results?

These are struggles they may not admit to, but they are not trying to be difficult on purpose. Don't think of you and your client as being on opposite sides: they are just human too. Maybe they're not aware of their own bias, or perhaps they feel ashamed for not being able to work as data-driven as the ideal scenario would require.

Rather than continuing to push your clients for approval, ask them instead what their reasons are. Ask them 'why' questions until you understand, such as why would they rather not focus on SEO? Try to understand their logic first; perhaps they will show you why SEO isn't the highest priority for their company after all. Are you still convinced SEO is important, or does this give you new insights as well? If you're still certain, then ask further questions to help them see why it could be worthwhile pursuing and work together from there to look from different perspectives. It all stems from this one starting question:

Why is it logical for my client to act this way?

Remember, thinking like your client is only one part of the equation, you need to ask them what THEY think too. Make feedback a vital part of the process.

The second part of Being Them is to put *them* in the spotlight rather than yourself. The minute the wins of the project feel like they come from your client's team, it will drive excitement. It will get people talking and motivated towards creating growth, and this is infinitely more valuable than claiming the win as your own. Claiming it as your own may bring you short-term recognition for the project but sharing the win will drive long-term success.

2. Be Real

The idea of Be Real is to be continuously realistic and honest in what is and isn't possible.

Sometimes growth hackers get a terrible reputation. The stereotype shows them as being super hacky and black hat in their techniques - "Do you want my secretive, never-seen-before hack that can drive your growth up 326% overnight? Click this link for more!". The minority are ruining the majority's reputation. At the same time, marketers, in general, struggle to be seen as trustworthy because it is their very nature to sell and use psychology to reach a goal.

However, a good relationship is built on trust and honesty, and the same goes for consultant/client relationships. Sleazy techniques will not get you far and will be picked up by your client very quickly.

Instead, try to be your client's partner in crime: working together to achieve your mission. You want to *Be Real* with each other about what is realistic and what is happening. Please don't promise endless quick-wins and mountains of gold, unless you know that you can deliver.

So, how do you do this? In our experience, it starts with the following examples:

- Follow through on your promises.
- Always be realistic in what you can and can't deliver.
- Indicate when something is not possible immediately.
- Let them know when variables change during the process and impact the potential.

Basing everything on the data is a massive part of achieving the Be Real principle. You want to work backwards from the data together with your client so that the data tells the story and your arguments become far more persuasive. It also allows your client to understand the underlying reasons, so you can work together to solve the growth challenge at hand. They will be able to give their suggestions, "I know we can't test the hypothesis this way, but wouldn't this work instead to test what we see in the data?" Build a relationship where you challenge each other based on the data. Your client is the expert in their niche, their product and their audience, so they will often come with the best ideas. Don't be scared not to be the one who brings the best ideas to the table, instead be afraid to not have the best ideas on the table at all. Your role becomes invaluable when you can make everybody else in the room more valuable and drive their ideas to execution.

So, always try to Be Real: be realistic in your promises, be honest about the reality of the given situation, and base your work on that reality aka be data-driven.

3. Be Open

Next to being real, it's crucial to Be Open in your process: what are your next steps and why? This relates, of course, to Be Real but takes this further by helping your client understand the full process, walking them through it step-by-step. We hate consultants who try to keep their approach, their tactics and their tools secret. If you are continually learning and moving forward, what does it matter if you share what currently works?

Being open starts with ensuring you aren't irreplaceable in terms of hands-on work but that you're focused on being extremely replaceable for the areas you've already set up. Encourage your client to take those areas over. Any repetitive work should either be automated or transferred to your client's team; your client will appreciate that you are considerate of their budget. Demonstrate to your client that you are adding strategic value. Whether that be devising new experiments or identifying bottlenecks - show your worth. Your client hired you for your way of thinking and approach, and to help them take the next steps not to keep running their campaigns for the coming years. The strategic value is actually far more challenging to replace than the hands-on work, and it will also drive far more ROI.

Also, don't keep all of your knowledge to yourself in fear of staying valuable to the client. Look at it from this perspective: every time you answer a question in its fullest, you can move on from that question, and for sure the next question will be more advanced and thus more valuable. Every time you make them smarter, your next hour becomes more valuable.

We believe that the best consultants are transparent by sharing the how and what for existing areas it allows you to focus on new areas rather than the old. By sharing knowledge with your client, you save time answering questions. You end up with longer and more sustainable client relationships as you continuously add value both in terms of results and knowledge, a double win for them and you.

To make sure that you are being open, ask yourself the following questions:

- Is this what is best for my client?

- Would my potential impact be 10x higher if I extensively explained the processes and the benefits?
- If I taught them along the way so that they can take over certain areas, would this free up my time to work on other opportunities?

Another part of being open is the frequency of your communication; you can never communicate often enough to a client. Update them consistently about the status of running tasks and what is happening. Both of us have never had a client say, "You communicate too much" or "Shut up already", and we both are avid updaters. If you're doing your job right, a lot is happening, and your clients usually want to be taken through the process. We have heard clients say there are too many hours in the overhead, that there is a 'meeting overflow'. That's not what we are suggesting. If you keep the updates small and authentic, you can Be Open without extra meetings. There are many ways to achieve this:

- Schedule status updates.
- Have short standups.
- Automate weekly KPI shares.
- Email back immediately to confirm you received their email and will look into it.
- Send them further analyses you've done to share the exciting insights.

But it's so much more than that. It is also about all those little moments:

- Send them additional ideas of what you've been thinking about; maybe you saw something cool online or discussed with a colleague, which could benefit your client.
- Send them a text for small updates, e.g. "The ads are live!", "FYI: I'm still working on the issue" or "I cancelled our meeting because there were no big updates".

- Maybe even tag a contact person on LinkedIn in a post that would interest them.

The assumption with consultants is that they might not care as much or be as driven as someone working for that company. The best consultants are the ones that genuinely care. Little actions like the above show that their success is on your mind and that you are continually thinking about how to grow them.

Finally take them through the process unless their personality type suggests they prefer not to know about the process (more on this in Chapter 3: Different Types of Personalities of Clients). In the short run, it may feel like more work or hours going into communication, but in the long run, it saves time as it will build trust and allow you extra freedom with less discussion. Not only that, by working together so closely, you can avoid mistakes or missing potentially better ideas from your client.

4. Be Bold

Growth cannot be fuelled from a place of fear or timidness. Growth happens when we are bold, daring to test new things and pushing for action. As a consultant, a phrase you will hear all too often is "that can't be done". That should get you excited, rolling up your sleeves and ready to figure it out. It is up to you to look at the data and determine when the possible results make it worthwhile to push through. Rather than accepting a "can't", "no" or "won't", you can get creative:

- Be proactive and come with suggestions.
- Give your client options.
- Try out alternative routes.
- Brainstorm alternative solutions together.

Keep going until you find a way to get things done. We once had a client who would be perfect for Quora ads but to obtain permission to do so internally would take months, especially getting the payment details. At first, they said "leave it, we will have to do something else", but that was the last thing we wanted. So we suggested including the ad budget in our consultancy fee and setting the ad account and visuals up ourselves. Then once the results were positive, it was far easier to convince the rest internally of the potential and to get it set up correctly.

Next to that, being bold is about being confident. Now that is easier said than done. Our goal with this book is to fuel your confidence if this is an area you struggle with. You have shown that you are eager enough to read a book about improving your consultancy skills, so we trust that you are doing the same for your hard skills. That means that you probably know your shit, pardon our French. Confidence is vital because your client sees you as their partner in crime, showing them the way. Sadly, in the past, we have received feedback from clients suggesting the opposite happened. They felt their consultants were not assertive enough and would like them to share their opinion more often. Your client wants you to lead them in their growth journey actively.

Like we said before, you two are partners in crime, the last thing you want is your crime partner to hesitate in the middle of a heist. Before you know it, you'll see the flashing lights and sirens of it all being over.

Sometimes results can be faltering, or there are a few losses in terms of experiments, but this is part of the growth process. If all your experiments win, you are probably playing it too small or too safe. Now how do you ensure your client doesn't lose faith in those moments? Confidence. They see you explaining what has been learned and what the next steps are. They can see that you still have control over the situation.

It's also crucial to understand the difference between ego and confidence: someone with an ego is stuffed with self-importance and hates to be wrong. An ego-driven growth hacker (unfortunately, there are quite a few of them) believes that their way is the only way to grow a company. They look only for data to confirm their beliefs, rather than always trying to look at growth from all angles (confirmation bias alert!). A confident growth hacker (without a giant ego weighing them down) doesn't care whether they or someone else is right. What matters to them is that the results are achieved and that they are focused on growth, not on themselves. They can find more opportunities than they could possibly think of because they can look at growth from every angle - not just their own.

We will, of course, help you to build that confidence further throughout the book, but you already have the secret weapon in your pocket - the data and the insights of the end consumer. Don't leave it there; it will help you win the heist, or rather, grow the client. As a growth hacker, your confidence should stem from being the advocate of the end customer and by always backing your decisions with data.

5. Be Focused

If you haven't noticed it yet from your own experience, we are going to let you in on a little secret... clients are often chaotic. They have 10+ stakeholders pulling them in various directions. They have enough work for 80 hours that they need to shove into 40 hours. Oh, and they have a ton of ideas they've always wanted to test. Now if anything is a recipe for killing focus, it's this:

Stakeholders + Being too busy + Idea overload

The ideas are great (being too busy and having annoying stakeholders not so much), but growth demands focus. Imagine you are playing darts… blindfolded (please don't try this at home). The game goes like this, you get to see the target/dartboard for a few seconds then the blindfold goes on, and you throw a dart. You then get to peek to see how you did: did you even hit the target? Is the wall crumbling beside it? You walk a bit further and try the same with a new target, the next in line. You repeat this with five targets: throw a dart, look at how it went and move on to the next target. Once you've done this five times, you move back to the first target. The goal is to hit the centre for all five targets as fast as possible (a time limit makes this game extra fun).

Throwing darts to hit a target whilst blindfolded is hard enough, add the element of moving to a new target each time, it makes it near impossible to win at this game. Moving each time means you have to recalibrate, try to remember where you were and try again. It will take you far longer to hit the centre of each dartboard (and you will need a fair amount of luck too).

This is precisely how it works with growth hacking when you are experimenting with your sight between dart throws and your previous darts on the board being your data. The blindfold represents the fact that you never have the full facts and therefore know with any certainty what will work. You never know which dart will be the big win and hit the bullseye. What you do know is that you need to observe what is working and what isn't, that you need to keep experimenting, and that only through doing this will you eventually hit the target smack bang in the middle.

When working with a client, your client will want you to try to go for the first version; they will give you five different targets at the same time. They will ask you to split your time and attention between them.

Assuming that there is a wall left standing after your first attempts, let's play again. This time the rules of the game have changed. You can stay in one place and try the first dartboard again and again.

Only once you hit the centre do you move on. Wouldn't that be much quicker?

You know immediately from this example that it is better to hit one bullseye and then move on systematically. It's your job to show your client the power of taking it one dartboard at a time. Sure the switching makes the game more exciting, but this isn't a game of excitement, it is a game of hitting the bullseye of growth.

Not only does a lack of focus slow you down, but it is also a key driver for client scope-creep. Ever felt like the number of hours you had for a client were not enough? If you give a growth hacker 8 hours per week for a client, they will find work for 12 hours. Give a growth hacker 16 hours and magically enough work for 24 hours appears. We realised that even on the biggest projects (80 hours a week) there still wasn't enough time, even though the project initially planned for 20 hours per week! There will always be more things you can do or potential ideas you could test. Your challenge as a growth hacker is to bring focus to your client. We want to help you do so by helping you find focus and to show you how to balance delivering short-term wins and long-term building so that growth occurs.

The best ways to bring focus are through the metrics you use, such as the North Star Metric, One Metric that Matters and other metrics. We will also show you practical techniques for how to deal with tricky stakeholders and idea overflow.

Which of the five principles are most relevant for you?

After harping on about the necessity of focus, your first challenge is how to apply that to your learning. All five principles will be explored throughout this book but take a moment to focus on, which principle is the most crucial for you now. There will always be one that you are struggling with more than the other four, but this is the one that will take you the furthest.

> **Time for Action**
>
> Pick your worst characteristic (aka principle) and write it on a post-it to be kept in your direct line of vision on your desk. Take 5 -10 minutes to go back through the section on that principle and choose one action point for the coming week. Add that to your post-it and intentionally try to improve on it. If you focus on them one-by-one, you'll be able to improve your long-term habits.
>
> For example, you might write down "Be Bold" followed by "Always get creative with solutions" on your post-it.
>
> Even better is to identify the situations when you aren't living up to that principle, already the awareness of that will be a massive step in improving it. Let's say you lose focus when you get into discussions about new ideas. Whenever a discussion comes up, first think "Ah, I might lose focus here" and then have a solution such as "I'll always say we need to prioritise ideas first."

Enough talk, let's get started. Your first client project is starting in a few weeks. Now what? Well, let's start at the beginning; why is your client even hiring a growth hacker? Aka, what are you even doing there in the first place?

Key Takeaway

Start with putting yourself in the shoes of your client, Be Them. From there, start to build empathetic communication with them by Being Open and Real throughout the process. Then keep the Focus and dare to be Bold in your suggestions to drive action. Bring it all together, and you have the secret of a successful Growth Consultant:

Empathetic communication that drives your client to take action.

SECTION 1

Pre-Contact

CHAPTER 1

Why Do Companies Hire A Growth Hacker?

1.1 The changing perception of growth hacking

Five years ago, when we started as growth hackers, people would say:

"You know... growth hacking, isn't that a bit of a buzzword?"

Yes, of course, we knew that, but we would laugh and nod along responding something along the lines of:

"Yes, yes. It's a bit of a buzzword, but we like to use it as it focuses on being data-driven and more experimental in your marketing."

Perhaps it would have been better to have said nothing. When at a party and someone asks "So what do you do?", it's an annoying question. Throw in a profession that no one knows, and you almost want to sigh at the mere mention of this question, you end up saying "I'm a marketer" or even "I'm a data-driven marketer" if you are feeling incredibly daring. You just don't feel like explaining growth hacking for the next twenty minutes while they sip their foamy beer and feign both interest and understanding.

Nowadays, the above couldn't be further from the truth, every company knows what a growth hacker is, and everyone wants one.

Yet, the reply we've been giving to sidestep lengthy conversations, such as being a marketer, data-driven marketer or even growth marketer, brings its own risk. In the attempt to avoid an unknown definition or the lousy reputation growth hackers have been gaining, we often throw in the phrase 'marketer'. We talk about channels and traffic with excitement but forget to show that growth is so much more than that. So even though companies set out to hire a growth hacker, though most know it isn't all those hacks, they may equate you to a marketer instead. Which you most definitely are not. Perhaps the solution is to say "growth consultant" and if you aren't a consultant, then settle for "growth strategist". Yet, these are not standard terms, and the truth is that for now, companies do look for growth hackers. That is why we will use the term growth hacking consultants throughout the book but interchangeably with growth consultants. For us, growth hacking isn't about marketing. Growth hacking isn't about hacking. It is about analysing what drives growth, experimenting and building new strategies from there.

Now the international competition is fiercely growing, and alongside it, there is the rise of innovative startups. Companies are desperate to stand out, experience growth and look for a growth hacker. In other cases, growth hacking is seen as the solution to running on the treadmill. Companies that are always busy racing ahead from one thing to the next, they have their treadmill set to maximum speed. Yet, they are still not getting the results they want. Eventually, they end up lowering the speed of the treadmill, sweating and exhausted. They look around wondering: how will we ever truly move forward? Should we even be running this way? Perhaps there's a different way to reach our goals? That is when they Google "Growth hacking consultants/freelancers/agency". It's like wanting to get a personal trainer... after trying to do crunches for one day, but not seeing any results.

It's essential to understand what drives a company: what is the tipping point that made them look for a growth hacker? Only then can you figure out how to best help them. We will cover how to get the answer from them, but first, you need to dive into the mind of your client.

Imagine for a moment that the company (your potential client) has an issue:

- They aren't growing fast enough.
- They don't have time for growth.
- They've hit a ceiling and stopped growing.
- Or maybe, they've seen their competitors skyrocket ahead, leaving them in their dusty wake.

All they want are results to be proud of, to know they are growing and on the right track. It is almost a strange reassurance that their company is on to something, that what they are creating is what customers want and need. They are not wasting their time with this whole business, as that is something, we all secretly fear at times. What if no one wants my product or service? What if this is all for nothing?

So, the marketing department hires a growth consultant. Yes, you read that correctly, the marketing department. Wait, didn't we just throw a temper tantrum that a growth consultant and marketer are not the same things? Yes, we did, and yes, we see them differently, but as we hinted at before, sadly most companies don't.

Arnout Hellemans, a growth consultant with 13+ years of digital experience, explained it when we interviewed him for this book:

> "95% if not 100% of the time you probably get hired by Marketing. When you get hired via the CMO or marketing team, you get stuck with marketing. That means product/engineering, where you can probably make the most impact, is in a completely different

> department. When their list of to-dos is overflowing, and marketing is overflowing, your improvements like changes to increase site speed or fix technical SEO issues get skipped. The ideal solution is to get hired by that department from the beginning. If not, you need to see at least how you can get closer with the other departments." - Arnout Hellemans

So, if possible, when your client is hiring, you indicate that you should actually be with the product department, as that is where you can make the most impact. If that isn't an option, we will walk through how to improve your collaboration with the various stakeholders in Chapters 20 - 26 (there is a lot to cover). For the most part, we will assume your contact person is the marketing manager and that you have joined via the marketing team as that is the reality in most cases.

1.2 Internal culture or internal resistance?

Often, it's the case that the internal culture at a company is the primary reason their growth is stunted. This is not something that happens overnight but was developed over the years. As a result, you need to understand which challenges stem from the culture and how to shake things up. The good news is they hired you; this confirms that somewhere in the organisation, there is the awareness that change is needed and a desire to make it happen.

We have often seen one or more of the following internal challenges by companies.

Internal Challenge	Explanation
People are feeling stuck	They feel like the current way is the only way, and they don't know how they can change things anymore.
Management is always changing direction	One day the management says X, the next day they say Y and a week later it will be Z. A fickle management team creates uncertainty within the organisation so people stop trying to push for change and growth falters as a result.
Lack of priorities	It is not only management that can lack focus; often, the marketing and product team struggles to get their priorities straight. As a result, they only work on the ongoing business, which rarely brings significant results. They stick to what they know and what they feel must be done (e.g. post on Instagram, build extra features) whether or not it delivers results.
Lack of skills	Sometimes the marketing team doesn't have the skills or mindset that are needed for growth. This makes it tough to beat companies with more knowledgeable growth hackers. Skills can be taught, of course, but only with the right mindset, which is crucial to fix first.

Holy planning of the tech team	You have some organisations (okay... many) where the tech team is only working on maintenance/own priorities. They don't make growth a priority. "How dare you ask for extra resources when you know how busy development is?!". Growth suffers when the tech team has no time or is seen as the king of the planning. What is within the marketing team's control, usually acquisition, will only get them so far.

A client will sometimes hire a growth hacker as a result of one or more of these issues. Perhaps they are aware of the problem they have, but more often than not, they have a feeling that growth isn't happening fast enough but don't know why.

As a growth hacker, you are an investigator that needs to figure this out through the questions you ask. We will cover crucial questions in Chapter 6: The Kickoff.

1.3 Why did they specifically hire a growth hacker?

We know the challenges that limit growth, but what we don't know is the reason they think a growth hacker is the solution to the problem. Why the sudden surge in the demand for growth hackers? Did the growth hackers do something to create exponential growth in their own demand? Or perhaps there are reasons for companies to realise growth hackers might be the solution, such as:

- They don't want to spend more ad budget, they've tried that.
- They want someone to look at what is and isn't working based on proof: data.

- They know they need someone who isn't afraid to try things outside the box. Someone who won't waste hundreds and thousands on only branding campaigns.

They want a growth hacker; someone who will shake up their organisation and bring results. They want *you*.

We have covered just a few of the main reasons an organisation might hire you as a growth hacker. You know that they are facing one or more internal challenges that you are there to help fix, yet an organisation consists of many individuals. An individual's reasons to hire you can be very different from the collective's.

Your contact person is the main person that you work with throughout the project. When we use the phrase 'client' we mean the organisation in the broader sense. We will use the term 'contact person' for your main point of contact. Finally, 'customers' will refer to your client's customers. Phew, got those definitions covered. Hopefully, that will avoid a bit of confusion later down the line. Now back to that contact person. Usually, you discuss and decide with them what to do and how to approach the project. You'll need to dive to a level deeper with them and also understand how they work to be successful, which is what we'll cover in the upcoming two chapters. We will start with their overall drivers, what we like to call their ABCs, followed by the four key types of client personalities.

Why do Companies Hire A Growth Hacker?

> **Key Takeaway**
>
> Growth hacking used to be a new buzzword, but now it is considered to be the solution to the challenge that a company is not growing fast enough. Clients see you as a magic fix yet give you only the reins of the marketing department. Your job is to go in there and understand their internal challenge by asking questions. From there, you can start to figure out how to gain broader impact best to drive results.

CHAPTER 2

Your Contact Person's ABC

2.1 The ABC Model

The principle Be Them not only applies to the company but also your contact person. They have their background: who they are and what they want to achieve at that company.

Understanding what drives them as an individual will help you to collaborate better. It will show you how you can set them up for success which will make you victorious as well. It is about finding a win-win situation.

It's not only what drives them but discovering what holds them back along the way is just as important. What are the barriers that keep them from getting to where they want to go? This could be anything from a lack of time to a lack of knowledge. Knowing these can also help you to communicate in the right way.

That is why we like to think of it with a model, your contact person's ABCs. Let's make understanding them as easy as ABC, 1-2-3 (anyone else hears the Jackson 5 in their heads). Anyways… this looks like the following:

1. **Awful:** Something is making your client feel **A**wful (or at least a bit uncomfortable). Without this, there would've been no reason to take steps to hire you or want your help.
2. **Barriers:** But to get to that desired place, they will have to overcome many **B**arriers: challenges, beliefs and struggles which will hold them back along the way.
3. **Cravings:** They have a **C**raving for something they want to achieve/how they want to feel/how they want to be seen. Like food cravings, it gnaws at them in the background while they try to get on with their day to day work.

See it as a person who is trying to get from point A, past their B-barriers to get to destination C.

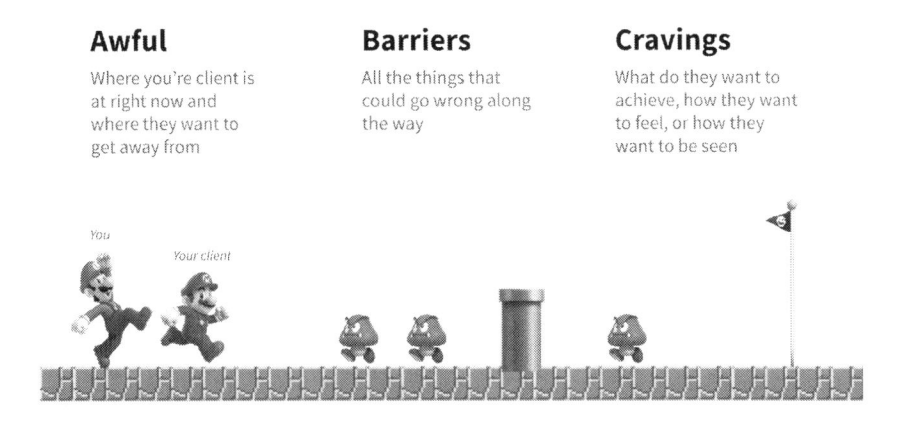

Awful
Where you're client is at right now and where they want to get away from

Barriers
All the things that could go wrong along the way

Cravings
What do they want to achieve, how they want to feel, or how they want to be seen

Don't worry if it feels a bit theoretical right now, by the end of this book you'll have no trouble with your ABCs. We will practice each letter a few times until you are fluent. For now, just be aware that your goal is not only to help the organisation reach what they crave (growth) but also to help your contact person in achieving what they desire. Whilst they will, of course, also crave growth, they also have other intricate cravings, which we'll discuss a bit later.

Now, of course, we realise that not every contact person is the same, but we will look at the 20% of ABC that will apply to 80% of your contact people. Very often, your contact person is a marketing manager, growth manager or innovation manager. We're going to walk a few pages in their shoes now, join us in entering the mind of the marketing manager. They are not the highest ranking in the organisation but also not the lowest. They are responsible for creating growth and results by growing the brand and driving conversions. But much is out of their control, such as project and development. They have loads to do and never enough time. So, what do their ABCs look like?

2.2 The Awful

So, what is the Awful? What are the fears that keep them up at night? Where are they at the start of the collaboration? Well, growth is likely not occurring as fast as they would want (it seldomly is). Otherwise, they wouldn't have hired you to be their partner in crime. They are probably worried that the company or their product won't grow. That they won't hit their targets... What if colleagues see them as a failure? What if they made a mistake in hiring a growth hacking consultant? What if they don't get the promotion they were hoping for? What if, even worse, they're let go? These are the Awful that your client wants to move away from; this is what keeps them up at night.

To discover these, you'll need to have a sincere one-on-one with your contact person. Suggesting that you want to get to know them at the start of your collaboration is not weird at all: you could propose planning an hour face-to-face during lunch or a separate meeting just to get acquainted. Ask them about their job, what work is like at the moment and ask them for advice for your job: What are aspects of the workplace that you'd need to avoid? What are the extra things at work that they'd love to see changed during your collaboration? Sometimes a stranger in an organisation can pick up on things that your contact person can't, so that is a great way to reach out with a helping hand.

The Awful can also be aspects of their personal life, struggles they have outside of work that impact their work performance. Enquiring around more personal aspects of your contact person's life (and being equally open about yourself) will reap benefits because you show a genuine interest beyond 'the job'. Understanding and showing compassion on a more personal level allows you to build a relationship to the point whereby you will receive a more honest response.

2.3 The Barriers

Now, what is getting in the way? Probably a lot: no one said growth would be effortless. Perhaps some of them look familiar:

1. Stakeholders that need to be on board, give approval and of course have a say.
2. There is also the legacy that gets in the way and the general frustrating slowness of the company.
3. There are those five other projects that demand your contact person's attention.
4. As well as a team to manage and take care of.
5. Oh, and probably a busy personal life.

Phew, that's a lot! And that list is only the beginning… It is enough to make your contact person feel anxious and uncertain, which can result in a bit of ego or fixed mindset. Maybe they think they know best and don't want to listen to your advice at times even though you both want the same thing.

As you can see, the barriers are a mixture of personal challenges and those associated with managing other stakeholders. You want to show understanding for the above and be considerate of them in your approach. This can then help you to bring your contact person closer to what they Crave.

To unravel their Barriers, you could ask them about previous attempts on growing the business: what went wrong before? What are typical frustrations during a process? What influenced the outcome to be less ambitious, bold or innovative?

2.4 The Cravings

So what do they Crave? What do they want above all else? Next to growth, there is also a natural desire to crave appreciation and recognition. It is even the fourth level of Maslow's Hierarchy of Needs:

Self-actualization
desire to become the most that one can be

Esteem
respect, self-esteem, status, recognition, strength, freedom

Love and belonging
friendship, intimacy, family, sense of connection

Safety needs
personal security, employment, resources, health, property

Psychological needs
air, water, food, shelter, sleep, clothing, reproduction

Maslow saw the importance in esteem, a primal need that can only be fulfilled once psychological, safety and love requirements are achieved. Esteem even outranks an individual's drive to become the most that you can. Maslow suggested that individuals want to accomplish something; they want to gain status and recognition for what they've done.

The importance of esteem can translate to more tangible forms of recognition: a raise or promotion with this project as a stepping stone to grow themselves. You were brought into the company to create growth, to ensure this project is successful. It's only natural for your contact person to crave the rewards of that success as they worked hard for it too. They could even crave the pride that arises as a result of the growth created, that feeling that we all know and love of having been able to make a difference.

Try to bring up their future and ambitions during a one-on-one conversation: even if it's just a quick question when you're walking to the coffee machine together. Understanding how they see their future will give you great insights into what they're craving. You might feel more comfortable first asking how and when they joined the company: what was their reason for joining? That again gives you insights into their drivers.

2.5 Practising your ABCs

Yes, it is time for action; a passive reader forgets and doesn't implement what they have learnt. An active reader translates the new knowledge into action and improves as a result of it. Hello active reader! It will take you five minutes, okay, maybe ten. Don't worry, we made a little cheatsheet for you, you can find it at growinghappyclients.com/resources.

Now grab a pen and some paper and start writing the old-fashioned way.

> **Time for Action**
>
> Choose either a previous contact person or a current one. Write out the following.
>
> 1. **The Awful:** What are your contact person's struggles? How could you take them away? How could you help them realise that you can solve them?
> 2. **The Barriers:** What are your contact person's barriers? How could you make the barriers easier to manage? How could you work around the barriers?
> 3. **The Cravings:** What are your contact person's cravings? How could you show your contact person that they can trust you to help them achieve them? How could you set them up for success, to satisfy their cravings?
>
> Remember the four other principles of the model: Be Real, Be Open, Be Bold and Be Focused. These can all help you to figure out how to support your client with their ABC.

All done? We hope you managed to come up with a few ideas, but no worries if not. This book is intensely focused on helping you to Be Them and understand your contact person's ABCs. It will come back in many of the chapters that follow. However, we can imagine that it would be nice to have some concrete examples already to get the wheels turning. So, let's get that car revving and drive through a few short examples:

1. The Awful

This is all about being Open and Real on the road to growth by showing them what is possible and what they can expect. Often fear stems from uncertainty: the way is foggy and unclear. A clear roadmap and goal (Be Focused) can help take that away. That doesn't mean lying if something is not realistic, but instead, it is showing them what is possible and what is needed to achieve their goals. The Awful is a lot less Awful when you see a bright future ahead.

2. The Barriers

This requires you to Be Bold. You need to make things happen, no matter what the barriers are that block your way. It could be sending several reminders to everyone in the team to ensure experiments get live. Then your client doesn't have to do that, as they are already swamped and can trust that you are on top of things. It could be coming up with creative solutions to get experiments live despite legacy. Dealing with Barriers also requires you to Be Open, so communicating to different departments and getting them on board.

3. The Cravings

There is this superb principle, "praise publicly, scold privately". Try to praise your contact person publicly and frequently. This not only encourages specific behaviour that drives on the road to growth, but it will also give the feeling that you are helping them achieve their Cravings. Put them in the spotlight, and they will bring you into it as well, as the person who put them there. This could be mentioning the achievements of your contact person in a growth meeting, for example, "Joan had this great idea of how to test our hypothesis" or "Shaun ensured that those two experiments went live yesterday". Now remember to Be Real: nothing is worse than a fake suck up. Bah, gross. Give honest compliments you believe in, and focus on everything your contact person and other team members are doing well. They hired you and set up all the foundations, so without them, you would not be able to help create growth. It is only fair that you both give and help them to receive the recognition they deserve. Another great example is providing them with presentations to send to their boss that show all that has been achieved; we will cover this in-depth in Chapter 17: Presenting Your Results.

Now we've covered why a company hires a growth hacker and how to understand your contact person, we'd encourage you to come back to these two chapters often. You will handle situations differently as a result, as it will stop you focusing on what you want and instead think from their perspective. Of course, no contact person is the same (that would be easy and boring). That is why we want to dive a bit deeper into the different types of personalities we often see using a framework; this will again give you the 20% that covers 80% in terms of the kind of clients out there.

> **Key Takeaway**
>
> Don't get so caught up in understanding the company's needs that you forget the individual that hired you. Knowing their Awfuls can help you show them you both understand and want to help solve them. Knowing their Barriers means you can proactively remove them or fix them. Knowing their Cravings helps you communicate through what matters to them.

CHAPTER 3

Different Types of Personalities of Clients

3.1 The Insights Discovery Personality test

We've talked about the company, and we've talked about your contact person. Now it's time to get to know your clients even better, to get to know them personally, the next step in embracing the principle: Be Them. We will talk about the following framework in reference to your contact person but note we did call this chapter "personalities of clients". No, we aren't getting our terminology mixed up, it is that you can definitely use this framework all the individuals within your client even if we focus on the contact person.

You might have already heard people say "I'm very Red" or "he is so Green". Now, this isn't a weird colour fetish but an insightful test known as the Insights Discovery Personality test (among other names, for some reason everyone calls it something different). We digress, whatever you call this colour test it will tell you a lot about someone's leadership and relationship style. It looks at people's attitudes (whether they are more introverted or extroverted) and their rationality (whether they think or feel more when making decisions). Using this, it divides individuals into four overarching colours:

- Red
- Yellow

- Green
- Blue

Each colour has a different approach, and not one colour is good or bad.

No one is entirely one colour, they are usually a mix of two and in some cases three. In fact, their colour might even change depending on the situation, especially in stressful scenarios. That said, most people tend to be more of one colour than the rest hence those people that say "I'm very Red" (also such a Red thing to say). Their primary colour reflects in their way of working. Take a Red person, they may be demanding, but they are also incredibly driven and great at getting things done. Whilst a Green person tends to be more relaxed and patient, they rarely give feedback which can make it difficult for you to improve.

Your client's good sides

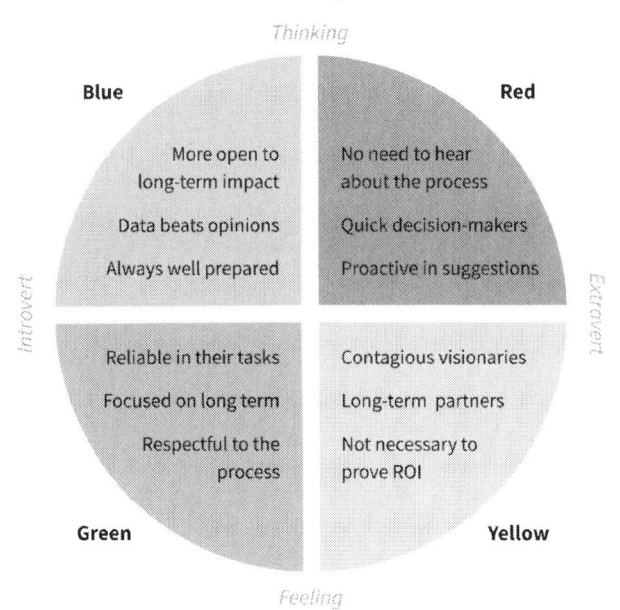

Thinking

Blue
- More open to long-term impact
- Data beats opinions
- Always well prepared

Red
- No need to hear about the process
- Quick decision-makers
- Proactive in suggestions

Introvert — *Extrovert*

Green
- Reliable in their tasks
- Focused on long term
- Respectful to the process

Yellow
- Contagious visionaries
- Long-term partners
- Not necessary to prove ROI

Feeling

Your client's ~~bad~~ could-be-better sides

Thinking

Blue
- Be prepared for follow-up questions
- Don't just take a leap
- Overthink/Over-analyze

Red
- Priorities can change quite sudden
- Undervalue process
- Deadline is 'Yesterday'

Introvert — *Extrovert*

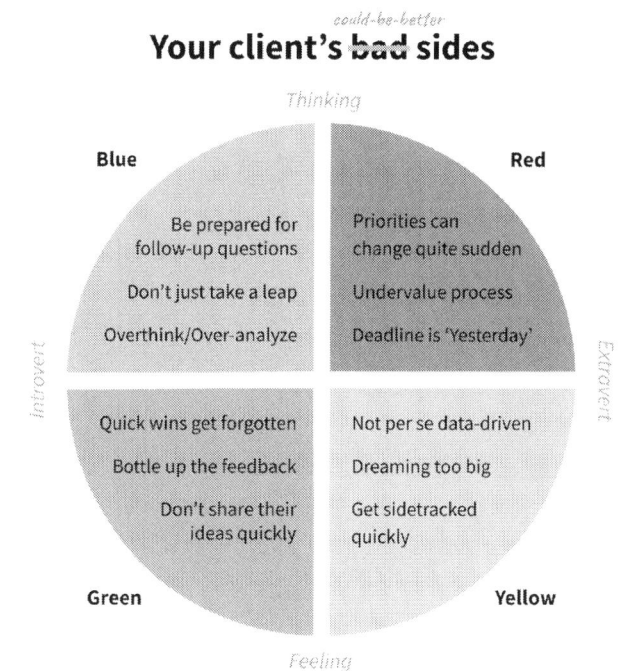

Green
- Quick wins get forgotten
- Bottle up the feedback
- Don't share their ideas quickly

Yellow
- Not per se data-driven
- Dreaming too big
- Get sidetracked quickly

Feeling

Knowing and understanding what your client's dominant colour is can be beneficial so you can then adjust your way of working to suit them. That does not mean being something, or some colour, that you are not, always remember the principle Be Real. Instead, it is about appreciating their needs and preferred way of communicating.

> **Time for Action**
>
> Ideally, you would ask your contact person to fill in the Insights Discovery Personality Test, but that might be a tad awkward. Luckily we have an alternative: take the test yourself. If you work at an agency, ask colleagues to take it too. It's 100% free.
>
> The reason that we recommend this is that it will give you a reference point. As we started learning more about the differences in colours, it became almost a game for us as consultants. You begin to think about and realise what your previous clients were. You'll try to figure it out with new potential clients too. One of us asked a potential client when they wanted something done and were informed "yesterday". All that goes through your mind, once you know the framework, is "Code Red, Code Red, I repeat".
>
> Keep your colour(s) in mind when reading the personalities that follow. You may notice that your most prominent colour isn't completely accurate, which is good because it never is. The idea is to give you an indication of what motivates you and your contact person, and not to place them into a specific box.
>
> In the resources section, we also include a link for you to do the test yourself: growinghappyclients.com/resources.

We will start by explaining how to identify your client's colour. Next, we will dive into essential tips for dealing with the various personalities. Finally, we will cover each personality type per colour and explain both the advantages and disadvantages of each type as well as how best to deal with a Red / Yellow / Green / Blue client. Spoiler alert, you'll even get a cheatsheet.

Again, we are not saying you can fit every client into a box, as every client is unique. Instead, this is a framework to understand better a significant part of how they work.

3.2 Identify your client's colour

The first step is to identify your client's colour. You could bluntly ask "You are definitely Blue, right?" and receive a very puzzled look in return, or hand them a quiz to fill out immediately. Neither option is ideal, particularly when you're just getting to know someone. Luckily, there are a few smoother ways to do this, such as:

1. **Ask your client what their fears are about the new collaboration.** Try to find out what they are scared of, e.g. too much focus on building the foundations rather than results or no insight into the data. This can help you to relate it to their primary colour by using the upcoming explanation of each colour.
2. **Listen to the type of words they use.** If they are always talking about the data, they are probably Blue. In contrast, someone who favours the softer side, the involved people and collaborators, will likely be Green.
3. **Look at their way of preparing for meetings.** A Blue will be super prepared whilst a Yellow will be less so and instead excited to talk about the bigger picture.
4. **Ask what they hope to get from the growth hacking project.** Based on their answer, you can identify their colour, for example, a Yellow will be focused on the long-term vision whilst the Blue more on working from data.

52 Different Types of Personalities of Clients

We have set up a little overview to help you figure out what colour they are based on how they communicate, prepare for meetings and what they hope to get out of the collaboration:

Identify your client's color

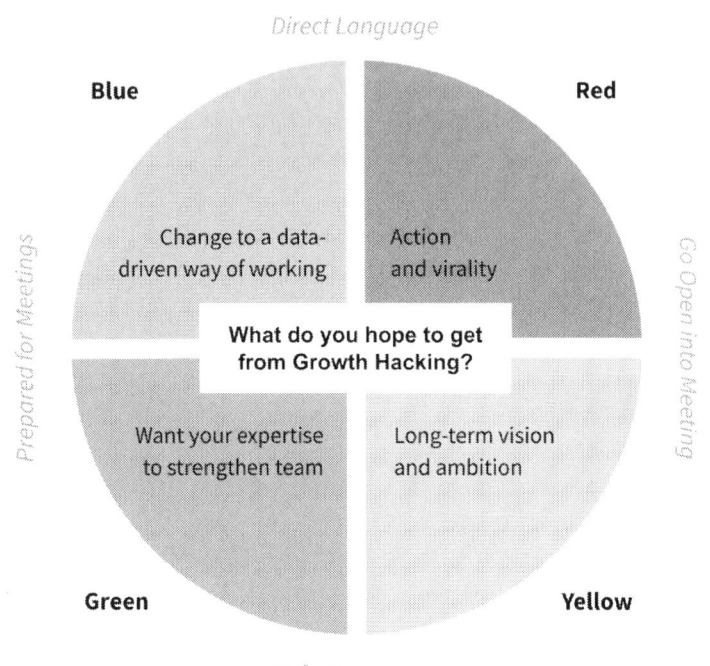

Direct Language

Blue — Change to a data-driven way of working

Red — Action and virality

Prepared for Meetings

What do you hope to get from Growth Hacking?

Go Open into Meeting

Green — Want your expertise to strengthen team

Yellow — Long-term vision and ambition

Softer Language

How they communicate will hint towards what their dominant colour is. Once you start to understand what colour they might be, you can begin to adjust your approach accordingly.

3.3 How to deal with the colours

The first step is always understanding their colours, the good and the bad. We will discuss that in more depth in a second, to help you know each colour as well as specific actions. There is some general advice we'd like to cover first about dealing with the various colours:

1. **Counter their behaviour with the opposite colour.** A good collaboration is always a balance between all of the colours rather than too much of one colour. It can be easy to assume someone who is Red wants to hear only about the results and move forward. Imagine a growth hacking strategy that is focused solely on moving forward and results (Red), that Red person might not place enough weight on ensuring the team feels a part of the success and are appreciated (Green). This would bring in less long-term results in the end, so it is crucial not only to respect what they want but also sneak in what the project needs.
2. **Speak in their language.** This makes communication far smoother. A Yellow likes to talk big picture whilst a Blue likes to communicate with data. This may seem like a contradiction to the previous point of countering their behaviour; we promise it isn't. We are not suggesting you forget the Blue side but instead consider how you bring your point across as it is much easier to do this using their language.
3. **Be aware of their flaws.** You can secure the project's future if you already know the pitfalls and act accordingly. Take a Green client, who will rarely give feedback; they may be annoyed or upset about something for weeks before you find out. If you know your client is Green, you can work extra hard on making sure they feel comfortable enough to provide feedback.

Now it's time to dive deeper into each colour, the advantages and disadvantages of each type, as well as practical tips for successfully working together.

3.4 Red: Goal-Oriented Clients

The colour red usually signifies stop or error. We see red daily with red traffic lights, warning us to halt. Ironically this type of person is the complete opposite. They are extremely goal-oriented, ready to go-go-go and get the results they want, this means:

1. **They are quick decision-makers.** They will not think endlessly and hesitate about every tiny decision.
2. You don't have to explain much, just skip the long explanations and get on with it. They don't want to hear much about the process, only the results.
3. **You don't have to come up with all the ideas yourself.** They already know what they want and will communicate this to you. They may also have ideas that they want to test.

If you need to create results fast, a Red client will be your fuel. However, as with everything, there are downsides too:

1. **They are quite impatient.** To the question Like the client we mentioned earlier, who wanted the task done "yesterday", a Red has no time to waste, so neither do you.
2. **They are quick to change their mind.** Today the Red client want A, tomorrow it will be B, and maybe next week it will be C.
3. **They may undervalue the process or getting the basics in place.** For example, they may see little to no value in a robust measurement setup or extensive pre-research. Get to the chase already, where are the results? This can make it harder to explain why specific actions take

longer, especially as they will see little to no value in work in progress.

This last one can be especially tricky when the client's infrastructure is not where it should be. Growth without the basics is near impossible. You will need to guide them actively in seeing how the process leads to the end goal.

When dealing with Reds, the following approaches can be beneficial:

1. **Always be proactive.** Have a plan and speak up about what that plan is; this is how you speak their language. Reds already know what they want and just want to see how it will happen. They like to see someone who is also ready to take action.
2. **Use action-focused language.** "To get there, we'll need to do this first…", show Red clients how you will get there and what you will need to do to reach the destination.
3. **Be direct in your feedback.** Reds don't want to "beat about the bush" instead, they want to get it done and move on. Sugar-coating (which is rarely a good idea) is a big no-no with a Red.
4. **Don't slip into the "Yes sir/madam".** It is easy when someone is so forthcoming to move into saying yes to everything, especially if you are shyer or less confident. You may think you are doing what Red clients want, but it will only irritate them over time. They want someone proactive and forward-minded like them. They don't mind pushback so long as it is thought through and still focused on getting more results.
5. **Pull them back to the process board.** Reds have their eye on the goal and don't always see what's necessary to get there. If you don't tell them, they won't understand why it took you so long. As much as they hate the process, you do have to show them why it is necessary. Just be sure always

to relate the process to the end goal, "We will take some extra time here, but that will bring us faster/better results in the future. The alternative of not doing this would impact the results".
6. **Ask them about their goals, never about their process**. That said, they expect you to figure out the process. They know where they want to go, but often don't want to know what needs to happen on the way there. So you should take that weight of arranging the process based on what their goal is instead of expecting them to arrange it.

The soft approach is not the right one for a Red client; instead, focus on the principles of Be Focused and Be Bold.

3.5 Yellow: Visionary Clients

They are the big thinkers of the world, the dreamers; they see what is possible and are excited to go there. When you listen to a Yellow individual talk, you will almost see the shiny future they paint before you, that is how real they make it. Your job with a Yellow client is to break that vision up into manageable actionable chunks. What makes Yellow clients enjoyable to work with is the following:

1. **They think big, so you rarely need to prove anything.** It's not weird for Yellow Clients to go all-in or take a risk, even though you haven't fully shown the potential/ROI of an idea. It is often easy to convince Yellow clients of long-term strategies such as content marketing.
2. **They are full of enthusiasm.** Nothing beats an enthusiastic client; enthusiasm is contagious after all. They will be thrilled about your ideas and input, and you can have endless conversations about all the possible opportunities.

3. **They want to work together to the goal.** Yellow clients want to work together to achieve the goals meaning they value the collaboration side of it all. Yellows won't expect you to do all of the work and brainstorming either, as they are happy to work as a team.

Now before you put up a sign saying "Looking for clients with Yellow personality type", we should keep things realistic and present both sides of this argument. Yellow clients may seem ideal, but be sure to keep in mind the flip side:

1. **They get side-tracked pretty quickly.** Yellows are visionaries, so if they 'see' something in the future, they want to make that happen right now... despite all the things that you have been discussing the last few months. You will need to keep them on track continually.
2. **They might dream too big to make it happen.** A big vision is terrific, but it needs to be realistic and relevant to the current size of the company. They may want to go all-in even though you are not sure yet if that is the right direction.

So now you know the good and bad of working with a Yellow, and you can face it head-on. But exactly how do you best collaborate with a Yellow? Don't worry; it isn't just by playing the realistic 'party pooper' the entire time. Instead, follow these simple steps to stay on track with your Yellow client:

1. **Give them a strict process to be creative within.** Try to give Yellow clients limits to work within, so they don't get side-tracked but can still be creative. For example, when brainstorming, be specific about the topic and the time they have. Don't brainstorm about 'content' and end up going down one rabbit hole after another. Instead, you could brainstorm what content could improve brand awareness among their target audience. If you are working

out the strategy, stick to frameworks. You could use a Strategyzer canvas when discussing strategy (just Google "Strategyzer canvas" to see the various templates, we've also linked the Strategyzer books in the extra resources: growinghappyclients.com/resources). That way, you only need to fill in the template by checking those boxes instead of getting side-tracked and ending up in unimportant discussions.
2. **Dream big, but act small.** These clients tend to go too big because of their visionary ideas, so make sure to keep things actionable. Break up action points into mini-steps: what is the smallest way you could test a new hypothesis?
3. **Don't bore them too much with in-depth analysis.** Yellow Clients are happy with enjoying the win; they don't need to understand the rationale behind success. Cut corners by keeping the statistical significance and analyses for the Blues.
4. **Always keep it data-driven.** These clients get distracted quickly by shiny new things, so you need to pull them back to your prioritised backlog. Try to make the prioritisation-framework as objective as possible by asking clear, data-driven questions. When discussing the potential of an idea, don't ask "What could this idea bring us?". Instead ask questions such as: "Does any hard or soft data show that this is a real bottleneck to focus on right now?", "How many people do we expect to reach with this?" or "Is this very different to the way that we solve this right now?".

It's all about the principles Be Real and Be Open. Help them feel like they are taking steps towards the dream… whilst you sneak in the structure and keep it all realistic. Be their reins but not their stop sign.

3.6 Green: Process-Oriented Clients

And now we move over to the left side of the chart, the more introverted side, starting with Greens. We mentioned that Greens might seem very relaxed and straightforward to work with as clients, after all:

1. **They are often people-pleasers.** So if you ask them to deliver something, they will. You can rely on a Green client.
2. **They try to understand the process behind it all.** Green clients do their best to understand your process in-depth and adjust to it. The process interests them (finally a process fan!).
3. **They are focused on the long-term.** Greens are more focused on long-term success & a friendly collaboration. They won't mind some short-term failures; that's a part of it.

Being so easygoing may lead you to think the project will seem like a breeze, but please don't get too comfortable. The silence could be a good thing, or it could be a lack of speaking up. With Greens, it is crucial to keep the following in mind:

1. **They rarely give feedback.** Since Green clients value the process and people so much, they are unlikely to critique you. They genuinely don't want to hurt your feelings or damage the relationship. The danger in this is that if they're dissatisfied, they won't tell you... until the very last moment when they need to cancel the contract. Which obviously is too late for you to fix it.
2. **They won't be quick to speak up with their ideas.** They don't want to overpower others, and so they won't share their opinions in fear of limiting your creativity or expertise. They may need to be pushed to share their thoughts.

3. **Their focus on long-term might side-track the project of quick, short-term goals.** Long-term actions are usually what results in more significant impact. However, only focusing on the long-term might distract from hitting immediate, short-term goals. Greens can be patient around that, but their bosses might not be. You will need to ensure that potential short-term wins don't end up forgotten.

Unlike Reds, a softer approach can work well here. Actually, Reds and Greens often clash because they have such different ways of working. With Greens, it's all about getting an open and frequent dialogue going. Critical tips for working with a Green are:

1. **Talk fears.** Talk about what they fear about this project early on in the relationship. Make this an open topic to encourage them to share what they feel.
2. **Keep them involved.** Always be proactive, ask them for their ideas/opinions/thoughts. They won't speak up by themselves.
3. **Learn how to give emotionally sensitive feedback.** Green Clients put a lot of value on the relationship so how you give feedback is vital. Don't lose their trust in your two-way collaboration by giving too harsh or super direct feedback.
4. **Show them the long-term, full impact that the project is having.** Green clients also see a lot of value in intangible outcomes so actively share them. They are interested in improvements such as trained employees, improved customer happiness and increased experiment speed. So mention these elements regularly in meetings. Where possible, try to add an anecdote (e.g. what did a customer say) to engage them and take them through the overall story.

5. **Keep both of you aware of the importance of short-term goals and deliverables.** You will need to be the one that ensures short-term improvements also end up in the planning.
6. **Help them to give push back internally.** Setting priorities means saying 'no' to other lower priorities. Yet, saying 'no' also means possibly hurting other people, which is very hard for Greens. Help guide them in finding the balance of being considerate but focused.

With Greens, it's essential to Be Them and Be Focused. Understand their struggles and help them along the way to balance both the short and long-term.

3.7 Blue: Researcher Clients

Well, hello, fellow data lover! Ready for some nerdy discussions? Blue clients love the numbers and understanding the whole process. They are super involved in the data side; this means:

1. **Numbers persuade them.** Data speaks for itself. They won't bring in their own opinions and assumptions to overrule proven results as data stands central for them.
2. **They naturally have their data in order.** They know their CLTV, CAC and CR's by heart, which will save you a lot of time in working this all out in the beginning.
3. **They think ahead, so they quickly see the long-term value.** This makes your potential impact a lot bigger if you can talk about the long-term ROI of your experiments/learnings. Show them the numbers, and they will go for the long-term improvements.

It might sound lovely to have someone who gets and appreciates the data, finally! A dream come true. So come on, what is the catch this time? Ok, there are a few to your fellow data nerd:

1. **They will always ask follow-up questions**. They want to deep dive into your data analysis to a painful extent which may slow down the overall process. You may have to do far more in-depth reports than you usually do and also walk them through this. Also, don't be surprised if they want to double-check your calculations during a meeting: "Are you sure that you took X and Y into account?".
2. **They tend to be risk averse.** Blue clients might decline ideas if you can't prove them making improvements such as "Work on the overall brand" hard to sell.
3. **They might overthink/over-analyse situations.** They want to have things done correctly, and that way, they might put perfection over speed.

So how do you find the right balance between their strengths and weaknesses? You can do this by keeping the following in mind:

1. **Make sure to have your numbers ready.** When your Blue client asks more in-depth analytical questions, have the answer available. If possible, consider taking an extra team member with you to meetings. Then when detailed questions get asked during the session, you can continue the meeting whilst the other person can look into it. That way, you can get through the meeting topics in time and avoid having unnecessarily long meetings. Do that or make sure you have an extensive appendix/details of the analyses in your slides at hand.
2. **Share your planning.** Blue clients value 'being organised' as a critical success factor, so show your most organised self to them. Consider putting some extra time in preparing a solid overview of what you want to do. The spare time you spend on this will benefit you in terms of more trust and speed later.
3. **Remind them of the 80/20 rule.** Blues tend to be perfectionists, which can slow down your progress. In

reality, you'll often grow a lot faster with MVP-level work versus robust, perfect-looking work. So feel free to challenge them if that extra step is vital in their language: "How big would the downside of this be if we go live with an 8/10 instead of a 9/10?". But get ready to give a well-thought-out answer, because as we said: they always come prepared, so you need to be prepared as well.

If you are prepared, data-driven and organised, you can manage Blue clients with ease. If we look back at the principles then Be Open is critical, they want to be walked through the process. Next to that Be Them, try to understand what data they need to be comfortable.

3.8 The Client Colour Cheatsheet

To make it easier to remember the tips for each client type, we've compiled it all in one cheatsheet to show the key points we covered per client. You can download it at: growinghappyclients.com/resources.

With your current clients (and your future one's!) grab this cheatsheet and try to figure out which type they might. See how you can further take into consideration their needs by understanding their way of working.

During the last few chapters, we've talked extensively about getting into the head of your client and your contact person. What type of growth hackers would we be if we didn't appreciate customer insights in driving success? You've learnt about why companies hire growth hackers as well as the drivers and concerns of your contact person. You've learnt the four colours that represent different types of clients. You understand the client and your contact person. What more could we possibly want to share before we kickoff walking through the project from A-Z? The risks and pitfalls. This is a huge challenge for new growth hackers: how do you prevent Captain Hindsight from going "I should have realised that all these different stakeholders would be an issue." or "Why didn't I push to improve the measurement setup?". Before you get stuck in and excited about a new project, let's make sure you understand which risks to watch out for so that you can tell Captain Hindsight to shut up once and for all.

> **Key Takeaway**
>
> Now you already have the cheatsheet to remember the various elements of each colour. So in this takeaway, we want to remind you of the biggest mistake you could make with each colour:
>
> 1. **Red.** It is not giving enough pushback on deadlines or ideas that wouldn't move the needle.
> 2. **Yellow.** Getting so caught up in the big picture that we underestimated the importance of the short-term results for the rest of the organisation.
> 3. **Green.** Not coaching them enough in giving feedback leading to them bottling it up and not sharing until it was too late.
> 4. **Blue.** Not pushing for the 80-20 rule and getting caught up in endless analysis and data reporting as a result.
>
> These were not their flaws but ours in how we handled the situations.

CHAPTER 4

Watching Out for Risks and Pitfalls

4.1 Let's keep it realistic

By now, you've probably noticed that we are realists through and through. We are not going to pretend that your client is perfect, neither are you, and neither are we. We can create a whole beautiful theory of how things should be and should go, "Follow this process and your clients will love you!". But that, quite frankly, would be naive and utterly unhelpful; it is better to be realistic and honest about the type of challenges you might face. Better to help you to be prepared for them before they occur. Which is why we are covering the risks and pitfalls early on in this book. What issues are actually risks? How do you know if something is an issue?

That is where our experience comes in handy. We always carry out a post-project analysis to identify issues, when they occurred and what signs we missed that should have told us trouble was brewing. What were the signs? We will summarise below the critical warning signs for future project challenges allowing you to be ahead of the game when they occur and know what to do. We've divided them into orange and red. It is like a traffic light, where hopefully you know that orange means "Hey, you should slow down" and red means "Stop right now".

4.2 Orange traffic lights to slow down for

Whilst orange traffic lights aren't showstoppers they do get in your way. They come in many forms from too many stakeholders to growth being just a side project. So you need to know what they are and how to solve them best. The *how* we will go through in detail during Section 4: Ups and Downs. For now, we will focus on showing the potential risks and pitfalls at a high level, so you know how to recognise them. As well as covering what the exact risks are if they occur:

1. Too many focus points, too much choice

Definitely one of the most common issues we see. Clients have started with growth hacking; they are beyond eager. Like children in a candy shop, they're running through the rows of experimental delights, and they want to taste everything. But this doesn't sound like a bad thing, your client is excited, isn't that ideal? Not when you need to be the annoying parent who tells them they can only choose one or two sweets (focus points). You'll notice this is an issue when a client is struggling to set a One Metric that Matters. They may have many projects going on or want an extensive scope meaning you need to live up to the principle Be Focused. If you don't, you risk making very little progress on all fronts. Remember our darts analogy in the Five Core Principles chapter? Don't hesitate to put your foot down; they can choose two sweets and nothing more.

2. Too many stakeholders, too many opinions

Are you having meetings so big you need to book larger rooms? Is the number of individuals involved so high that you have to make a list to remember them all? Uh oh, these are telltale signs that there are too many stakeholders involved. This issue is common in large corporations or organisations with an overload of egos; lots of people who feel their say is critical. All those approvals slow down the pace through a constant discussion on how to approach experiments. Whilst some debate is healthy, don't forget the 80/20 principle with it. Next to that, it may be hard to set priorities because everyone sees their area as the priority, impacting focus. You'll need to set up simple approval structures (we will show you how). If not, then gaining speed will be challenging, and you risk the client feeling output is low.

3. Experiments are on the side

Sometimes growth is perceived as a side project, a little extra boost. You will notice this is the case when people don't show up to meetings (they had "other priorities" or were "too busy"). Everything feels a bit rushed, and you get warned not to use up too many resources. If you don't fix this, you risk your experiments not getting prioritised and results faltering. It is almost like a self-fulfilling prophecy. They think your project is not important and growth hacking won't work, so you end up unsuccessful. You want to ensure growth is not a project but *the* project.

4. Any slower and we'd be going backwards

Even though all of the previous issues impact speed, speed is that important that it receives its own point (and chapter). It can be about culture ("It has to be perfect when it goes live") or even legacy ("that will take ages to change"). Whenever you see that the first experiments take ages to go live, it is crucial to dissect the cause. Speed is a competitive advantage that your client needs.

5. Silos with big walls

Every department has been trudging along, doing their own thing, and a new cross-functional growth team will not magically solve that. You know this is an issue when this is the first meeting that everyone is together or there are different conflicting KPIs. Even worse: that departments talk badly about one another the moment the other is gone, it is like high school all over again. Silos can impact the effectiveness of working together as one team. It can also make giving priorities to the right areas challenging.

Each of these orange issues will receive an own chapter later on. For now, you must know that they don't have to be deal-breakers but that you do need to deal with them early on in the collaboration. You might need to slow down at first to solve them so that you can speed off the moment the traffic light is green again.

4.3 Red traffic lights to stop for

Note we say stop in the title of this section, you need to really pause to tackle them. Whilst red traffic lights suck (there is no other way to put it) they don't have to be the end of it. If you keep an open dialogue and work together with your clients, many can be solved. But the same cannot be said for actual traffic lights. Here are some of the red traffic lights we see the most often:

1. Fixed mindset

Let's rip off the bandaid and start with the worst: a fixed mindset. A mindset wherein failure is terrible, feedback is not appreciated, and things just are the way they are. You will notice this when there are always arguments for why certain things shouldn't be changed. Again, don't confuse this with a healthy dialogue about ideas. The difference is that the first is not the result of actual data but purely gut feelings or opinions with phrases like "I don't think we should do this, I know that A/B testing will not bring us results". Following that, you may also notice adverse reactions to the first lost experiment. The worst is if a key stakeholder or your contact person has a fixed mindset, but luckily this is rarely the case. They didn't get to where they are now through a fixed mindset. More often (and more manageable) is that it is one or two individuals in the team. This red flag is so crucial that it will have an entire chapter dedicated to it.

2. A lack of Product-Market Fit (PMF)

Imagine you have a bucket that has holes. When you try to fill it with water, it will be far slower and more challenging than a bucket with smaller or fewer holes. Companies sadly focus on filling the bucket rather than fixing the holes. If a company has not tested for PMF, does not have PMF or has low retention, then this will kill your growth. You need first to double-check their PMF. In a small company, this might be the traditional Sean Ellis test. For a larger company, it may be more analysis of cohorts and retention rates as well as reasons for churn. If they lack Product-Market Fit or struggle with retention, you will need to steer them away from acquisition. That will be a waste of budget, and both their time and yours. You need to see if they are open to working on improving their PMF. Often what helps is having your client join interviews with the end customer to hear this from their perspective.

3. Low growth knowledge on their side

Clients have hired you for your skills and experience, meaning that for your area of expertise, there will always be a knowledge gap. However, when the difference grows too large, e.g. they are not able to pick up anything themselves, or you spend hours explaining what you are doing, this is a risk. An example is a client we had with very ambitious growth goals of increasing revenue by 50% per month yet; we ended up rewriting every piece of copy written for the website and email. Every single design and ad needed triple checking. This lack of knowledge slows down the speed and means everything requires far more hours to go live. In such cases, you either need to focus on teaching, helping them bring in additional knowledgeable individuals or arranging additional hours to pick up the extra work.

4. Missing people in the team setup

Sometimes there is no specific individual for an area within the organisation, usually the case with smaller clients. Or there is, but there are no resources available. The lack of resources could be for development, design or even copywriting. Depending on the focus area of your project, this may or may not have a significant impact on which experiments you can set up. There either needs to be a change of focus (assuming there is another area you can drive equal impact) or you either hire or outsource the required work.

5. Terrible measurement setup

Measurement seems to end up chaotic with some organisations having a considerable amount of legacy in the structure, or unable to measure crucial elements. Another major one is that they want a OMTM on end customers but that last part of the funnel is not yet measurable, making it hard for you to show the real impact of your work. The solution for this is all about determining the 80/20 in measuring. If you try to get it perfect immediately, it will cost too much time and momentum, frustrating both you and the client. Instead, see what the must-haves are. What do you need to be able to measure to base your decisions on data? If this is not possible, see if there are workarounds or proxies you can use. For example: can you send the UTM as a hidden field to the CRM system? Can you use a proxy, e.g. 15% will become customers? Not an ideal or a long-term solution but allows you to move forward whilst fixing the setup. The greater risk is if your client doesn't value investments in setting up measurement correctly. You should then consider whether it is worthwhile continuing the collaboration.

6. No customer insights or research

This applies when you ask at the beginning for the customer research but hear there is little to none available. Or yes, there are personas but we made them two years ago and never use them. No customer insights are a red traffic light because it is likely that a lot has been done based on assumptions. Lack of research should make you very sceptical of whether the client has Product-Market Fit. The first step to solving this is for you to start devouring customer reviews if they are available as they will give you a great insight into the current state: are there raving fans? What is the most common feedback or issue? Start with any form of data you can get your hands-on industry data, social media comments, competitor reviews. From there, it is time to start gathering customer insights, ideally through interviews. The lack of customer insights is only a risk if they aren't open to you spending time gathering extra insights.

Finding and understanding orange and red traffic lights can be tricky. That is why we want to talk about an additional skill that will help you before moving on to dealing with the specific orange and red traffic lights. This skill may seem simple, but it is so powerful: asking the right questions.

4.4 Finding the real underlying reasons

It starts with the basics: just ask questions. Yet, it's not about asking them in the first place; it's about the way you ask those questions. It is all about the 'how' as this will significantly influence the information you receive. That information, in turn, may potentially affect your end success. They say great leaders ask great questions, but we would like to rephrase that:

> Great consultants ask great questions

Why is that? Well, that's because great questions can help you uncover the real reasons behind actions, the actual causes. They get your clients thinking, triggering them to realise what is needed or missing to be successful.

Too often, when consultants ask a question about what can and can't be done, they accept the first answer, i.e. it can't be done. Well that's it then, better find a new focus point. Or when you ask if all those stakeholders really need to be involved, yup they do, well I guess I'd better make a list of them all and start checking off next year's experiments. But that isn't the case, that isn't the end of it.

It's not that your client is explicitly lying to you; they honestly believe that it is not possible or realistic. They have their context and framework shaped by time and the organisation. Yet, when you push further and ask more profound questions, you start to find the real reason beneath it all. You can only open a client to possibilities once you discover the underlying cause and understand it better. Never accept a 'no' for face value, always try to dive one step deeper.

Realise that every person in this world can only judge the world based on what they know of it. That goes for our clients and us: we might not have even known that their industry existed before we heard about their business, whilst our clients can't judge as effectively as we can how difficult a task is or how quickly it can be done. They are probably not aware of all kinds of workaround that you've already experienced, and maybe they would scope things differently if they heard about your experiences and the nifty tools you work with. Share your view of this world with them, and suddenly you'll be able to talk to them on a new level.

Asking great questions is a valuable skill that will help you throughout your entire collaboration with a client. Starting with using that skill to identify risks and pitfalls as well as getting the right information to solve them.

So how do you ask great questions? Let's start with the obvious: 'Yes or No' questions are a no-go — especially when dealing with challenging issues or changes you want to make. Of course, you could ask "Are you open to adjusting the landing page?", they respond "no" to which you ask why. However, that first "no" can be demotivating for you, even subconsciously. It also sets them in the mindset that it can't be done. Try to ask questions that dig deeper instead such as "What are potential challenges we could face if we change the landing page?" or "What changes have you made in the past to the landing page?".

The other main issue we see is steering questions. Consultants often try to guide their clients to do what they want. Don't do that! Be Real and Be Open instead. Try to avoid questions and statements that start with phrases like the following:

- "It is obvious that it would be better if we..."
- "Don't you agree that..."
- "I feel strongly that we should do... do you agree?"

One of us was once in a meeting where an individual said: "it would be stupid of you to think that way", talk about controlling opinions. Perhaps steering the conversation works in the short-term, but in the long run, it will ruin the trust. You want to know what your client thinks, not what you want them to think.

Now those are two things to avoid, but what should you do to come up with great questions? These are three of our favourite techniques:

1. Focus on the end goal

Too often, people get into an argument about the potential solution even though they both align on the end goal. You both have the same destination in mind, so fixated on that aspect. Remind both your client and yourself what the end goal is. Keeping this aspiration in mind opens up the dialogue to alternative solutions. Take the example we used earlier of adjusting the landing page, what if you had said: "Okay, it is difficult to adjust the layout of the landing page. What are other ways we could improve the number of sign ups?". Now the focus is on the number of sign ups again, not the landing page.

2. Use the ladder technique

The ladder technique is a common interview technique that focuses on diving deeper. You may have used it for user interviews before; it is just as suitable for your client as well. The idea is that instead of taking the first answer, you ask the *what* or *why* behind it to keep diving deeper and deeper. Remember how as a kid, you would keep asking your parents "Why?" to every answer they gave—time to play that Why game again. So if the client says they don't think CRO is essential right now you should ask "Why do you feel it is not important?" and "What do you see as CRO?". They explain that they see it as optimising the whole customer journey for success (if they say testing different button colours, you have a whole other problem on your hands). They tell us that they did a few tests that weren't successful. So we shoot back with "Why do you believe those tests were not winners?". By diving deeper each time you understand the client a little more, and see what the actual reasons are.

3. Offer alternatives

Your client may not be a fan of the first 2-3 ideas you offer, that is okay; it's merely brainstorming. You don't execute every idea you come up with; you look for the best ones. Try to understand what their concerns are and keep looking at the problem from different angles:

"Maybe we can test a Linkedin lead ad instead and send users there?"

"Perhaps we could start with improving the copy on the landing page and see if that improves the signups?"

Your client will appreciate your creativity. They will also understand that you are not pressuring them to select the only option. Often doing this will also encourage them to start thinking and come up with suggestions too. Giving alternatives is far more productive than asking about a single idea; sometimes, you even end up back at the first idea, after all. Additionally, you have the added possibility of the Decoy Effect, offering alternatives that you know your client won't choose to help make them happier with the original option. It takes seeing the other options for your client to realise that the first option is quite an attractive one.

So consider this for your client engagements. If your client says no or isn't giving you the information, you seek, then how can you better ask questions? How can you dive deeper to understand what is needed?

Now that you've managed to understand what is going on, it is time to consider how to deal with the orange or red flag you've identified.

4.5 How do you deal with orange and red traffic lights?

Don't panic if you notice one of the above; at least 60-70% of our clients have had one or more traffic lights. In most cases, we managed to make it work, especially when we tackled them early on. As we said, no one is perfect.

When haven't we been able to solve it? When there has been no room for a dialogue about it with no possibility of working together to solve it. Suppose you don't have the trust of your client even to discuss it, then matters become difficult, but let's hope that is not the case here. So let's walk through five concrete steps to work on orange and red traffic lights:

Step 1: Find the right timing

You might be sharp and have already spotted an orange or red flag in the first minute of the conversation. Whilst you should not gloss over it, don't be too quick to bring it up. Mention you would like to look into it (e.g. the measurement setup) as it is crucial and discuss it thoroughly later. Doing this gives you the time to firstly start building trust with your client, and additionally to dive deeper and look into potential solutions. Try to ask as many questions as possible to understand the dynamics of the situation. Say there is a Silos issue, ask who sets the targets? Once you have done that you should plan one-on-one time with your contact person to walk through it all. Never bring up an orange or red traffic light in a meeting with everyone present. Firstly talk to your contact person and only then extend the conversation to the full team, if relevant.

Step 2: Start looking for workarounds

Clients hate having a problem brought to them; they hired you in to solve things. So whenever you spot a risk, consider potential solutions first. For example, if there are missing people in the team: did you notice someone else in the group who can take it over? Do you know external individuals who you could hire to solve it? Your contact person may have a solution, but they haven't mentioned it yet, such as "Yes we are missing a designer, but we have a new one starting in two weeks". Either way, it is still beneficial to have a backup plan ready.

Step 3: Let your account manager know (only relevant for agencies with account managers)

If you work for an agency, rather than as a freelancer, make sure to notify your account manager. We've often seen junior team members who felt like they needed to solve all of it on their own, while this is what account managers are specifically here for. They are the ones who sold the project to the client and are there to keep the client happy. They need to know if there are risks in the project and can likely help you in dealing with the challenge.

Step 4: Open a dialogue about it one-on-one

Once you've prepared potential solutions, it is time to talk. Depending on how severe the issue is, you might choose to ask the account manager to join as well. Make sure to keep the conversation open and honest, explaining how to solve it. Hold your client personality type in mind to determine your approach. Should you go in-depth, focus more on the results or be extra empathetic? Show your contact person that there are options, but also indicate which option you'd advise and why.

Step 5: Determine a long-term plan to improve it together

If all goes well, it's time to work out a short and long-term plan. Show what is needed; not only in the short-term but also in the long run. Let the client know what the implications are for the hours/investment in the project (if relevant). Make sure there is a clear step-by-step plan that you can refer to if the issue isn't improving or going as intended.

4.6 Should you end the collaboration?

This question is a tough one, but we feel it necessary to raise it. Right now, this is in terms of stopping early in this process, but much later (all the way in Chapter 34) we'll tackle when this question arises further down the line. Let's start with why this question is so difficult to answer.

The first reason is that far too often, consultants are made to feel like they have to 'take' certain things. The client is the queen/king, and we should respect their wishes or way of working. Yes, they are acting horribly, but they are paying for our time and ensuring we have an income.

The second reason is that it feels like a failure; it feels like you have failed to do your job when choosing to give up on a client. You couldn't grow them, and you didn't do everything you could to make the project a success.

The third reason is that financially, it may not be an option to stop, especially if you are a freelancer. This reason is very subjective, so if this is the cause, we cannot speak for you. But when it comes to the previous two concerns, we have an answer in mind: both reasons are both absolute bullshit :-).

When it comes to accepting whatever the client throws at you or whatever they want, you don't have to. That does not mean being arrogant, but instead Be Bold and show your client what is needed. You've heard of 'Mother knows best', well welcome to 'Consultant knows best'. Do they need to make culture/infrastructure improvements first? It is your responsibility as a consultant to indicate that. We have had talks with clients who came to us too early as they first needed to fix certain areas and appreciated our honesty in that. Maybe you can work together to solve it, but that depends on what the challenges are. You should never roll over and blindly do what they ask; this will only backfire because then you will have to work twice as hard for a situation that you are aware probably can't succeed. It's also a lose-lose situation, as you will ultimately get blamed for not mentioning the problem earlier on when offering it as a reason for failure.

Next to that, if your client is treating you horribly, you don't have to take it. Sadly, there are people out there who do not treat consultants and others well. In our careers, we've been lucky enough to only come across one or two each. We hope you never come across one. If you are an agency, we hope they put the team's happiness over that client and choose to kick them out. We have so much respect for agencies that dare to fire clients and believe that the best agencies always do. If you are an individual, we hope you have the financial possibility to say 'no'. The short-term financial gain is not worth this. Try to prevent this from happening by focusing on getting better clients rather than more.

Ward worked as a freelance growth hacker for many years knowing the discomfort of an unstable income that comes with being a freelancer. He has had to make the tough decision of saying goodbye to customers and wanted to share the following advice:

"From my experience, I've always seen my time working on my freelancer brand as most valuable. Of course, you need clients to pay the bills. But at the same time that I'd be working on one client,

I could also create a piece of content, a campaign or a lead magnet which could bring in five clients in the upcoming years. So for €100 paid by client A, I could also be ensuring €500 in the future from clients B, C, D, E and F. You need to be able to pay your bills, but know that that time spent on your work could be even more valuable.

Next to that, realise that most freelancers determine their hourly rate, based on the concept that they'd earn enough in eight months to sustain themselves for twelve months. This enables you to create a financial safety net to ensure that you have the financial freedom to turn down clients when you need to."

If you still aren't convinced by us maybe Craig Sullivan, a CRO Consultant, can do the trick:

> "If you fire your clients, it is a competitive advantage. They will go to your competitors and make them miserable instead." - Craig Sullivan

Reconsidering? We hope so.

Still, think it's a failure to turn down a client? We hope not. As a consultant, you have a particular span of control that involves all the areas that you can change/influence. Many consultants underestimate their span of control. Take a lack of development resources, is that outside of your span of control? Maybe, but you can probably convince your client to get extra development resources if you show them the benefits of it. You could use workarounds to require fewer development resources. If you've tried everything to solve a red or orange flag, then it would be a more significant failure to power on. That is just a waste of their resources and time. As the meme goes... ain't nobody got time for that. While you don't need everything to be perfect for growing, you do need the absolute basics in place. Then the only failure possible is a lack of communication.

We hope it doesn't come to the above. Ideally, you will have amazing clients and never need to use this advice, but just in case, you now know where to find it. When a challenge arises, you know how to press pause, or even stop when needed. We are now ready to start with the step-by-step process of a new client, to go from meta to reality. We will be commencing with your first contact moment; it is time to begin your project.

Key Takeaway

It is not a matter of if there will be a red or orange traffic light but rather what it will be. No organisation is perfect. Focus first on understanding which traffic light is present and the underlying reason. From there, be proactive and start looking for solutions. Don't be afraid to start a dialogue and equally don't be scared of it not working out. Some matches are not made to be, and that is better for both sides.

SECTION 2

Starting Off

CHAPTER 5

The First Contact With Your Client

5.1 A new client!

The moment has arrived; you have a new client. You feel a nervous excitement rushing through you, a new playground to explore and enjoy but also a new challenge. Unless you've sold the project yourself and not within an agency, you usually have no idea what to expect. It's like a first date; you're conscious of everything you say or do, even in the contact before the first meeting and at the same time, you're hyperalert of what they say or do. So how should you approach it all? How do you kickoff the project? We believe that covering the following will help you get off to a good start and prepare for the actual date:

1. Setting the scene
2. Understanding their growth
3. Getting ready to go

In this scenario, your first date is your official kickoff. We will walk through each of these moments in turn.

5.2 Setting the scene

The first crucial part is setting the stage to give them an idea of what they can expect from you. One way to do this is to ask for a quick 30 minute call to walk through the first steps, starting with the process:

"Hi Rachel, I just wanted to call to walk you through the next couple of weeks, so you know what to expect."

This shows you are there to lead them through the process with confidence. Also, it allows you to immediately avoid misalignment in expectations, walk the contact person through your way of working and the high-level planning for the coming weeks. From there on, you can start planning in the first meetings:

"I would also like to plan the kickoff and a few other meetings if that's ok? There we will go through the desired goal of the project in more depth. As well as the current challenges and way of working."

You want to find the balance between leading them and giving them plenty of room for their questions and input. Ask them questions such as:

"Are there any topics you'd like to put on the agenda of the kickoff?"
"Is there any other data or information you feel is important for me to have access to before we start?"
"Do you have any other questions?"

 If they aren't sure, then encourage them to send it over later:

"No worries, if you think of anything, feel free to email it to me later. I will be sending you an email anyways to summarise what we discussed and what the first steps are."

Don't see the above as a script to follow but rather an example. Find the right way of phrasing and walking through the process that suits you.
You want to try to plan in:

1. The kickoff
2. The North Star Metric session (more on this later)
3. When sprint/planning meetings will take place
4. Any other meetings you would like to have, e.g. meeting key stakeholders or maybe an informal one-on-one with your contact person

Do this as soon as possible; the last thing you want is that the project is off to a slow start because everyone is too busy to meet. It's useful to agree on a set time for your sprint/planning meetings. Also ask them how they prefer to communicate, e.g. do they prefer calling or emailing? Do they want a standard weekly one-on-one call next to the full team meetings? Ideally, you also want to agree on the main communication channels and where you will store documents. Will you use your communication channels or theirs? In which drive will files be kept? These sound like minor areas but are crucial to aligning and avoiding the project getting messy.

This should help to clarify the general way of working, when key meetings are and what they can expect. Then you can move on to questions around understanding their growth and getting them ready to go.

5.3 Understand their growth

In the beginning, you must try to understand the company and their growth as much as possible. Thus, your conversation continues:

"I also have a few high-level questions that I wanted to talk through with you now. These are to try and understand what data you already have. That way, we can ensure we hit the ground running and start faster."

There is specific data that you need to know if the company already has; these include:

1. Who is their target audience?
2. What research have they already done around this?
3. Is there any other data that would be good to look at?
4. Have they got an overview of the current customer journey?
5. Which tools do they use?

We highly recommend asking them to send over the research they already have on their target audience. Requesting this has double benefits. Not only do you get insights, but you can also immediately gage their current maturity. Seeing how up to date this is and how it is structured can tell you a lot. Clients who say "Oh we have these personas we made two years ago, but we don't use them", are not actively using customer research. A lack of up to date user research will make getting new data crucial in the beginning. You may choose to cover some of these questions again in the kickoff with the various stakeholders present as discrepancies in answers tell you a lot too.

Next to that, you want to understand their growth:

6. Do they have an outline of their current growth strategy?
7. What have they already tried?
8. What is stopping their growth at the moment?
9. What's their biggest bottleneck?
10. Where do they feel there are potential improvements?
11. What big things, product or marketing related, are on the agenda that might have a significant impact on the project?

You will need to dive deeper into the data for this and discuss it extensively in the actual kickoff. Asking such questions is mainly to become aware of anything that can give you hints of where to place focus. We usually like to request this via the phone rather than email after talking a little bit. Some clients might get defensive or insecure if they don't have this, so doing this via a phone call allows you to comfort them if need be:

"No worries, I just wanted to check in case. We can also walk through what you are focusing on right now in the kickoff."

Now that you have a better idea of what is in place and a general direction of the project, it is time to get practical.

5.4 Getting them ready to go

The one thing that is always underestimated is getting access to tooling seeing as each tool has a different way of giving access. Even within the Google tool suite, there are differences - why Google, why? Add the fact that each client has a different set of rules or setup about providing access, and this part is always fun. Yes, that was maybe a bit too sarcastic. Don't be surprised if they aren't sure who is Admin or how giving access works that is all a part of it. You need to make sure that you calculate enough time to sort this out before the kickoff. Again, there are two essential benefits here.

The first is to get the hassle out of the way. The kickoff is a party, a celebration of your new collaboration. You want to get going and started, not do the equivalent of a boring background checklist on the first date. By having the access understood and sorted beforehand, it will be far easier to make the first steps after the kickoff. The client can then see that you are starting to make progress. Not only that, if there are issues with giving access (Facebook, it's almost always Facebook!), you can double-check that. You can reserve a bit of time at the end of the kickoff and help them figure out what is going on.

The second reason is to get a sneak preview of the setup and what is happening. Just like the customer research, it gives you clues as to the current status. Whilst you can't pull everything out without more context, it can give you the chance to do a quick check. Having a look into the tools will help you to know how much the focus on hygiene factors vs growth is. You might notice that nothing is measured or that they did not set up conversion tracking correctly. That suggests that you will need to focus more on solving that in the beginning.

The easiest thing to do is to have a standard email with explanations of how to provide access to all the tools. Consider this when writing out that email the first time, so that you can save it to reuse it in the future. Then you (or together with your team) can always copy and paste this template rather than explain it again each time.

Next to that, it can be handy to ask them to already think about a few key concepts that are often tough to answer on the spot. These are concepts such as the North Star Metric and Lifetime Value. We have listed the ones we find crucial below. We have also added some guiding questions per area to help them understand the concept. Feel free to utilise our list or adjust accordingly to your client.

> [I/We] would like to discuss a few areas in the kickoff as well as the following meetings. The following questions will help [me/us] to better understand [Company Name] and focus my/our actions accordingly. [I/We] don't expect you to send back a full answer to every question straight away, but if you could send over what you already have (or start

thinking about the following concepts) we can discuss it further in the upcoming meetings:

1. **North Star Metric (NSM). What** is the high-level goal we are striving to attain? What purpose guides every action? Ideally not in terms of revenue but rather something that reflects value for you and your end customers. If you are struggling to determine this, no worries, we will have a session to discuss it. In the meantime, an excellent guiding question is: What is the reason the company was started?
2. **The One Metric that Matters (OMTM).** What is the shorter-term goal we would like to achieve together in the coming 2-4 months? What is the biggest bottleneck(s) to solve?
3. **Lifetime Value.** What is the average value of a customer across their whole lifetime? Do you work with an overall average or different ones per customer segments?
4. **Cost of Acquisition.** What is the average cost of acquiring a new customer? Do you use an overall average or different ones per customer segments? Does the current cost match what you would like to strive for?
5. **AAARRR.** AAARRR stands for the various phases of the funnel: Awareness, Acquisition, Activation, Retention, Referral and Revenue. For each stage could you explain: what this stage looks like, how you measure it and where possible, the drop off rate.

Just see which parts you are already able to send over and if you have any questions, feel free to email me. The rest we can discuss or look into in the coming weeks.

The above is one part of your first email. Your email following up on all of the above should cover:

1. The agenda for the kickoff (asking if they have anything to add).
2. Key dates of various meetings.
3. The agreed way of working.
4. Data you would like them to send over, e.g. previous research.
5. Which tools you would like access to and how to provide access.
6. Starting questions for them to think about.

For your convenience, we have added a full template email to growinghappyclients.com/resources. Of course, it will vary a bit per engagement, but having such a template can save you time and hassle in the beginning. Remember this is just before your first date and first impressions count!

Time for Action

Now it's time to take what you have learnt and put it to action. Do this even if you don't have a new client starting soon, just take some time to do the following:

1. Make a list of everything you would need before starting. What things would you like to know in the beginning, but might not be easy to answer on the spot? What do you need during the process to do your job? Preparing this will help you look more organised, speed up your process throughout and will give you a lot more confidence in your way of working.

2. Set up an outline for the first call.
You don't want to script out that entire first call but take some time to consider what you would like to discuss in such a call. What is the goal of the call? What questions would you like to ask?

3. Set up an outline for the first email.
Write an outline for the first email, including the six areas we mentioned above. You will, of course, customise this email a bit per client but that way you'll have an outline ready to send. Feel free to use our template to get you started.

Even if you already have these set up or your agency does, review the processes, stay critical, the best processes are updated regularly.

Now it's time to kick things off with the kickoff.

Key Takeaway

That first contact gives you the first opportunity to start strong. Do this by walking your client through the process, communicating clearly and beginning to get everything in place for growth. The kickoff is much smoother when you don't have to worry about the nitty-gritty details like getting access to tools.

CHAPTER 6

The Kickoff

6.1 Why is the kickoff crucial?

The kickoff is likely to be the first time you get everyone working on the project together as a new growth team. It is your chance to get everyone on the same page and running towards the shared goal. That comes through not only building enthusiasm for the project but also through getting right up and personal with the business. It is one of the few meetings where you will have many of the key stakeholders in one room, don't underestimate this golden opportunity. They are the ones that will help you understand your new client's business inside and out to figure out what makes it tick.

For this chapter, we couldn't resist asking Craig Sullivan for his advice. For those who have not had the chance to meet Craig, he is a CRO consultant, who has been optimising and creating websites for 20+ years. He has even developed a whole course about running a CRO agency on CXL Institute which is definitely worth checking out. When we got the chance to talk about the kickoff, he explained it as machinery:

> "Every online business has or is a machine. Understand that machine and the type of business on top; then the rest is then just details around it. What is the machinery of the business? It could be a simple machine, selling a subscription where X leads come in, Y% convert to paying customers, leading to

> revenue and profit. Once you know the key data points and how the model works, you start to understand the whole machine. See it as a watch; everyone focuses on the numbers on the front of the watch rather than the cogs behind it. Those cogs are what makes the whole business work, e.g. conversion rate, churn, returns. That is where you can find the cog with which you can have the biggest multiplier effect." - Craig Sullivan

How do you understand the cogs behind the business? There is no rocket science to it; it all comes down to asking questions and really asking why, why, oh and why again, to get down to the true cogs of the business. We will give you a list of questions to do this with but it is up to you to listen to your client.

6.2 Agenda for the kickoff

The following is the general agenda we like to use in the kickoff. Every client is unique, so please do adjust it. If you've already worked with the client before and this is a second project, you can probably skip a bit of the introduction and way of working. Our usual agenda is as follows:

1. Introductions
2. Desired outcomes
3. Understanding current growth and history
4. Way of working
5. Roadmap

That middle section is crucial, that is where the breaking into the watch comes in and fiddling with the cogs. Let's go through each one in turn.

1. Introductions

The kickoff is likely to be the first time you get everyone who is working on the project together, time to introduce yourself and don't be afraid to Be Bold. When Daphne used to introduce herself, she would mumble a few things about being their growth consultant, a few years of experience, mumble, mumble, mumble. She was there to grow their company, turn things around, but do you think such an introduction gave those clients the confidence that she could be the one to do that? Daphne noticed how she introduced herself made a difference in how clients viewed her and valued her suggestions. Now that doesn't mean that you should monologue about all your achievements for the next half hour. Like we said before, "ain't nobody got time for that" and frankly no one cares that much. Instead, be proud of what you have done and show what your specialities are. More than that, let your passion and enthusiasm shine through, as enthusiasm is rather contagious.

> **Time for Action**
>
> Take 10-15 minutes to write out a short introduction for yourself to use in the next kickoff. A general guideline is to cover the following (the order is up to you):
>
> - Who you are
> - Your background
> - A few of your past clients (optional)
> - What you are specialised in / passionate about
> - Something a bit more personal about yourself to break the ice
>
> Here is an example (companies are imaginary).

> I'm Charlotte, I've been a growth consultant for the past four years. My background is in psychology, which helps me dive into what the end customer wants and needs. I'm specialised in conversion optimisation, which makes the psychology background very useful.
>
> I've worked mainly with several large health and fitness companies such as WeFit, Dream Juices and Hello Health. So this project fits perfectly with me, also because I'm an absolute workoutaholic with my current obsession being kickboxing.
>
> Write your own and run through your introduction a few times until you feel comfortable saying it in kickoffs.
>
> You don't do introductions often so it isn't crazy that you would first practice this a few times at home, even consider recording it and watching it back. Remember, your confidence gives your client confidence.

Listen carefully to how everyone else introduces themselves and make sure you understand their roles in the project. Ask if there are any other key individuals for the project who are not there right now. What will their role be?

2. Desired outcome

You can never go back to the reason why you are here often enough, as Simon Sinek would say "Start with why". Go over what the goal of the project is because that's what keeps everybody motivated if results don't happen. If you are not sure what that is, ask your client probing questions like:

1. What does success look like?

2. What was the reason for you all to start this project?
3. What would allow you to be satisfied with this project three months from now?
4. What changes would signal to you that this project has been a success?

We have given you a few different variations to help you find the wording that fits best for you. Your client has hired you for a reason, figure out what that is. Note how we also are talking about success and not results. It is not only about the hard figures but also about organisational changes. That will have a far more significant impact than any single experiment you could run. We have often heard answers like:
"Success would be that we're running experiments in a regular and structured manner."
"Everyone is actively working together to one goal as one growth team."

Often if results are not going as fast as you would've hoped, this is what buys you some extra time, that the client sees the other softer goals that were reached, that you are taking steps in the right direction.

Once you know the desired outcomes, it is also crucial to see what risks there are that may prevent success:

1. What could stand in the way of us reaching our goal?
2. What could be potential challenges or blocks in reaching our goal?
3. Imagine we are three months later and there is no growth, what would be the cause?

We especially love the last one as it is forcing the client to imagine they are further down the road and looking back. Also note the use of the word "our" with the other two questions: you must give your client the feeling that even you see it as your goal. Whichever phrasing suits you, it is crucial to get all the key stakeholders to name the risks early on. If needed, go around the room and ask everyone for potential risks.

Try to understand the underlying reasons for a risk. We've never heard a client casually drop "Our organisation has such a fixed mindset". Imagine that? Instead, they may give a clue that there is a fixed mindset, "Some people are less enthusiastic about this problem" or something like "Some people in the organisation do not see the need for a new way of working". Remember that you want to be looking at the cogs, not the surface of the watch.

3. Understanding current growth

The kickoff is also the perfect time to dive deeper into the history of the company and the current strategy. To figure this out, it can be beneficial to ask questions such as:

1. How and why was the company set up?
2. What is the background for this specific product/service?
3. What is the current growth strategy?
4. What are the key channels that drive growth right now?
5. How do different channels work together right now?
6. What are the channels you have tried in the past? Why did you stop using them?
7. Do you know the Lifetime Value of one customer?
8. What is the Cost of Acquisition for a new customer?
9. How do you attribute customers to channels?
10. What does the current customer journey look like? What are the key touchpoints?
11. What KPIs drive you on a daily/weekly/monthly basis?
12. Who is your key target audience?
13. What are the 20% of clients that drive 80% of your revenue/profit?
14. What does the funnel look like right now?

15. What do you think is holding you back from growing faster right now?
16. What customer research and insights do you have right now?
17. What tools do you use now for qualitative research? E.g. interviews, surveys, heatmaps, session replays.
18. Who do you see as your key competitors?

You pick and choose which to ask and which to skip according to your customer. The goal is to understand the business and its growth; the questions are but mere tools to get there. Some answers you may already know because of your previous contact, e.g. customer research. We included it again because if you haven't got those answers yet now is the time.

Whilst there will be a certain level of subjectivity in the answers you reccive, it will still tell you a lot. It will show you how the team sees growth. Discussions and disagreements may even start within their team about how it works now. Again this can provide tremendous insights (please do stop it before it drifts too off-topic though!).

The purpose of covering this area is not to find the answers. You are trying to discover the crucial starting points as you did in your first phone call.

4. Way of working

Growth is not only about what you do but also how you do it. You can have the best ideas, but if you can't find a structured way of implementing them fast, then driving results becomes challenging. We would suggest starting with explaining your general way of working to the client: what the client can expect from you and what you expect from them to be successful. It is always useful to have a few slides that walk through this. You should have an idea of what their preferred way of working is from that first conversation but don't be afraid to double-check it. You want to make sure you understand what channels they prefer to communicate through, who you need to keep in the loop and what the sign off process is.

The way of working is not just about using email vs calling but about how you approach growth. Do you first improve the foundations, which means that the initial results will take longer? Or do you start with a few quick wins whilst fixing the foundations so that they see that the ball has started rolling? Explaining your way of working is the first part in managing the expectations of the client.

If it is a large team, it is also essential to discuss roles and responsibilities, who to check off with and for what. Discussing roles may seem simple enough, but as you will see in Chapter 30: Too Many Stakeholders, Too Many Opinions it isn't. Not having one person to check off with for something can hugely slow down growth. We will give you an approval matrix in Chapter 30 that you can use in the kickoff if relevant.

5. Roadmap

The last topic on our agenda is usually the roadmap: where are we now and where are we going? The roadmap helps your client see what the next steps are and what they can expect.

You may also choose to summarise the first sprint or priorities for the coming week or two here. You want people to leave the kickoff with energy about where they want to go to but also clarity regarding what is next. If the kickoff ends and the client has to ask "So, what happens next?" then there has not been enough time spent explaining the roadmap and following steps.

And in the end, always make room for any final questions.

6.3 The secret to a successful kickoff

Now we could explain every question you could ask in a kickoff, go even deeper into what the agenda should be, who should be there and all that jazz. It won't help. That is not the recipe to a successful kickoff. As often in life, the real secret to success is easy to explain but hard to do: listen. Let them do the talking. Analyse inside and out what they are and aren't saying. Not only will that give you the insights you need, but it is the first step to building trust with the key stakeholders:

> "If you leave the meeting with the senior people feeling like you want to get under the skin of the business, that begins to give a degree of trust. This shows them you know that technology is just a means to an end and not the solution." - Craig Sullivan

They will realise you know what drives success and that it is not a random growth hack. It's about understanding what makes the watch tick as we said in the beginning. The only way to do this is to stay curious and ask why.

Key Takeaway

We will let Craig sum this one up perfectly with the best advice he ever received on the subject:

> "I got told by my mentor the following was the key to success: ask good questions, shut up, listen and repeat." - Craig Sullivan

CHAPTER 7

North Star Metric

7.1 Navigating with a map

Imagine that you have a treasure map, and your whole company wants to get to the X on the map. Now, the X is quite far away, a dream you all are working towards. There are many of you in the company, and you are all starting in different places. When working like this, you might slowly progress towards X, but it will take a while. You won't necessarily take the quickest route because you don't know how to get there.

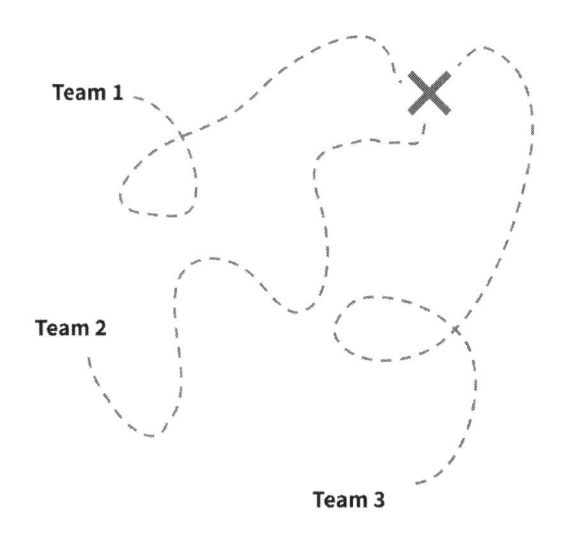

That said, it's already brilliant that you know you want to go to X and that this is your primary goal. The clearer you make it how and why you all want to go to X, the easier it will be to keep your company motivated on their challenging journey.

When we talk in terms of a map, it seems logical to know where you want to go. Yet, if you compare this analogy to organisations, the reality tends to be the polar opposite. Most people in your organisation won't know what X is, let alone that they'll have any idea what the steps are to get there! With all the best intentions, they are running towards where they think they need to go. Yet, they are never 100% sure whether it is the right way, or that they are doing the right things to create growth.

Having an X on a map is the same as having a North Star Metric (NSM), it will help to guide your client through the map of growth. Now, what about the steps to get there? Let's go back to our map example.

It makes sense to create markers along the way as these are your milestones, and you hit them on your way to X. Especially if it is a long journey, and X may take years to reach. Those markers will also help navigate your team effortlessly in the right direction. It assists them in finding the quickest route. It will indicate that they are making progress so that they don't accidentally double back or lose hope.

When we talk about our map, it seems logical that you set smaller goals until you reach the primary goal. In growth hacking, this is logical as well; these smaller steps are your One Metric that Matters (OMTM). They will bring the team step-by-step towards your NSM (if set correctly).

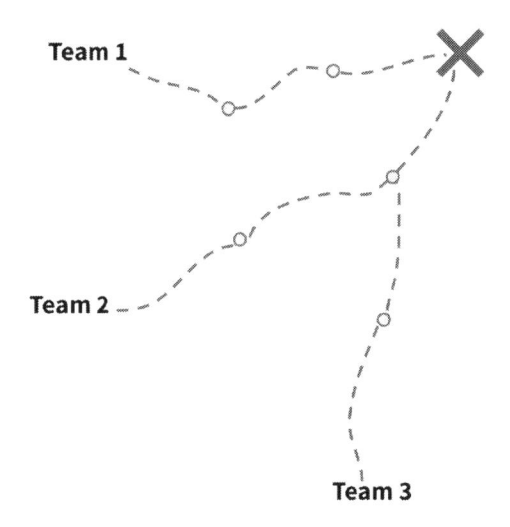

Now the truth is that even though it is a point on the map, it is a treasure map. You may never find the treasure, but it's the idea of the magical pot of gold that guides your movements and direction day in, day out. That is the power of the NSM. Our talk with Ethan Garr about the NSM for this book perfectly summed this up. Ethan Garr works with teams to accelerate growth and creates the Breakout Growth Podcast together with Sean Ellis. Ethan stated the following:

> "A well-considered North Star Metric can unlock a company's ability to accelerate expansion across its full growth engine. Because the metric inherently captures how the product delivers value to end-users, it aligns teams so that they can meaningfully focus all of their optimisation effort towards a shared mission." - Ethan Garr

We have stayed away from growth hacking theory until now because we wanted to focus on giving you the soft skills. However, one crucial soft skill is being able to help a company set a robust NSM and OMTM. That is why we want to ensure that you first understand these metrics so that then you can help your clients with them. There are many opposing definitions out there of what a NSM or a OMTM is. Heck, the two of us don't even fully agree on the one for a OMTM (more on that fun little argument in Chapter 9). We've managed to align for the most part and will walk you through our vision, that said, feel free to create your approach. We don't mind whether you call it North Star Metric, Vision, the Why or Big Hairy Audacious Goal. The key takeaways of this chapter are not what a NSM and OMTM are. It's about knowing how to apply these principles, how to create a map for your client.

In this chapter, we will focus on the NSM and how to set it. In Chapter 9, we will dive deeper into what a OMTM is and setting short and long-term priorities. You cannot determine the short-term goals, the OMTM(s), at the same time as the NSM. You first need to know clearly what the NSM is before taking the next steps.

7.2 The North Star Metric

We believe it is crucial to start with a NSM, that is the far-away X you want to reach, the pirate's treasure waiting to be discovered by you.

Your NSM is your high-level metric that aligns all teams in the organisation; it's the star on the horizon that you want to go towards, the reason for the existence of your company. Sean Ellis summarises it perfectly in his blog post "What is a North Star?" on growthhackers.com.

> "The North Star Metric is the *single metric* that best captures the core value that your product delivers to customers" - Sean Ellis

It should not be revenue, but rather something that brings value to both you and the end customer, something people, are aspired to achieve. Some great examples are:

- Spotify = Time spent listening
- Airbnb = Number of nights booked
- Uber = Rides per week
- Quora = Number of questions answered
- Facebook = Monthly active users

Notice how all these examples summarise it in just three or four words. That is not a coincidence. It is that simplicity that makes it possible for teams to rally around it, that makes it clear to everyone in the team.

Note again, none of these metrics are revenue. Of course, these metrics result in revenue. If people actively listen to Spotify, they are more likely to keep their subscription. More subscriptions mean that artists and Spotify earn money. However, revenue is the result of the value created rather than the core focus. If revenue would have been the focus, Spotify could double the number of ads or double their prices, but then the chances of people retaining would be exceptionally slim, and that would hurt the revenue. Focusing on value ensures you keep the focus on the customer, which provides the long-term success of your company.

> **Time for Action**
>
> Consider what the NSM could be for the following two companies:
>
> - Nike
> - Slack
>
> If you are struggling, reading through their mission and vision statement can help guide you. Try to come up with a 3-5 word phrase that encompasses what drives the company forward.
>
> We will give you our suggestions for both at the end of this chapter.

7.3 Setting the NSM

Now that you know more about the NSM, it is time to get to the critical part: how do you help your client set a strong NSM?

Setting the NSM is so essential that we'd advise you not to rush this and do it during the kickoff (especially if you don't have the data yet). Instead, take the time in a separate NSM session for this. We once had a three-hour meeting to set the NSM; it was long but brought so much clarity to everyone in the room.

All the key stakeholders should be at this session so that you get a holistic view of the company's needs. An excellent exercise, to begin with, is to go around the room and ask each individual:

> Why did you join or start this company?

The answer to this question gives you an idea of their deeper drive and where you want to go, but it also provides a great picture of the value you are adding to the lives of your customers. From there we have an eight point checklist you can walk through with your client to make sure you have the right NSM. You want to be able to say yes to these eight questions about your NSM:

1. **Does this help the customer reach their end goal?** Does it help the end customer get the intended result they want from the product/service?
2. Does this apply to all the customers? Does it add value to all the customers?
3. **Is it measurable for you?** Can you quantify it and measure your progress towards it?
4. **Does your NSM grow frequently?** Is it a metric that you see growth in on a daily/weekly basis? Otherwise, it will be hard to adjust.
5. Do we know what the best frequency (day/week/month)) is to measure this on? Is the NSM time-bound? How often should you check in on it?
6. Do external factors have a minimum impact? Is it within your control?
7. **Is the NSM growth tied to business growth?** Is it not only great for the end customer but also you as a business?
8. **Does the full AAARRR funnel impact the NSM?** If you improve one part of the funnel, will it help you towards your NSM?

If the answer to these eight questions is 'yes', then chances are you have a powerful NSM. You will notice that revenue doesn't make it through these questions: it isn't what helps customers reach their end goal or focus on the full funnel.

It can be easy to get caught up on what the exact metric should be rather than whether it drives value. Ethan Garr said the following about developing your North Star Metric.

> "When you work to develop your North Star Metric, focus first on value delivery, not the metric itself. The more you understand about how your product works to delight users the easier it will be to pick an actionable metric that can help you grow." - Ethan Garr

So once you know what drives value, the metric will naturally follow. Next, make sure the NSM doesn't just stay with the people in that room: everyone in the organisation needs to know and focus on it. We talk a lot about being focused and driving growth. In reality, though it is not the focus alone on growth that drives growth, it is the focus on a greater purpose, the why.

Now you understand the *Why* we will show you which basics to get in place so that you have enough data and insights to set the OMTM(s).

Time for Action (Answers)

Earlier on we asked you to come up with the NSM for Nike and Slack. Here is what we think they should be:

Nike
Nike is all about inspiring athletes; their vision is "To bring inspiration and innovation to every athlete in the world". Thus it would make sense to have a NSM that captures that they inspired someone through Nike. The NSM could be Active Nike Fans, so the number of individuals who have purchased Nike in the last year. Whilst this doesn't capture whether they wear the Nike items they bought and therefore gained value but comes as close as possible.

Slack

Slack's vision is to "make work life simpler, more pleasant and more productive". They do this by creating easy communication and having people actively use their platform. Their product is effective for both Slack in terms of value and for the end-user when they use it regularly. Therefore, a NSM around Daily Active Users or Messages Sent would be ideal.

Key Takeaway

The NSM is the most important metric you can set; it is the why of the whole project and broader than that, the company. It captures when the value is delivered and has the power to align the various teams within the organisation, almost like a Trojan horse for Silos.

CHAPTER 8

The Crucial Basics to Get Into Place

8.1 Why do we need to get the basics in place?

Unfortunately, too often, businesses miss the basics needed for growth. Us growth hackers are all about the basics, from robust customer profiling to measurement systems. It is a bit like fixing up a car: the fixing up will help your car drive better and go further, but during the fixing up, you are not going anywhere.

The question for you as a consultant is how long do you fix it up before you start driving? What is good enough? It is tempting to get caught up in fixing and creating the perfect car. However, the measure of your success is not perfection. It is about being able to drive a reliable distance within a time limit. But on the contrary, if you start driving too soon with a lousy setup; your car may go a few kilometres before stuttering and sputtering to a halt. So how do you find the balance?

We believe this comes down to three factors:

1. Knowing what the basics are.
2. Ensuring the value of the basics are understood.
3. Figuring out the 20/80 of the basics.

That first part is the biggest challenge presented by the basics; they are not sexy or flashy. No one likes fixing up the car; they like driving at breakneck speed. It is only when the car breaks down that they consider perhaps they should have spent a bit more time on the fixing part, oops. Too little, too late. For each basic, we will show you how certain elements differ not based on the size of your client but the phase. You can't and shouldn't go from no measure of Lifetime Value (LTV) to a predictive model of LTV. Start with one LTV and build it up from there. Again, as always, adjust according to your target audience.

8.2 Which basics are essential for (almost) every client?

Clients are like snowflakes, not only in how careful you need to be in handing them, but also in that they are unique, and with that, their basics are also individualised. We want to avoid leaving you with only that vague answer, so we put our heads together and came up with twelve elements that are essential for almost every client. There will be exceptions, edits to be made, but generally speaking, you can get started with this list. These twelve elements are:

- North Star Metric / One Metric that Matters
- Lifetime Value (LTV)
- Cost per Acquisition (CAC)
- Awareness, Acquisition, Activation, Revenue, Retention, Referral (AAARRR)
- Basic measurement
- Customer research
- Competitor insights
- Experiment overview
- Current marketing assets
- Overall roadmap

- One-on-one with the primary decision-maker
- User-friendly experience

There is no need to feel overwhelmed when looking at this extensive list; we will explain each one in turn. We will also give examples of how this may differ depending on the phase that your client is in. Note that we say phase and not size, try to do everything step-by-step.

1. North Star Metric and One Metric that Matters

We have already talked about the NSM in-depth and will cover the OMTM that matters in the next chapter. So, for now, we will say that this is key for creating focus. Next to that, you need to have a measurement system for this to work out the correlation. If it is complicated to measure all the way through to the NSM, e.g. customers, we would recommend starting with a proxy in the meantime. For example, if you can only measure leads, you can assume 20% become a customer. Then use this to calculate the Cost per Acquisition. It is not a long-term solution, as you need to be able to measure whether or not you are driving impact on your NSM, but a proxy will buy you time to fix it.

2. Lifetime Value (LTV)

The LTV is the value that a single customer brings in over their whole lifetime, some growth hackers work out the total value and others minus the costs. One of the challenges in setting this is that a client will say they cannot calculate it or that it depends. They'll claim that every customer varies so much, one buys €20 worth and the other €200. What if you spend €30 on a €20 customer? In the beginning, it is not about the individual; it is about the average. In the future, you can work with a fancy prediction model that shows the potential of a customer and what they are worth. We would dare to argue that 99% of clients are not there yet. You start with an average LTV if there is none and then build it out from there.

If the client claims it's impossible to set an average, since some of their customers differ so much from others, split it into a few different target groups and give those each an average LTV. You need *something* to start working with.

3. Customer Acquisition Cost (CAC)

CAC is simply the cost to acquire a new customer. It is not only the current costs per channel but also what the ideal cost per acquisition is. Often this is calculated based on the LTV, usually around 20 - 25% of the LTV. For a basic setup, you have one CAC. If you have many different products or services, you might work with a few CACs based on that or the customer type.

4. Awareness, Acquisition, Activation, Revenue, Retention, Referral (AAARRR)

We love the traditional pirate funnels and metrics. It is crucial to understand how they measure each phase and what the KPI is of that phase. We have added Awareness as we feel that growth hackers often forget this. Don't underestimate the impact of having a strong brand and in turn, the effect brand awareness can have on growth. Now a customer journey is rarely a straight funnel. The goal is not to oversimplify it, but understand what each phase is. Sometimes you might need to split the funnel into seven or eight steps, or define several funnels, but don't make it too complicated, to begin with.

5. Basic measurement

It is difficult for us to tell you what the necessary measurement setup looks like for your client. It's dependent on the customer journey, the type of business model, and tooling. We would say that you must be able to measure the four metrics mentioned above (NSM, OMTM, LTV and CAC). If not, then you should have at least worked out a proxy. You need to be able to trust the measurement setup. Bad data is as useless as no data. So you have walked through it, and no significant errors or bot traffic appeared. We would always recommend doing a quick measurement audit at the beginning. As a growth hacker, you need to be able to trust the data. Arnout Hellemans, who we also referred to in Chapter 1: Why Do Companies Hire Growth Hackers, takes it a step further:

> "For the first month, I focus on measurement, making sure everything is set up correctly. What I mean with this is to fix all your Analytics because, by default, it's broken. Set up proper dashboards to talk about the North Star and the supporting metrics. Do nothing else. Then ask your client: How was your month? Was it a good one? Was it a bad one? What's your feeling? Because in a lot of cases, they didn't measure it correctly. So now you can tell them what last-click PPC brought in, what SEO brought in, what social did, etc. By just being able to set a benchmark, because you didn't do anything for a month apart from measurement, you can then start improving on the rest of the basics. Because this will get you the buy-in at a later stage as well." - Arnout Hellemans

By knowing what is happening and what impact he is having, Arnout can be far more effective in knowing what to focus on. **You'll need to guide your client** to be able to convince them of a month of measurement, but if you can, and you start figuring out how to fix other basics, e.g. site speed, technical errors, then you'll be able to drive further results from there.

6. Customer research

Customer research seems so obvious to have in place. However, often clients have done some research here and there but do not have one clear overview. It could be having one or more personas or customer journey maps based on data. We specify 'based on data' because we too often see these awful fluffy personas. They contain details like "has three cats"... How does that relate to their purchasing behaviour of a laptop? Does it need to be cat-proof? (One of Ward's three cats decided to lay down on Daphne's laptop at one point so it could be an area to look into!).

There are two aspects that you want to cover. Firstly, what drives the individual? Think back to our chapter on the ABC of your contact person. Try to get into the head of your customer. To that, you need to understand the journey of the customer, if possible, online and offline. You can create a customer journey map (also known as a customer experience map) which is a combination of a persona and journey. Here you show not only the channels that play a role in each step of the customer journey but also the emotions, questions, pain points, and tasks to be done. This turns a very flat persona into a 3D individual who changes over time as they move through the customer journey.

Again, try to balance this out. If you have no persona, then start with analysing the 20% of the target audience who provide 80% of revenue. Get to know and understand that customer. From there, you can always build it out—the same for the journey. Perhaps you start purely by using the multichannel report of Google Analytics. Later you interview individuals and build it out from there.

Getting the basics in place with customer research is not about doing another huge one-off piece of research that gets dusty in a desk drawer or some hidden folder in Google Drive. No, it is about building a system to get regular customer feedback. It is far better to interview a few different customers every month than interviewing twenty once a year. Build a system where they are talking to customers every month.

7. Competitor insights

We could have a whole chapter debating how much you should or shouldn't focus on what your competitors are up to. We will save you that entire debate and simply leave you with the conclusion; better safe than sorry. It is beneficial to know what your competitors are doing. It is not to copy them but rather to understand how you can distinguish yourself in the market. The basics are knowing who the key competitors are and what their main value proposition is. The next level is trying to understand their marketing strategy. You can learn a lot through competitor tools, analysis and SEO tools (e.g. BuzzSumo, iSpionage and Semrush, just to name a few).

8. Experiment overview

Sadly the benefits of tracking experiments are often undervalued. The result is a chaos of questions such as:

- What tests are we running?
- How many winners did we have in the last six months?
- What are the biggest winners?

Trust us in that trying to create an overview of the last six months in one go is more problematic than a Sherlock Holmes investigation and a lot less fun. We will explain the full benefits of tracking in Chapter 16: Structured - Tracking Experiment Progress. We will also provide you with a template for tracking this. We consider a system for monitoring experiments, whether a tool or a simple Google Sheet, to be a crucial basic.

9. Current marketing assets

Customer marketing assets are not a basic for you to set up but rather something to get access to. It is beneficial to have access to the current marketing assets to know what is in place already. That way, you know what will need to be set up for potential experiments and can better measure the time required to set up an experiment as well as what has and hasn't been tested before in terms of messaging, visuals and videos.

10. Overall roadmap

We will walk through various methods for structuring your working process in Chapter 12: Planning and Preparing your Work Process.

For now, know that some form of structure is vital. It is not about planning out every little action for the coming three months. We understand that some clients request this but please push back. It's honestly a waste of time; you can not predict what you will need to do in two months. Instead, tell them what your intended outcome is and the high-level steps or focus areas on getting there. Based on your approach (e.g. sprints or deadline-based), you can then map out the significant milestones for your client encouraging your client to think more long-term rather than getting too stuck on what the results from the first two weeks were.

11. One-on-one with the primary decision-maker

Again perhaps a strange one for the basics list but hear us out. Your contact person isn't necessarily the primary decision-maker. We have seen all too often that the whole approach was agreed upon with the contact person. Then a mere month later their manager (or whoever the critical decision-maker is) takes a look. They do not agree in the slightest with how everything is being approached. All your work up until that point is... wasted! That is why we would highly recommend taking the time to sit down with them. Walkthrough the roadmap and the plans, and get everyone on board.

12. User-friendly experience

When we started writing this chapter, we were very much focused on the basics you need in terms of documents, KPIs and data. Yet, talking with many growth consultants opened our eyes to the truth. We would be doing you an utmost disservice if we didn't stress the importance of the experience for the end customer. It is tempting to get focused on the big experiments immediately but have you got the basics of UX in place for the website/platform/app? This includes technicalities:

- Is the site speed up to par?
- Does it work on all devices and browsers?

- Are there any broken links?
- Does the website have a clear hierarchy?
- Is the website accessible?

As well as everything involved in the flow and experience of the website:

- Is there always a clear call to action?
- Does every click to and within the website have pre/post click relevancy?
- Have you lived up to the basic principles of persuasion by Cialdini?

We once did a check of a client's website across different browsers and devices only to find out that a bug on tablets (for once it wasn't Internet Explorer) costing them around €20,000 per quarter. The review module was overlaying the add to cart button. You can even calculate and show the impact of such fixing by working out what the value would be if you increased the conversion rate for that browser.

Time for Action

Go through the list of basics for a new or an existing client. Tick off which you have:
- North Star Metric / One Metric that Matters
- Lifetime Value (LTV)
- Cost per Acquisition (CAC)
- Awareness, Acquisition, Activation, Revenue, Retention, Referral (AAARRR)
- Basic measurement
- Customer research
- Competitor insights

- Experiment overview
- Current marketing assets
- Overall roadmap
- One-on-one with the primary decision-maker
- User-friendly experience

Now for each of the areas you are missing, write one or two sentences of what this would look like for your client. From there, prioritise and plan in each action item.

So, you know the basics you need, and what is missing for your client, now it is time to start getting them into place. It is time to rev that engine and get driving, time to figure out where the biggest bottleneck will be on the road to growth.

Key Takeaway

It is easy to forget or rush through the basics in the desire to focus on more tangible actions. Please don't as these are what truly drive growth in the end. In particular, measurement and creating a user-friendly experience are the most commonly forgotten but crucial ASPECTS OF your success.

CHAPTER 9

One Metric That Matters

9.1 OMTM

Having a goal as high-level as a NSM is excellent, but how do you get to such a big, far-away goal? How do you not get lost in the day to day and forget about what you want to achieve? That is where the markers we talked about in the NSM Chapter come in: those milestones. They are the markers on the map that guide you and your client in the right direction. We call them OMTMs: One Metric that Matters. Your OMTM is more short-term than your NSM; it is usually for 2-4 months. It is in line with your NSM and is a leap towards it. Depending on your viewpoint, you may have one or several within the organisation (more on that later on). Whether or not you have one or multiple OMTMs within your organisation, each team should only have one OMTM to stay focused.

How specific your OMTM also depends on the size of your organisation, for example:

- Startup - 40% retention of new customers after seven days.
- Scaleup - 40% retention of new, freemium customers after seven days.
- Corporate - 40% retention of new, freemium customers for product X after experiencing the WOW moment.

You'll notice that with larger organisations, they get more specific.

9.2 Why is it essential to set a OMTM?

As you saw in the original map analogy, things get hectic without set clarity. Everyone may know where they want to go but lose sight of it or get lost on the way. A company may think they know where they are going but until you get everyone in the same room and start breaking things down, you can't be sure. Ask seven team members separately what the most significant bottleneck is right now and you'll get seven different answers, it is worse than a game of Chinese whispers. By ensuring they know the OMTM as well as the NSM it creates a tremendous amount of alignment and focus for the team. Everything they and you do should be related to the OMTM and in turn the NSM. Always be asking yourself, does this bring us closer to our OMTM and NSM?

The reason we suggest having OMTM(s), as well as a NSM, is that a NSM alone is too high-level. It gives focus but not enough on which part you should improve to reach the NSM. Your OMTM should be nothing more than the most significant bottleneck (more on those later) to achieving your NSM. Often the long-term gets forgotten in the hurry of short-term actions, which is why you also need to have a clear NSM. By working backwards and having a simple NSM, you can keep that in mind at all times.

9.3 How to handle conflicting KPIs?

When we walk clients through this, we often get the following reaction:

"That sounds great and all, but it is impossible for us to have one metric. Our business is too complex for that."

We get that, OMTMs are output metrics. They are the result of what you want to achieve:

NETFLIX

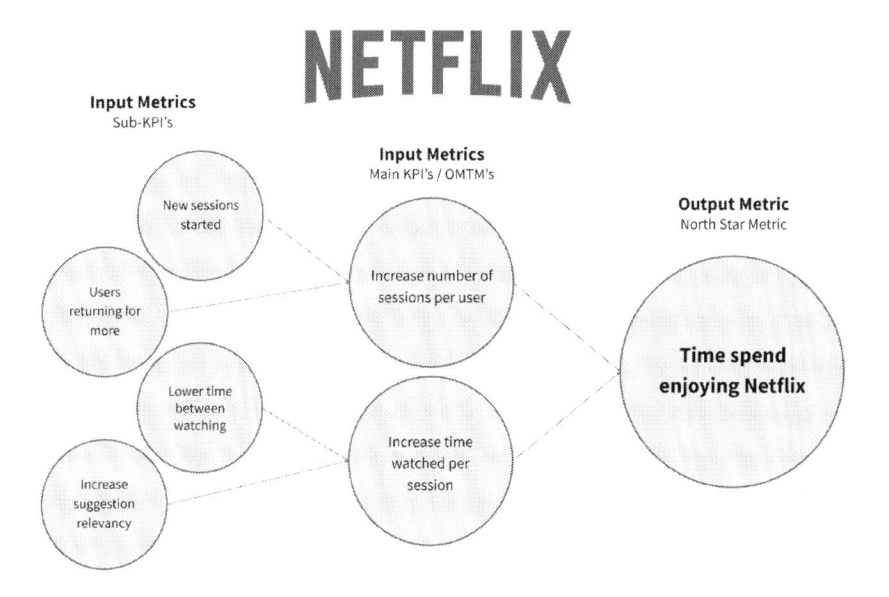

Input Metrics
Sub-KPI's
- New sessions started
- Users returning for more
- Lower time between watching
- Increase suggestion relevancy

Input Metrics
Main KPI's / OMTM's
- Increase number of sessions per user
- Increase time watched per session

Output Metric
North Star Metric
- **Time spend enjoying Netflix**

It doesn't mean you have only one metric but rather that you look at whether other metrics are inputs for the output you want to achieve. If not, this shows you are focusing on a different goal. Take Netflix as an example, their output goal may be time watching Netflix. Increasing the sessions (aka binge sessions of Netflix) helps to reach this goal. Meaning it is important also to increase this to escalate time watched. The key is understanding the relationship between those input metrics. Then work backwards from the NSM and the OMTM. It is not just whether or not the input metric helps you achieve the OMTM but also how closely they correlate with it. One way to create a clear overview is to set up metric tiers:

Input & Output Metrics

Example: Ecommerce Store

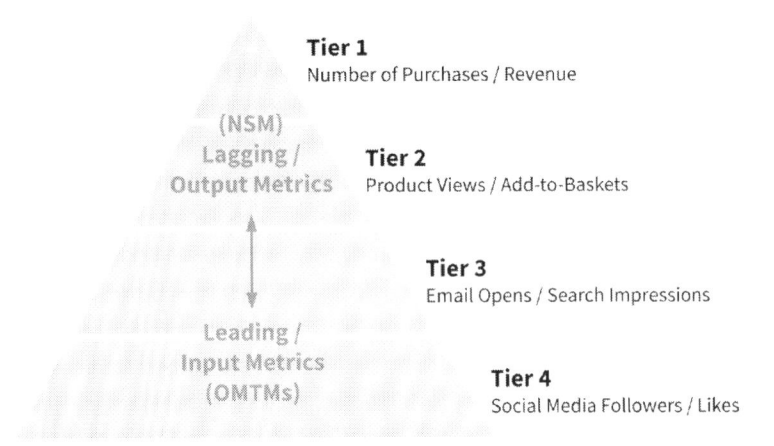

Tier 1
Number of Purchases / Revenue

(NSM)
Lagging /
Output Metrics

Tier 2
Product Views / Add-to-Baskets

Tier 3
Email Opens / Search Impressions

Leading /
Input Metrics
(OMTMs)

Tier 4
Social Media Followers / Likes

Doing this shows the strength of the relationship between the Input Metric and the Output. Take our ecommerce clothing store, yes, followers help gain awareness but that alone doesn't directly lead to sales and purchases. By understanding the relationship, it makes it acceptable to work on different Input Metrics so long as the following is clear:

- Do they correlate to the NSM and in turn OMTM(s)?
- What are the biggest bottlenecks in achieving the NSM at this moment?

9.4 Can you have multiple OMTMs?

Here it comes... our biggest argument: can you have multiple OMTMs? Long before the idea of this book was even born, we loved to discuss this topic over-and-over. We realised the minute we started writing this book that we would have to figure it out once and for all so we spent a fair amount of time on video calls discussing this. We totally did not follow the 80/20 rule in the amount of time that went into this, but it was fun, kind of. We managed to align on all of the above, but we couldn't bring ourselves to agree on this point. Therefore, you get both of our views so that you can make your own decision, consider it to be bonus content.

Ward's view on multiple OMTMs

When you have numerous growth teams working with just one OMTM, it's too tricky, either your experiments or your resources are conflicting. It makes far more sense to identify several OMTMs, one per team, based on the worst bottlenecks. These work parallel to each other to reach the NSM. For example, one team may have a retention OMTM, while the other team is focusing on another critical bottleneck: improving organic acquisition. Every 2-4 months, the teams will set new OMTMs once they've significantly improved their OMTM and should start focusing their attention on other bottlenecks with more potential.

Daphne's view on multiple OMTMs

One Metric that Matters means one, it is not known as the Four Metrics that Matter for a reason. The fear I have with numerous OMTMs is that there may end up being competitiveness between the teams. Within a larger organisation, you have the OMTM and then you break that down further per team. You give each team different input metrics to work on to reach the OMTM. As a result, your OMTM may be a bit broader; for example, it won't be focusing just on organic traffic. You can define your OMTM further by specifying the input metrics that need to be improved to reach it. One OMTM reduces the risk of internal competition and misalignment.

Yes, we realise it almost comes down to the same thing, but it allows us to agree to disagree on the terminology.

9.5 Setting the OMTM

Your OMTM needs to be SMART (Specific, Measurable, Attainable, Relevant, Time-Bound) with a significant focus on Specific. Too often a OMTM is set but isn't made concrete enough, which leaves far too much room for interpretation. Take the goal of retention for an e-commerce store:

- Are customers retained when they order a second time? Or is it that they order X times per period?
- Does it matter what their order value is?
- What happens if they return the product the first or second time? Are they still retained?
- What if they order a second time just outside of that period? Do we then count them as a new customer?
- What if we see orders from the same address but a different name? Do we measure retention on an individual level or a household level?

All these questions may seem like nitpicking, but this is how specific you need to get. Only by understanding all of these types of questions do you know whether you are on the right track.

Next to that, it is crucial to consider the other elements. A big challenge for consultants is when the client says "I want 1000 products sold by January 2021" and you're inclined to agree, promising that you could reach it. In the back of your mind, you are wondering if they could even sell 1000 products, as you need to take into consideration factors such as:

1. Start up time
2. Seasonality
3. Budget available
4. Time available
5. The current funnel
6. Logistics of that value

It can be so tempting just to say "Yes, let's go for it". Please, please don't. We have seen this come back to bite growth hackers in the arse multiple times. We know it is challenging, but you want to Be Real, meaning you don't make false promises to keep your client happy but are always looking at the data. Then based on the data you can indicate what is and isn't possible.

Rather than be a killjoy immediately, ask them more about why they chose that goal. Then say you'll look into it and get back to them. It is far easier to discuss whether or not it is realistic once you've had the time to look into the six points above. A good starting point for many OMTMs is looking at what it would cost to achieve that goal at the current cost of acquisition. If they want to re-activate 500 old customers and it now costs €20 per re-activation, do they have around €10,000 to spend on this? Try to get all the information possible on why they feel it is realistic as well as what is available to make it happen. Once you've dived into the data, if you still think it isn't possible, indicate what is and why. Find a metric you are both happy with.

Part of doing this is also managing the expectations of what a OMTM is. Too many consultants explain it as if it is a promise, we will guarantee 100% to keep our pinky promise. With the complexity of businesses, it is tough to pledge such a goal. The alternative is setting the goal far lower because you are scared of not making your promise, this is also not ideal. When you get so caught up in under-promising and then hoping to overdeliver you lose your client's trust before you even have it. They will just start to question why they are paying so much for so little. Not only that, but you begin tackling low goals as high goals. High goals force you to think and work on a more strategic level to achieve them. They encourage you to look at bigger changes to create true impact. Instead treat the OMTM as a strive goal, an ambitious goal that your client and you will work together to achieve.

Make sure you do continually re-evaluate it as you go along, especially if you set it for a more extended period (such as six months). You want to be critical of whether or not it is the most important element and that it remains a good stretch goal given where you are:

> **Key Takeaway**
>
> Ward is right that you can have multiple OMTMs.
>
> Jokes aside, it is worth taking the time to set the OMTM and continuously being critical of it depending on changes that occur. It will not only encourage proper focus but force you to really determine where you can bring the most significant impact. It also pushes you to set expectations and manage priorities. Yes, that is tough. That is why we spend the whole of the next chapter helping you figure out how to do that.

CHAPTER 10

How to set the Right Expectations and Priorities

10.1 The importance of managing expectations

Too many clients think growth hacking is like a magical weight loss pill: "Take this every day, and you will lose twenty kilos!". But growth hacking is more like a balanced diet and workout regime: it requires discipline and focus in both the short and long-term, to see the results of your efforts. If you haven't worked out before or are a junk food addict, it will take time to get used to it all. You will have to start with the very basics first. You won't try to run 10 kilometres immediately but instead, learn how to do squats and lunges.

Why all this talk of working out? Even though you are in constant communication with your client, from discussing goals to the next action points, there's often a misalignment on what's possible and what isn't. They think you are that magic weight loss pill when actually they need their workout foundations in place, the exact reason we spent the last three chapters talking about those foundations. Measurement is the perfect example, if you can't measure correctly, you might be running multiple tests but be unsure precisely what the results are. Setting up the foundations can take some time though, which makes it crucial to keep managing your client's expectations continuously and to help them understand what to expect. Help them not to get discouraged after those first tough gym sessions. It will take time and a bit of muscle pain, but the results are well worth it.

10.2 How to manage expectations

After the kickoff and NSM meeting, it is good to have a session focused on managing expectations (just don't call it the 'managing your expectations' session). Often in the kickoff, you don't have enough information to push back on expectations. Now that you've got more insights, you should go through the data and understand the setup better. That means you can figure out if the desired OMTM(s) is realistic. Did you spot any of the orange and red traffic lights we mentioned earlier?

Don't feel like you have to know everything already, of course, there is most definitely more crap you don't know about. It is like cleaning out a cupboard: the deeper you look into a cupboard (especially one you've had for a long time), the more crap you find. The same goes for data analysis: don't strive to know everything but trust your instinct and the data on what you feel is possible. Buy yourself time when you are missing that data by saying "I'd have to look into that before I can make any promises".

Managing expectations is one of the hardest parts of being a growth hacker; it was one of the top things that growth hackers indicated to us that they wanted to learn about in this book. How do I manage expectations? How do I tell my client 'no'?

We will give you different methods and techniques to do so, but if you don't do this one thing, the rest won't help: be confident. We know, easier said than done. It is something that comes with time and practice. Just know this: nine out of ten times your client's reaction will be better than you expect, even more so if you use the following techniques. We often make situations bigger or worse in our head. It takes a while to get used to it, practice and that in turn will translate to confidence.

Now, let's walk through some concrete tactics in the following sections to help you build that confidence.

10.3 Start with the deliverables and the definition of 'done'

The first part is to determine what the deliverables are:

- What can you realistically promise or not?
- What are the potential risks of those deliverables?
- Are there other risks related to the project in general?

Let's walk through this step-by-step starting with: what is realistic? That is a tough one to work out. You have to be realistic in two senses, in terms of time needed and output. To figure out the required time, it is very much about breaking tasks down and being observant of how long things take vs. the reality of it. It can help to have an excel sheet with all the tasks and time needed to see how that differs from reality.

Next, in terms of output, this is very much about weighing what is and isn't in your control. That is why it is crucial to understand the risks too. What could all go wrong? Do you have any way to prevent that? Do you have a back-up plan? Finally, consider what else could get in the way, e.g. fixed mindset, lack of time.

It can be beneficial to indicate it as follows:

"We can get the new email campaign live on Thursday if John can have the images ready by Tuesday and we only do one round of feedback."

Here you limit both the impact of the reliance on John and the chance of too many feedback rounds.

We'll go more in-depth on all the obstacles that you might run into, in the 'Ups and Downs' section of this book.

Not only that but what is the definition of 'done'? The definition of done is a great concept we've borrowed from Scrum. It suggests that you don't just define tasks, but also what does 'done' look like. This technique is so powerful. What you think 'done' looks like and what your client thinks it looks like, might be completely different.

Let's look at the example of working out a content strategy: you may see this as working out the type of content per stage of the funnel, the structure of the blog and backlink strategy. Your client, on the other hand, may expect the plan to include a full promotion strategy so even though your content strategy covers a lot, they could still be disappointed. When you bring it back to a definition of done, the conversation can go a bit like this:

You: For the first part of this month we will be working out the content strategy. Content will be crucial in building up long-term traffic for the platform.
Client: Great, super excited to see it.
You: In the content strategy I plan to cover the type of content per stage of the funnel, the structure of the blog and the backlink strategy. Is there anything you are missing?
Client: Oh, I thought you would include a promotion strategy too.
You: I can understand that, what do you define as a promotion strategy? Is that a full strategy detailing every platform we cover when promoting a new piece of content?
Client: No, just a checklist, how are we going to promote each piece when we put it live.
You: Clear. That shouldn't be a problem to include.

In this small interaction, there were already two misinterpretations of expectations, and we could've even asked for more clarification on how specific they'd want it or at what the difficulty level the checklist should be. Merely trying to understand what done looks like can avoid a lot of wasted time and frustration.

10.4 Relate it to your client's ABCs

Take it a step further by always trying to relate what you focus on and deliver back to their ABCs:

- What are the Awfuls that keep them up at night?
- What are the Barriers that stand in their way?
- What do they Crave to achieve?

From there you can look at how an action will benefit them. Again, let's work with an example, this time a Google Analytics audit to check their measurement setup. "I'm going to do a Google Analytics audit" doesn't sound sexy or convincing in the slightest. Your client is probably thinking "Ten hours to analyse our whole measurement setup?! No thank you!".
But what if you phrased it differently?

"We will analyse the Google Analytics setup, so that you can get far clearer insights as to where sales come from. That way, you can say with more certainty that the data is correct, rendering it easier to make decisions. Not only that but it will save hours for your team in the future in analyses where they try to piece the data together to understand what is going on."

That sounds far better, same analysis but different messaging. Your client now knows what they can expect and what the benefit of it is on a personal and business level.

We've talked to many growth hackers who struggle to convince their client of audits, even channel-specific ones. That this is tough makes sense - an audit hardly screams benefits. But think about it: why would you do such an audit? Often it is to develop a strategy or specific action points. A Facebook strategy or Facebook action plan sounds far better than a Facebook audit. Again, same thing, different packaging.

10.5 Let the data talk

Once Daphne was interviewing a growth hacker for a job position and asked the classically clichéd question "What's your biggest weakness?". The individual hesitated at first and honestly admitted "Low confidence". It was a surprise; she had nine years of experience and knew her stuff inside and out. So Daphne asked how she dealt with this when trying to share ideas. Her reply has stayed with Daphne ever since "Through the data". It lit her up to talk and show how data guided her to the right actions, data gave her the confidence to share her ideas. By basing her opinions on data, she knew what had priority and to manage expectations, leaving the low confidence behind and forgotten.

It can be challenging to know that what you want to do is correct. To just go up to a C level executive who wants you to focus on acquisition and say: "We have an activation problem. We need to solve this first before increasing ad spend." might sound a bit unsubstantiated. But data, well that can help you to be more confident in the suggestions you make, even if they are C Level.

Think back to our example of the interviewee: she loved data because it gave her the confidence she needed. It helped her to tell the client what had to happen and what the focus should be even when it's challenging.

Now, this doesn't mean randomly looking for some data that shows your opinion and pushing that forward - hell no! Don't torture the data to see what you want to see. Instead, look into all possible causes to present the full picture and to be sure that you found the real reason behind the problem.

For example, let's say you see that the conversion rate increased after an experiment. Don't immediately jump around, screaming "We have a winner!". First, do robustness tests:

- What else could have caused the change?
- A change in device mix?
- A change in new vs returning sessions?
- Is the channel mix still the same?
- Were any other tests running on that part of the funnel?
- What about any promotions (maybe more individuals in the one variant had the code than the other)?

Of course, you're never 100% sure or able to check every tiny possible cause. It is again the 80/20 rule: check the most critical alternative reasons. The more significant the investment in the action or the bigger the risk, the more it makes sense to put in the extra time to double-check it.

Now, whilst data can help indicate the priority, it's not just any type of data or metrics that should be chosen. Too often, we see people communicating conversion rates and click through rates. These are very logical and exciting metrics for you, but not for the rest of the organisation. We could turn off all paid traffic and skyrocket the conversion rate whilst end sales decrease.

Also, these metrics are not indicative of the result. Most clients, especially clients with Red personalities, care far more about another metric: profit. What does this bring to the bottom line? Too few growth hackers talk about profit.

Growth hackers do not always talk about profit because of one simple reason: it is not available in our analytics tools or dashboards. It's far easier to use a metric we readily can access, and that can measure our improvements. That's why you must set up at least a proxy for profit, some measure of it. A proxy is a substitute measure of what it approximately is, e.g. 20% of revenue. Even if it's not exact, it's still better than to pretend there are no costs at all. That way, you can ensure actions are worthwhile. And also don't forget: your time as a consultant will cost them money too.

10.6 Calculating the potential impact

To calculate the impact of an experiment, you can't just look at the upside of what you're doing, but you also have to look at what you plan to do. You can calculate what your actions will bring in terms of the bottom line and in turn use this to decide if it is a priority.

A great example of this is when you want to set up push notifications for an app. If you know how many users your app has you can calculate opt-ins with industry benchmarks for your type of apps (there are plenty of benchmark reports out there that show this).

Once you know the opt-ins for Android and iOS, you can calculate the traffic and in turn the revenue (e.g. ad revenue, sales based on conversion rate), based on the number of pushes you send per week/month.

Now that you have the revenue, work out the costs by looking at:

- What is the cost of setting up and sending notifications?
- What are the costs of the tooling?
- What are the costs of your time as a consultant in setting it up?
- What are the costs of your time as a consultant once it is up and running?

Once you have the costs you can work out the profit and benefits of it.

What you'll also see is if you look at the results per month that in the beginning, the value will go up slowly. More costs tend to go into the setup and you have fewer opt-ins. As you gather more downloads and opt-ins and through learning when it is best to ask for an opt-in, the value will grow.

Conclusion of the example

Now how does this relate to managing expectations? You could tell your client something like this:

"If we want to test the value of push notifications truly, we will need to test it for at least six months. Based on my calculations, the first two to three months will not be profitable. After six months, I expect the average monthly profit will be around €7,000."

Gone is the panic after one month of push notifications - "It isn't working, we are losing money. Turn it off!". Instead, you can check if the results are in line with the expectations. From there, you can recalculate and adjust expectations accordingly.

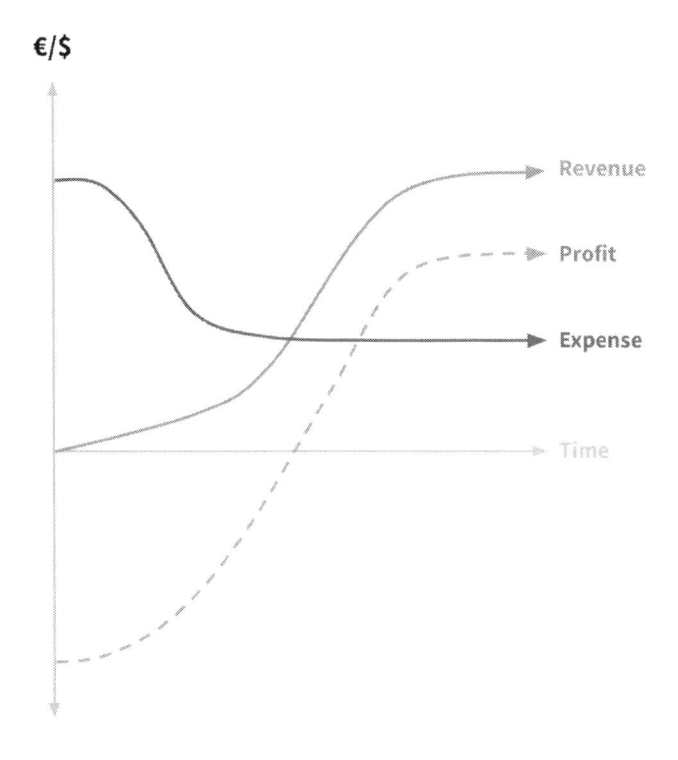

Now it is time for you to give it a go. Not ready quite yet? No worries, we have included an extra example in the resources section (growinghappyclients.com/resources). This time we look at the impact of optimising an existing channel. Optimising can be tricky because of two things: the first is that you could do it endlessly, but are all those optimisations worth it? When have you hit the point of diminishing returns? How much time should you spend trying to optimise? The second is that it is not very tangible for the client: "Okay, you want to optimise Google Ads, what will this bring?". Good question, client. What will it bring? We can calculate it as we did with a new channel, this is the example you'll find in the extra resources section.

Okay, your turn.

> **Time for Action**
>
> Now we realise this is tricky to understand from just reading about it. To understand it, you need to put it into practice.
>
> Take an existing channel - e.g. Facebook, Google Ads, Browser Notification - that you want to try out for a client. We would advise not to pick content marketing / SEO for now. Organic channels can be a bit trickier to calculate, so keep it on a paid channel for now.
>
> Next, look at what you feel could be optimised, e.g. volume, targeting, ads, copy, landing page, etc. Understand which metric this would impact and improve. From there, calculate it back to profit.

This technique has another powerful benefit as it helps to convince your client of what not to focus on. They may be raving that Facebook needs to be optimised but if you show them that another channel will drive more impact, it's much easier to convince them what the priority should be.

A little bit of time spent researching upfront will save you hours down the line. One of us (won't mention who, ahem, Daphne) once made the mistake of conducting a four hour Google Ads Audit for a big client, where she saw loads of improvement points. Wanting to be data-driven, she tried to show the impact of each optimisation, what if we optimise age targeting, what will it deliver? Each time this was only €100 or €200, not much. Finally, a frustrated Daphne looked at what the impact was of optimising the overall account for profit. Maybe that would be worthwhile? What if the Click Through Rate and Conversion Rate both increased... just €900 extra profit per month? For a large company, that's not worth it. If she had taken half an hour to calculate this overall potential at the beginning, it would have saved hours wasted. Oops - but that taught her a great new insight (and a little story for this book).

Now one final option of how you can use this method. Let's say you run an experiment, and it wins or loses. In both cases, you can calculate the impact it would have had in the following three months. For the winner, it is the expected gains, and for the loser, it is the avoided losses if you hadn't tested it first.

Imagine you had just 'assumed' your variant would work better and had implemented it without testing. It decreases the conversion rate by 5% meaning that revenue has also dropped by 5%. With an e-commerce store earning €500,000 per year that is a €25,000 drop in revenue per year! If you explain this to your client they'll see that you not only bring in revenue, but also prevent mistakes that would potentially have cost them a loss in revenue of €25,000.

Suddenly losing variants become learnings and also added value. Suddenly the value of your way-of-working is clear: it's worth taking the extra time to run experiments because it makes sure that such losses don't happen. It also helps you show the value of testing first, not just in wins but also in avoided losses.

10.7 Always look for alternatives rather than saying no

Whenever you are managing expectations and priorities, you are also indicating what is and isn't possible. One of the hardest parts of which is saying no.

Luckily, we don't have to say no as often as we think we do. There is an alternative option, rather than saying no, you can say:

"Not for right now."
"Instead, we can do this."
"We could do that but differently."
"Right now this has more priority."

It is not like you are going to do nothing, you are choosing other priorities. What if all the hours are finished though? Don't you have to say no then? Even then, there are options:

Do they want to spend more budget?
Do they want to pick it up themselves?
Do they want to use future hours sooner?

So, before you say flat out 'no' to a client and create a negative feeling, next time see how else you can phrase it.

By using these four steps, you do more than just managing the expectations of your client. You also help show them what has priority based on the data. Remember, throughout it all: confidence is half of it.

> **Key Takeaway**
>
> Managing expectations and prioritisation is hard. Let the data guide you in what the priorities are and get concrete through deliverables. Focus on those two elements first.

CHAPTER 11

Bottlenecks

11.1 Beer? A story about Daphne

For four years, Daphne taught a guest lecture on growth hacking to 2nd-year students at Erasmus University. The goal was to give them a brief introduction into growth hacking and hopefully give them a feeling of how it was to grow companies in reality. It was also a tremendous challenge, keeping the attention of five hundred students. Then she'd get to her favourite slide, the one with beers. The whole room would visibly perk up, did someone say beer? She would always show them a slide zoomed in on the top half of green beer bottles. As the slide would span across a range of bottles, she would then ask:

"What is this?"

The students, never that quick to call out in a lecture, were immediately enthusiastic. They'd start shouting various answers:

"Beer!"
"Beer bottles!"
"Heineken!"

Whilst all those answers were technically correct, they weren't the one she was looking for. In four years of teaching the class, the students never saw what she saw in that projected image in the lecture hall: bottlenecks. Bottlenecks are the end part of a beer, almost like a funnel, they slow the tempo and the flow of the beer.

If you turned a beer bottle upside down, it is the bottleneck that restricts the flow. It is also the bottlenecks that slow the tempo of growth. She wanted to show those students to think not of beer but understand growth bottlenecks. As growth consultants, we often get asked to bring more people on the website; traffic is the solution. Is that the real bottleneck? In reality, the bottleneck can occur anywhere in your funnel, or even the business, from low retention to lacking development resources. It is the potent blockade of your business's growth. Teaching the students to understand and find bottlenecks would help them far more than showing them a few fancy growth hacks.

Why our obsession with bottlenecks? Well, it is not just that they are a part of our love for drinking beer (just not Heineken!), but they are also crucial for growth hacking consultants. You come in as an external consultant with a birds-eye view and need to find your client's growth bottleneck. Only by figuring out the bottlenecks do you figure out how to create real growth.

11.2 Where are the bottlenecks?

As we mentioned, almost too often, it feels like clients believe that acquisition is their bottleneck. Rarely is that the case though, it is an easy focus as it feels more tangible. Of course, in some cases, it is getting more individuals to see your brand and onto your website. In reality, it is often in other areas, such as retention. Retention gets frequently undervalued because we have the naive belief that new clients will stay, but they don't. Not only is retaining a client usually cheaper than acquiring one, but as we said, it's less tangible. You are increasing lifetime value rather than the number of customers.

The focus of this book isn't whether or not retention is the issue. Retention is just a tangible example of a hidden goldmine. What we do want to show you is that it is crucial that you continuously think about bottlenecks rather than blindly perform random actions to drive growth. In that first part of your collaboration, you need to identify what the most significant bottleneck is. Even within an area such as acquisition, you need to calculate what the impact of improving A vs B is. Too often, we've seen a consultant focus on tidying up and improving Google Ads, just look at the example in the last chapter. When we calculate the improvement of that considering the costs and time required, it isn't what will drive the impact. You find bottlenecks by working backwards from the NSM to the OMTM. From there, you figure out why you can't reach the OMTM today.

11.3 Bottlenecks in the organisation

So, we know that there will probably be a bottleneck somewhere in the funnel but what about in the organisation itself? Yes, retention may be an issue, but if development takes five weeks to get a test live, that could be a far more significant bottleneck. How can you then improve retention if you can't get a test live? You need to look at what is preventing you from doing and achieving more within the organisation. We covered many organisational bottlenecks when we talked about the various orange and red traffic lights:

- A lack of focus.
- A lack of specific resources.
- Too many opinions for too small decisions.
- Legacy.

How do you convince a client that organisational blockers need to be solved? Whilst growth consultants often talk in terms of impact; it is important also to highlight the costs of not getting tests live. How much does a delayed test cost? How much does it cost to implement a winning variant three weeks later? By discussing it like this, it suddenly becomes tangible what the cost is. You can also show the potential impact of being able to test faster by using a calculation such as:

Extra value per week = Win rate x Number of additional tests per week x Average value gained per test

Clients like things to be made tangible. The above is far more powerful than saying development is slow. Let's say 32% of your tests win with an average lift of €22.000 per three months. You usually run two tests per week and want to run one more per week. That means the extra value per week would be as follows:

Extra value per week = 32% x 1 x €22.000 = €7.040

Not bad for an extra experiment per week.

11.4 Will the bottleneck stay the same?

The bottleneck will continuously change. You want always to be looking at what is slowing down growth the most right now. What is slowing down the progress? That is your focus area. Bottlenecks come in two sizes: short and long (term). You want to balance fixing both types of bottlenecks. Now let's consider why.

11.5 Long-term vs short-term focus

Let's say you tackled your bottlenecks one-by-one like in Growth Scenario #1, what would happen?

Growth Scenario #1
Tackling bottlenecks one-by-one

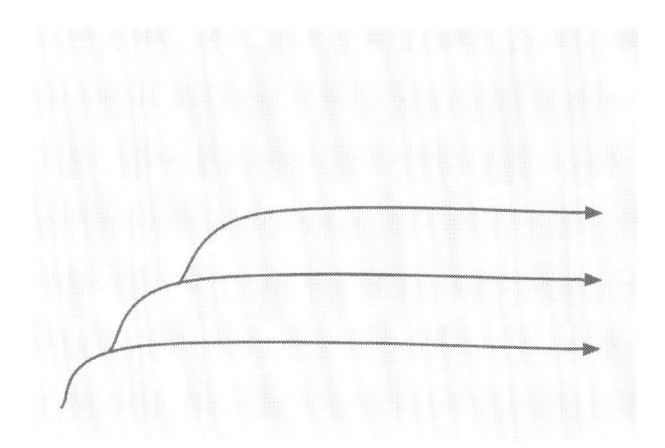

You would see growth because every time you tackle a bottleneck, the overall conversion rate goes up. Some examples are:

- Making sure that the website has no conversion blockers.
- Having all pages rank for branded search terms.
- Creating a consistent visual branding across the whole site.
- Adding some social proof on several pages.

Sadly it is not exactly what your client is looking for, because this growth is dreadfully slow, and honestly… these are basic fixes.

On the other hand, you could also decide to go for all quick-win tactics, and give the client what they want: fast and instant result, consisting of tactics like:

- Setting up paid search campaigns.
- Adding more paid social campaigns.
- Improving your email marketing.

- Setting up partnerships with big players.
- Trying to go viral on social or forums.

Focusing on the short-term feels lovely... in the short-term. If you do this, it will probably look something like Growth Scenario #2:

Growth Scenario #2
Go for quick-win/-impact tactics

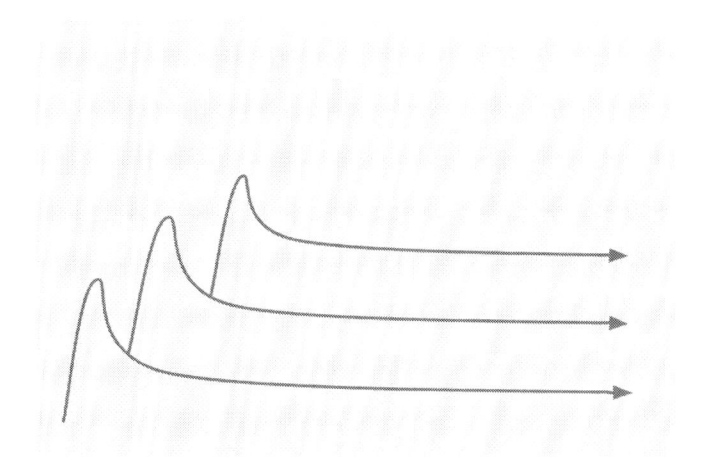

You see quick results; your client is happy, which makes you happy. Happy client, happy life, all is great in the land of growth. At a certain point, it will get harder and harder to drive scalable growth only through short-term actions. The results were great, but most of these tactics are one-time wonders, meaning that the next month, you'll have to come with another miracle to match the same results. Overall your growth starts to level out because you can only be as big as the miracle of that month. So this isn't the ideal route either, even though it feels more manageable.

Then there's a third option, which might seem like the best option because you're creating compounding marketing tactics. Meaning that you can set them up once and instead of plateauing, they get only more substantial over time. Think of tactics like:

- Content marketing with in-depth SEO.
- Building a well-known brand in the industry.
- Creating a big reach through organic social.
- Setting up a viral referral program.
- Or building a loving community of customer-fans.

The impact has no limits, and if these tactics work out properly, the business will become an industry example of 'how business should be done'. This will look something like growth scenario #3:

Growth Scenario #3
Creating Sustainable Growth Loops

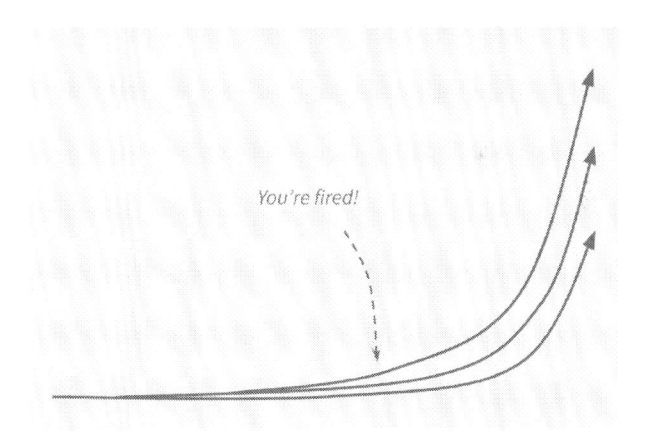

You're fired!

There is a dark side to it because for the first months it will look like almost nothing is happening. In reality, these strategies take time: Google needs time to accept you as an authority, a brand is not built on peak-quality, but through consistent quality, and your social media posts will only reach a lot of people if you have a lot of followers, but you need to reach people to get followers.

By this time, the client has fired you long ago. You were putting in hour after hour, but they did not see results yet, and there is no guarantee that this is a case of 'We're getting there', instead of a case of 'We have no idea what we're doing and need to stall for time'.

So how do you do it then?

Well, as always, you need a proper balance. The formula looks a bit like this:

- First, you'll have to fix the basics. If you don't, it's not worth attracting more traffic, because they'll be crashing on a concrete wall of low conversion rates. So first remove those obstacles.
- Second, once the basics are done correctly, you'll need to start pushing the gas pedal. If you don't show the sexy results that the client was promised in the sales meetings, then they'll have to start putting more pressure on you. So this is the point where you should show them that you have the expertise needed and they have nothing to worry about their future growth.
- Third, now you have to re-set the expectations: these kinds of spikes are impossible to maintain, and we should now start to look at the heavier channels, which take a lot of time and effort. Luckily, by now, you've built the credibility you need, and you've bought yourself enough time to stay in the game until that compounding effect kicks in.

If you follow this formula as the order of implementation for different types of tactics, you'll rock it!

This is how to grow
First basics, then impact, then flywheel

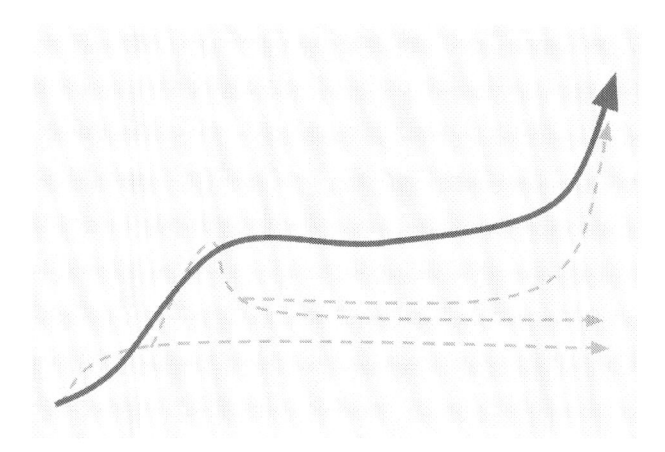

Next to that, be aware that with a short-term focus, you are only fixing small things rather than developing a foundation for growth. Such as reducing the checkout dropoff instead of creating a strong content strategy.

Whilst the long-term actions won't show results immediately, they are what drives scale. Not only that, but long-term goals are connected to your bigger why your NSM. When things get tough (growth stalls), it is what will keep people motivated and moving forward. So the ideal situation is to find a balance, you get the basics in place whilst starting on the long-term actions—the best of both worlds.

Depending on your client's personality (see Chapter 3: Different Types of Personalities of Clients again for the personalities) you might be able to shift your focus and process slightly. A Red client needs more short-term goals, whilst a Yellow client needs more focus on long-term goals. It is crucial to help your client see and understand the above relationship. Balancing the short and long-term not only helps to manage their expectations but allows you to create a far more extensive and long-lasting impact.

> **Key Takeaway**
>
> Once you start to see potential growth blockers as bottlenecks, you begin to understand their impact on growth. From there, you get the basics in place and play the crucial balancing act of the short and long-term actions that drive together in the end, sustainable growth for your client.

CHAPTER 12

Planning and Preparing the Working Process

Picture placing together multiple individuals with different projects, varying relations and conflicting KPIs... what happens next? A natural form of organisational chaos. We feel this is to be expected in large organisations; they hold such a complex network of individuals with thousands of connections. Then you come in as a consultant, and it is easy to get caught up in it all, like a leaf in the wind, you allow the wind to blow you whichever way you want. Instead, you want to be more like a plane. A plane has no control of the external environment but is continually recalibrating to adjust to it and stay on course. So how do you do that? How do you create order in the chaos? No magic formulas here; it is merely about structure.

Even if structure is not your 'thing,' you require a certain level of it. You may prefer one format to the other, or you may adjust your approach to your clients. We are huge fans of structure, but which you use is up to you. Unless you work at an agency, in which their standard way of working should apply. We will walk you through the two primary forms of structure that we see growth hacking consultants use as well as their advantages and disadvantages. If possible, try to experiment and test both. Speaking of experiments, should you be running them? Everything you read about growth hacking pushes an experiment-based approach. In many cases, this is beneficial, but not always, so we will also show you when it is and when it isn't.

12.1 Sprint-based approach

This approach is based on Scrum. We will briefly introduce Scrum in case you are not familiar. We know there are multiple ways to use Scrum, and everyone has their vision, this simply describes our experience with Scrum and the parts that work for us.

The idea of Scrum is that it is impossible to plan far ahead accurately as we are terrible at estimating how long tasks take and what is realistic within a certain period. Thus instead, you work in chunks, aka sprints, maybe 1-3 weeks per sprint. It will take a few sprints to figure out how much the team you're working with can handle within a sprint, so the first few sprints you might be completely off. The amount of work that can be done with the same team can differ per client, as some are simply more complex or are lacking proper communication etc.

Scrum centres around the 'ceremonies', the key meetings. There are a lot of meetings in Scrum, so don't worry if you don't have the time to do all of these meetings, we're sharing a few tips below. These are the various ceremonies of Scrum:

- **Daily Stand-up Meetings.** Short 15-minute stand-up that covers what was done yesterday, what will be done that day, and any impediments.
- **Sprint Review Meetings.** Here you show the client what has been achieved during the sprint as you don't show work in progress during the project.
- **Sprint Retrospective Meeting.** An evaluation at the end of each sprint to see what went well and what to improve.
- **Sprint Backlog Refinement.** A meeting to go through the backlog of ideas and to re-prioritise according to the current information.

- **Sprint Planning Meetings.** Decide what does and doesn't go in the sprint, also how you plan to tackle those tasks.

There is a Scrum Master who coordinates these ceremonies, but they should not be the Project Manager (aka you). The Project Manager is an impartial individual who ensures the project is running smoothly, and the team follows the Scrum process. The Product Owner is another crucial role in Scrum; they are the one who decides what will be picked up within the project. The product owner is usually your client, your primary contact person. The Product Owner is in the driver seat, you as the Project Manager sit next to them and provide guidance where needed.

There is another important feature of Scrum that you deliver at the end of every sprint. Scrum was created for development projects with the idea that within the sprint you deliver features, features that are usable at the end of the sprint. The features can be a minimally viable version or the full feature. Rather than work on twenty different things and half finishing them, your whole focus is on 'shipping' every sprint and increasing the output. That doesn't mean you can't go back and improve it further; you could deliver a feature (e.g. a new email flow) at the end of sprint 1, test it in sprint 2 and then in sprint 3 improve on what you built (e.g. adjust the emails according to what you've learnt). We like to use the same concept when using sprints for growth hacking.

A straightforward example: you are working on ten new Facebook ads throughout two sprints. Rather than set them all live at the end of the two sprints, you would put five live at the end of the first sprint. Then the remaining five at the end of the second sprint.

The above is only a brief introduction to Scrum. If this approach is new for you and you are curious to learn more, we'd highly recommend the book "Scrum: The Art of Doing Twice the Work in Half the Time" by Jeff Sutherland.

Many of the benefits of the sprint-based approach have already been mentioned indirectly. As you can imagine, working in such short time intervals makes you very agile, you don't have to plan everything all in one go in a way that usually never works out. If done correctly, it also ensures that you focus on shipping.

Next to that, as we already mentioned, people are terrible at estimating the time needed for tasks. Scrum uses story points; you calculate story points by comparing issue sizes relative to other tasks, rather than hours. After a few sprints, you can work out what your velocity is per sprint (how many story points are realistic). It naturally forces your client to make tradeoffs: only X story points fit per sprint, so if they want an extra task, what is going to be swapped out? Finally, it discourages last-minute tasks and planning. The idea is that once you have started a sprint, you stick to the sprint planning no matter what.

However, there are risks of working with Scrum. Firstly, it is easy to get caught up in individual sprints rather than in the big picture, you work sprint to sprint and forget to take a step back. You get caught up in the sprint and lose sight of where you are going; your client may even feel that too. Secondly, you cannot tell the client upfront about what they will get exactly. The scope can (and always will) change during the sprints, as new information becomes available. Finally, it can feel a lot like small random tasks rather than bigger goals to achieve; these smaller tasks can also cause the team to get tired of sprinting after a while. It begins to feel like the same thing, a different sprint which impacts the motivation of the group.

If your team is working on multiple projects, it can also cause tasks to pile up towards the end of the sprint. Let's say you have three projects with two-week sprints. The first week you have to finish the first two projects racing like crazy to finish everything off. Then the next week, project three's sprint ends. Uh oh, still got a lot of tasks left because last week you focused on the other two projects.

Of course, rationally speaking, you'd divide tasks over those two weeks. Yet if we all reasoned in this manner libraries would be far emptier the week before exams. Many people tend to leave tasks until just before the deadline, and as you can imagine, your client is probably not very impressed when this happens. Especially if there is an unforeseen issue, which means you can't complete the sprint.

Clients will also push for you to do more in the same amount of time which can result in you giving pushback. It is a difficult balance to find, plan too little, and you might not realise because work naturally expands to fill the time available (Parkinson's law). Plan too much, and you have a stressed-out team. It is about finding the balance throughout the sprint.

Scrum can be quite extensive for smaller projects. Say you have five client projects that would mean 1.25 hours per day alone of just stand-ups! There is a high proportion of time that goes into meetings, even if you only have one or two projects. So we would advise a lighter version instead by:

- Backlog refinement occurring less regularly.
- Stand-ups are once or twice a week.
- You may not have a separate Scrum Master, but you take on the role yourself (or have someone else in the team perform it).
- Planning and reviewing meetings are combined.

We usually say that if a project is less than twenty hours per week, it does not make sense to do a full-blown Scrum. For more significant projects, it could be a better option.

Now time to look at the other approach.

12.2 Deadline-based approach

With a deadline-based model, you start with the primary goal and work backwards from there to define the significant tasks to do. For each task, you also specify the deadline leading to a high-level roadmap of the coming period. It is commonly used for shorter projects, but can also work for longer projects. For longer projects, you will not only plan the full year but say the first three months roughly and the next month in detail. It is a waste of time trying to plan every little detail for the coming year as what happens in the short run will most likely completely change it.

A valuable part of working with a deadline-based planning model is that your client will know when to expect tasks as they can see a clear timeline of when they will be delivered and how you plan to get from A to B giving them a sense of control in the project. It also avoids the disadvantage we explained of Scrum, in that everything can get piled up to the end of the sprint. Deadline-based works exceptionally well with new startup-projects, where you often know that you need to do X, Y and Z to get it all set up, and you won't need to do much test-and-adjust along the way.

Now, as you can imagine, there is far less flexibility than with sprints. With sprints, you can adjust the sprint based on new information, and with deadline-based, you plan further ahead. Planning ahead allows you to think actions through and give your client insight into the future, but this isn't without consequence. Planning too far ahead can often land you in trouble; nobody has a crystal ball that can predict the future. Of course, you could just adjust based on the new insights, but the framework can make it feel less flexible. You have promised certain tasks or specific dates; you have a commitment bias. Even changing the order might feel challenging as you don't want your client to think that you are trying to get out of specific tasks.

Find the approach that works for you. We like to use the deadline-based approach with smaller teams or short-term projects. The sprint-based process works well when you are working on a larger project where you are mainly adding features, making improvements and fixes. Then you also have enough hours to spend on the project, since there are a lot of meetings. Then the structure saves a lot of time in trying to plan everything that needs to be done. It's also a great approach when working with experiments, as you can use the sprints to determine the experiment tempo, e.g. you commit to putting three experiments live per sprint. This brings us to the final part of this planning chapter. We've discussed how to run experiments but not even approached the question of should you be running experiments?

Ready for the typical answer: it depends. Don't worry; we will get more specific of when it does or doesn't make sense to run experiments.

Key Takeaway

Experiment with different techniques for structuring your project and find the one that works best for you. There is no perfect structure, but rather it is crucial to find a method that brings structure to the project.

CHAPTER 13

To Experiment or Not to Experiment?

That is the question, and it is a very valid question as everyone assumes that growth hacking is about running experiments continuously. What we mean is that every change you make should have a hypothesis and a clear definition of when it is a win. To answer whether or not you need to run experiments at all comes down to the core of what growth hacking is (at least for us). For us, experiments are nothing more than a tool for a growth hacker. Being a growth hacker is not necessarily about experimentation but instead working from data and customer insights to create holistic growth. For this, experiments are a great way to achieve this goal, but not the only way.

Some growth hackers get obsessed with the number of experiments and make every task an experiment. Doing this can be unnecessarily time-consuming and costs effort. With an A/B test on a platform, you need to design the experiment, write functional specs where required, build the test, do quality assurance, monitor the test and analyse the results. That is no small feat. Not only that there isn't always a hypothesis or the possibility to test, but sometimes people end up experimenting for the sake of testing. Take sending emails; you don't have to experiment with every single email. Yes, you'll learn, but at a certain point, you'll be choosing experiments just for the sake of it, and it may not necessarily be worth the ROI given the extra time it will require.

13.1 When not to experiment

The following list summaries the main scenarios of what doesn't make sense to run as an experiment:

1. Hygiene factors in the beginning

Some tasks are hygiene factors, such as setting up measurement systems or conducting user research. You can't create an experiment of running a Google Analytics Audit, is the experiment a win when you find ten issues? Especially at the beginning of a project, there are quite a few tasks like that which are just a part of setting up the infrastructure.

2. Hard to measure areas

This example slightly relates to the above as some hygiene factors; in the beginning, are indeed hard to measure. However, other tasks may also be tough to run as one experiment, e.g. improving branding, culture improvements, content marketing. You may have some measures of success that you use when say, building the brand, but determining the exact success would be difficult. With such tasks, it is more about making a case of why doing this will help you to reach the goal, the NSM. You'll often need far more time for this than a single experiment takes as most of these improvements take months before you see the difference.

3. Very high ease or certainty tasks

The concept of best practices is controversial; some people swear by them whilst others hate them. We aren't saying that all best practices are correct, but there are absolute basics needed for growth. Take Call to Actions (CTA), having a CTA is better than having none. If you have no CTA, the user will not know what to focus on or what the next step is. If you have no CTA we would just suggest adding the CTA without experimenting is possible (unless you want to measure the effect). If they are missing many of these basics and you want to run them all as individual tests, you'll be holding back the growth. That said, the best copy for the CTA or type of CTA may be something you do want to test out, also to understand whether it is worth playing around with the copy or type of CTA further.

A second example is remarketing. If you have no remarketing, you can be pretty sure adding it will almost always help your conversions. However, just like with CTAs, once you set it up, you may want to test various approaches to it. You don't want to waste money remarketing to someone who would have converted anyway.

4. Small clients

Not all clients have the data to run experiments. If your client has fifty conversions a month, they may not have sufficient data to test correctly; it would be too slow to run experiments. If you measured the time needed to see a difference, it would cost months and months to measure it. In those cases, data is your best guide as to what changes to make.

Let's say you have one or more of the above and choose for now not to run experiments as part of your growth project. What do you do instead? The alternative to experimenting would simply be called 'moving forward'. It's when you have a clear path ahead of you of all the things you'd need to improve, and you just put one foot in front of the other and make the company better every week/sprint. This way of communication also works excellent for Red personality clients, who might care less about experimenting and prefer 'just going' ahead. Keep in mind that you should always have your measurement systems set up correctly so that you can see what the impact is afterwards. That way if you don't see a difference as you move through the project, you can try to understand what is and isn't driving change.

Now please, don't think we are set against experimenting!

It's not that, but we simply feel like many growth hacking processes suggest always running experiments. We want to show you the nuances and let you know that it is okay to not continuously run experiments. There are many cases for when you should push experiments, in particular, when the following two requirements are met.

13.2 When to experiment

There are two requirements you first need to fulfil before you can even consider experimenting. They are:

1. Does experimenting justify the extra investment? Aka is there a positive ROI.
2. Is there enough traffic to test?

The first requirement means does the potential lift of experiments winning justify the extra time and resources required to experiment? Phrased differently, does the possible lift exceed costs of running experiments? The costs of running experiments are not only the tooling, costs of ads (for advertising experiments) but costs of time from you and the team. Often growth hackers (and team members in general) forget that their time is money. As a consultant, it is easy enough to calculate what your hourly rate is but for other team members on the project; you also want to know what their time costs. Even if it is just a guesstimate, e.g. €50 per hour. Calculating ROI on an experiment program is tough when you are starting; you might need to run experiments for a month and use the documentation to work out what the ROI was. Now the first month may not be great as it takes time to get into a good flow, but at least you'll see if you are on the right track.

The second requirement: is there enough traffic to test? You might want to experiment, but if you don't have the traffic, then you can't. We already mentioned this in saying you can't run experiments for smaller clients, but it seems growth hackers are too quick to assume there is enough traffic. Google "minimum sample size calculator a/b testing" and you will find tonnes of online calculators that can help with this. You need to look not just at the traffic of the website but the various areas to figure out what is and isn't possible.

There are still ways to test on low traffic setups or alternative solutions, e.g. testing before/after, driving additional traffic via ads, testing on micro-conversions vs end conversions. So if you don't have enough traffic, you can always consider one of those.

These calculations are quite advanced, but we feel obliged to mention it and encourage you to look into it further. We have seen too many growth hackers start running experiments without measuring the lift needed to see what the minimal detectable effect is. The result is a train of non-significant experiment results and that the client thinks the whole project is a failure. That is the last thing you want.

So if these two basic requirements are met, here are some main scenarios where you should consider running experiments:

1. Big investment

Changes that require a significant investment are worth testing smaller first. Try to figure out the smallest way you could test a substantial change before going full-on.

2. Low certainty of what will work

When you are not sure what will work or what is needed, experiments are a great way to find this out. It could be that an area is completely new for a client (e.g. Bing ads) or that you have not found consistent patterns yet for what drives growth.

3. Big potential impact

Sometimes you may have a lot of confidence in an experiment, and the potential impact is very high. In this instance, you might want to run it as an experiment. This decision is more tactical; you want to know the exact impact. Knowing that can help push your growth hacking project forward and gain internal buy-in.

4. Trade-offs/Limited resources

When you are very limited in resources such as development resources, the extra effort of experiments is worth investing. You have to be very critical in what you do and don't invest time in.

5. Variables

Many growth hacking actions have variables and options. Does version 1 or version 2 of the onboarding email convert better? The way to understand which variable works better is through experimentation. It also decreases your risk, if you set 2 or 3 Facebook ads live for an audience the chance of finding one that works and resonates is higher rather than just having one.

6. Messaging

We felt this was another key one to mention. Even if you base the copy precisely on what your customers say, messaging is still tricky. You often don't know what phrasing or value proposition will work best with which target audience. Even if you don't have the traffic to test this on your website, you could always test it via ads.

Once you have the basics in place for a client and understand better what phase they are in, you can figure out how to approach it. Whether you suggest to them that you focus entirely on experiments, or run some experiments whilst fixing the rest, or even not run them at all.

In the next part, we will focus on the real hustle. The project is up and running. A big part of this, whether you run sprints or not is deciding what will drive the biggest impact starting by building a healthy backlog of ideas and from there prioritising.

> **Key Takeaway**
>
> Please don't run experiments for the sake of it. They cost a considerable amount of additional resources so you should be critical of whether they are right for that type of task and project. That doesn't mean that you don't measure actions but rather consider what does and doesn't need to be an experiment.

SECTION 3

The Real Hustle

CHAPTER 14

Ideation - How to get new, great ideas and get involved

14.1 The challenges With ideation

Ideas occur everywhere, from flying in during meetings to stemming from an in-depth analysis. It could even be that you have a specific brainstorm or just a conversation at the lunch table. We've even had some great ideas for this book over beers. It doesn't matter where they occur, what matters is that there is always room for ideation as well as that you document ideas in a systematic and structured method.

Creating room for ideation is often underappreciated. People believe that ideas will occur in meetings and analysis, but by relying only on that we can guarantee the following will happen:

1. **Outspoken individuals often dominate the ideation.** There are always a few individuals who are quick to start with little data or are generally more outspoken. This means introverts or people who want more time to think first often don't get the chance to voice their ideas.
2. **The rest of the organisation doesn't get asked for input.** As the ideas are often discussed in meetings or result from analysis other team members don't always get the

chance to voice their ideas. The customer support team tends to have brilliant ideas but if they don't know who to tell they often get forgotten or never shared. By having a system where the room is united in brainstorming and gathering ideas, you can change this.
3. **Ideas get forgotten.** Ideas get forgotten when you don't have a structure for documentation. We don't care how you do it; from a wall of post-its to a project management tool, make sure that every idea is documented. Great ideas often occur during random conversations you have. They may pop up at the beginning/end of calls or whilst grabbing coffee. Too often, ideas are thought of or mentioned randomly and forgotten. Even if they aren't winners, others might see the hypothesis and come up with a better or new implementation.

A structured way of documenting ideas and brainstorming solves many of these risks. Not only that, but the more considerable backlog often increases the quality of the ideas chosen in the end. You are not selecting ideas for the sake of it but focusing only on the best ones.

14.2 Taking the time to brainstorm

We have already explained the risks of missing ideas. Now don't underestimate individuals who don't immediately rattle off ten ideas. Some people are not quick starters, as they don't start until they have enough information, they need more time to gather extra data or think, and then come up with ideas. You could assume they don't have any ideas but that is not the case. At Heights, Daphne has a colleague who struggles with coming up with ideas during brainstorming sessions, but that is because he needs time to see a problem from various angles and think it through. The ideas he comes with afterwards are always of high quality and have often proven to be winners. Don't let these individuals' creativity be underestimated; as a result, it is quality over quantity.

So how do you create room for these individuals?

The solution is simple but challenging to do structurally: have set, regular brainstorm moments. Having such moments focused on just one or two areas gives an opportunity to these deep divers. Even if the ideas come afterwards, like in our example, it creates time to provide the context of a problem and start everyone thinking about it. It also helps you to involve other individuals who are usually not part of the growth meetings. The brainstorm should not be a random "How do we reach the OMTM?", but instead very focused on one or maybe two areas. Often random ideas are suggested if there is a lack of focus, leaving the biggest bottlenecks unsolved. These ideas may be beneficial but are more wild shots rather than focused shots on the target. Make sure everyone knows what the brainstorming topics are ahead of the meeting so they can start to think things over and, if relevant, dive into the data beforehand.

There are many different techniques for brainstorming. We will only mention two of our favourites rather than list every method here. A simple search of "brainstorm techniques" will do the subject far more justice than we could attempt within the confines of this book. Whatever technique you choose, try to find strategies that avoid groupthink (one or two individuals dominating the room) and keep varying approaches. Varying the brainstorming method will get the creativity flowing and will bring out new ideas and ways of thinking.

The first technique we like is starting with individual brainstorming, everyone takes 5 -15 minutes to note down any ideas they have. Only then discuss various ideas and areas. By doing this, it helps avoid groupthink as if you start with discussion a few people will dominate the room and others end up just agreeing. It also gives time to think through all ideas that come to mind in a quieter setting. Afterwards you start to discuss the individual ideas and group them. You will even notice new ideas and creativity come up as a result of the discussions.

The second technique is to challenge the team to think without limitations. Too often, people don't consider ideas anymore because they believe they are not possible or out of scope. People give up suggesting things because they weren't possible the way they imagined it. When you start asking questions like:
"Imagine we could change anything on the website, what would you change?"
"Imagine if we rebuilt the product page from scratch, how would you build it?"

Suddenly you change the reference point. The team no longer focuses on the limitations, but rather the possibilities. It's the same as thinking about improving your own house versus building a new one from scratch. With the new one, your ideas are far more daring.

14.3 Documenting ideas

When documenting ideas, it is about finding a balance. You want to have enough information to understand the potential and concept of the idea. Too little and by the time you implement it, you have no idea what the idea was. You want it to be clear from the documentation what data a view is based on. You also want to know what the belief behind the hypothesis is (e.g. if we change X, we will see Y).

On the other hand, you don't want it to be a hassle to document. It's not necessary to work out a full growth experiment card per idea as that becomes overkill. Also, the specifics of an experiment

are often more relevant closer to the date of the experiment. Things such as:
"How long do we expect the experiment will take?"
"When are the results worth the time invested?"
Working these out too early not only makes documentation a hassle but it's a waste of time. If the amount of traffic has changed since you had the idea, you will need to recalculate the duration of the experiment anyway.

Next to that, the documentation should be in a location that you and the team look at often. Again we don't care if this is a project management tool or a bookmarked excel. Find a system that works for you and your client. Everyone should know where the ideas are and look at them regularly. Often seeing the ideas and data can inspire new ideas.

14.4 How do you know if you have enough ideas?

How many ideas do you need for there to be "enough" ideas? How stuffed of ideas does the backlog need to be to meet that criteria of "enough"? These are tough questions because there is no golden number of ideas to have. You could have a backlog of five high potential ideas that you can break down into smaller experiments. That may keep you busy for the coming months. You could also have a backlog of a hundred low quality small ideas and have no idea what to do next. That is why we won't tell you an amount but rather try to teach you our benchmark for judging a backlog.

You have enough ideas in your backlog:

1. **When there is excitement about all the potential ideas.** This is a clear sign that there are high impact ideas in the backlog. Note what we see as excitement, we don't mean "Oooh this is such a cool test, I've always thought it

would be great to test TikTok ads". No, we mean the excitement of the potential of ideas: "I feel like one of these will help us solve our product page dropoff!". It is the excitement that comes from knowing that the tests have the potential to improve an area, that you've thought through all the ideas to find the best one.
2. **When it's a matter of priorities and choices during the planning meeting.** If you are struggling to find what to test next when planning, it is a sign that extra brainstorming is needed. It is tempting to figure it out in the planning meeting, but planning is for prioritising, not brainstorming. You know that you have enough ideas when the discussion isn't "Does anyone have an idea of what to do next?" but "Which of these ideas have the highest priority?".
3. **When ideas start getting so small that the potential impact is little**. Sometimes you keep searching for more ideas around your focus area. Yet, everything you come up with has a low potential or impact. Whilst a hundred micro improvements will lead to significant progress, the time needed to test an idea should not be more than the benefits it might offer. First, try a different brainstorm technique or mix up the group. If the ideas remain small, you may have hit your maximum in that area or have covered the main ideas for now. Maybe you need to take a full step back (the second technique we mentioned for brainstorming) or see if this should still be the focus area, is this still your biggest bottleneck?

If the points above apply, you most likely have a healthy backlog. We'll mention it once more for good effect: it is rarely the case that organisations lack ideas. Rather they lack the time or structure to keep track of those ideas systematically. It's part of your job to solve this - to bring in a system and provide the necessary structure to grow your backlog quickly.

Key Takeaway

It is easy to get caught up in the day to day and not take enough time for ideation. This means you could miss a considerable wealth of ideas especially from people who are not part of meetings and/or are not quick to speak up. Create a system where all ideas are welcome and documented.

CHAPTER 15

Prioritising - More or Better Tests

15.1 A growth strategy without prioritisation

Once you have the ideas, the next step is to prioritise them. It may feel like you know what needs to be done, making it tempting to skip the prioritisation framework. Beware! Whilst this may save you time in the short-term, by avoiding work that you deem to be a hassle, it has several risks:

- You may not take the time to consider experiments in-depth as well as from different perspectives. Prioritisation often forces you to think an experiment further through: what resources do we need? What do we expect the results to be? This often results in a healthy discussion from which stems perspectives that may change your views about experiments.
- You create too much room for experiments based on HIPPOs (Highest Paying Person's Opinion). Without a framework for what experiments are chosen, it is tough to give pushback. It is easier to show a client that something won't or shouldn't be tested when it ranks low on the list.
- You would bear the full responsibility if it was more of a subjective choice instead of a carefully considered group

decision. That means that you alone will receive the blame if the results don't come in as you hoped.

Not having a prioritisation framework is risky. There is power in perceptions and discussions. Don't underestimate what you can learn from scoring issues. Even talking about why people would rate specific issues differently can teach you a lot. Especially if you take into account that you are an expert in your field of growth, but not in the industry.

In contrast, your client is working day-in, day-out with the people from the industry. They might know what works better with their target audience, which tactics have already been tried by competitors and what platforms are booming in the industry, all of which could be your springboard for growth.

15.2 How to prioritise

There are many different frameworks for prioritising experiments:

- ICE
- BRASS
- PXL

... And several other abbreviations. Just smash your keyboard, and we are sure the letters that come up will spell some type of prioritisation framework.

We are not here to tell you that one is better than the other. We have both used various frameworks, depending on the organisation and type of project. For example, with a project heavily focused on conversion optimisation, we love PXL. It helps to remove some of the subjectivity and puts weight on the data. In contrast, for the prioritisation of content, we usually make up a framework considering variables such as ease of writing, business value, search volume, and potential to rank. Choose a framework that you feel reflects the critical considerations for that organisation and don't be afraid to adjust it according to your needs.

For example, if it is time-consuming to get experiments up and running, you might put extra weight on the ease element. Whilst, if you need a win, you might put more weight on a component that reflects certainty. If you want to consider scalability you might prefer a framework like BRASS. Each project you work on should have its framework rather than a fixed one you prefer.

In general, be wary of subjective frameworks; the quality of your experiments is only as good as the quality of your prioritisation. Frameworks like ICE are incredibly subjective, meaning it may add little value. It is too easy to game the system and let your favourite ideas rank high. Do whatever you can to remove subjectivity:

- Base ease on time needed, e.g. <4 hours = 5, 4-8 hours = 4, etc.
- Make sure you include categories for what you consider to be high traffic to measure impact. What is or isn't a considerable amount of traffic in this case?
- Weigh ideas with multiple sources of data, backing them up more heavily. So give additional points to an idea based on user testing, Analytics and screen recordings vs an idea based solely on findings from a screen recording.

Next to that, prioritisation is not only about which framework to use. It is also about your process of prioritisation. Like everything in growth hacking, this needs a transparent system where you must consider:

1. How do you document the prioritisation?

Where do you document the prioritised experiments? Does everyone know where to find it? Do you document them all in one place and use filters for diving deeper, or do you divide up the experiment per focus area? The second makes more sense when you have different teams working on each focus area.

2. Who does the prioritisation?

You could choose to do the first prioritisation alone, and then you discuss it with the group in the sprint meeting. There are two other options. The first is to have a separate session where you score all of the items. A different session can be time-consuming but immediately provokes discussion. The other option is to allow several individuals to rank issues by building this into your prioritisation framework and then create an average as a result. It doesn't have to be that everyone ranks all of the issues but perhaps just 2-3 key stakeholders of which you use to take the average score. The consistency in who does the scoring is vital. If person A is scoring half of the issues and person B handles the second half, this may mess up the ranking. We would advise always doing the basic prioritisation before the growth meeting, as this avoids taking too much time prioritising, which can lead to long and less engaging sessions.

3. How do you determine which experiments you will do in the end?

The idea of a framework is not to let the framework pick the top 3 or 5 experiments; a framework is only a tool. It does, however, help bring order to an extensive list of issues from which you choose the absolute priorities. It could be that everyone has to vote before or during the growth meeting, for example, give each individual five votes on the top ten experiments. From there, you select the most popular experiments. You can also have everyone pitch an experiment and see how that goes.

15.3 More or better tests?

An intriguing discussion is whether you should be pushing for more wins or bigger wins. Some organisations measure the success of a growth program on speed, but the risk of this is that you end up focusing too much on small or quick experiments. You may skip over more significant, impactful tests because it would reduce velocity.

Others focus on win rate, and again this comes with its drawbacks. You have the opposite almost; you might be more scared of pursuing riskier tests. What if they fail? You can also become too focused on perfecting a test before running it, forgetting the 80/20 rule. The client may end up disappointed with the tempo and feeling that things aren't going fast enough.

Before sharing our views, we want to show you the benefits of both sides. That way, you can also look critically at your current or upcoming project to see what you think makes sense. After that, we will explain our advice in choosing an approach.

Firstly, what are the benefits of focusing on better tests, aka focusing on impact?

- **Higher quality of tests.** Often experiments are chosen on quality rather than quantity. Not caring about how many tests are run creates more room for high impact experiments.
- **More time to understand tests.** When you focus on the impact, it creates more room to set up the test correctly and analyse the results. When you focus on speed, not enough time is spent analysing and learning from previous experiments. It also gives you the time to do qualitative interviews with customers to understand why people did what they did.

- **Better use of resources.** Resources are limited in almost every organisation so by focusing on quality over quantity; you can make sure you use them as effectively as possible.

The benefits of focusing on more tests, aka velocity, are as follows:

- **Bring in more wins.** If prioritised properly higher velocity should increase the results. More high potential experiments should mean a higher overall number of experiments that win.
- **Avoids granular perfection.** It forces people to keep it simple and not spend more time than beneficial on a single experiment.
- **Limits scope.** It also prevents you from making experiments too big but always finding the smallest way to test a hypothesis.
- **Improves the foundation setup.** Focusing on speed forces you to stretch what the organisation is capable of. As a result, you optimise how you set tests up, for example, through automating specific tasks such as analysis or setting up a new test.

We would argue the following points when deciding. It's a balancing act between the two, with the importance of each depending on your phase. In the beginning, you want to bring up the tempo; you want to nail the mechanism of getting experiments live. It's about growing the mindset of testing in the organisation. That is particularly important if an organisation usually tries to perfect or overcomplicate things, then you should focus on speed to help force them to keep it small and straightforward.

From there, once you have the right tempo in place, you may want to focus more on your win rate. You may see lots of experiments going live, but there are not enough winners relative to the number of tests. It could also be that the win rate was high in the beginning, but as most of the low hanging fruit was picked up already, it is slowly flatlining.

If you were hoping that we would just give you the right win rate or tempo; unfortunately, we are going to disappoint you. There is no one correct rate; it is all relative to your organisation. An older organisation that has been experimenting for a long time will have a lower rate than an organisation just starting with testing. The key is to measure both metrics and agree on priorities together with your client.

We often talk about the results and the focus areas with our client but not the overall process. Even if growth hacking is not new for their organisation, it's essential to reflect regularly on the process metrics, such as:

- Number of ideas in the backlog
- Win rate (as well as the number of winners, losers, insignificant and discontinued tests)
- Velocity (number of tests per month/quarter)

If you are tracking experiments, this should be easy enough to monitor. We will cover more on how to track experiments in the coming chapter as well as provide you with a template for it.

> **Key Takeaway**
>
> Prioritisation is hard by nature because the frameworks are often subjective. Try to build a custom setup for your client and take the subjectivity out as much as possible to ensure the best ideas win.

CHAPTER 16

Structured - Tracking Experiment Progress

Documentation… wait, don't skip this chapter!

We get it; documentation is tedious and annoying to do. It can feel like an absolute waste of time because you don't need the documentation on a day-to-day basis. So you start slacking and not documenting the ongoing experiments.

But then... BAM! Suddenly, the client asks a question. Maybe it's for an overview of the growth program or how many tests were run during the last quarter because they are reviewing if they want to continue next quarter. You spend the coming hours scrambling around and trying to remember everything from the previous three months to pin it down on paper. You could have shown exactly how much growth you brought the organisation… if only you had documented it at the time.

Documentation, dreadfully dull, but essential.

First, let's run through the risks of not documenting and then we will show you how we track experiments (you'll get access to our framework as part of the book). From there, we will show you how you can leverage the documentation to get the benefits out of it. We will keep it short and straightforward as we realise that this isn't your favourite part. But please don't underestimate the value of documentation, or else you risk learning it the hard way like in the example above.

16.1 Risks of not documenting

Just to ensure the message truly hits home, let's go over some worst-case scenarios. We'll list them here so that you hopefully never have to experience them for yourself. If you don't note down experiments, you run the risk of:

1. **Losing sight of your KPI.** In the last chapter, we highlighted the importance of looking at specific metrics, like the win rate and velocity. That way, you can understand where and how you should improve your overall growth program. To know these metrics, you need to keep track of your experiments.
2. **Miss out on learnings between experiments.** You may miss out on specific findings and patterns you can find by looking across experiments, rather than at individual tests. For example, which types of tests often win or lose? Which part of the funnels creates the most impact?
3. **Running experiments for nothing, because you had no goal or the wrong goal.** Having a clear definition of a win sounds simple, but let's use an example of an email experiment: are one or two purchases considered a success? When is it worthwhile to do those types of emails more often? Far too frequently, experiments are run and only afterwards, it is unclear whether it was a win or not.
4. **Having to put hours and hours in preparing process meetings.** Every quarter, we advise taking a step back with your client to see how the last three months have gone. We call this the "quarterly zoom out" meeting. What should you focus more or less on in the coming quarter? We will talk more about this in Chapter 19: Quarterly Zoom

Outs. For now, know that documenting saves you a considerable amount of time preparing for those sessions. You can often copy and paste figures, rather than having to look everything up individually.

16.2 How best to document

Documentation can be done in many different ways. Some people prefer to do it in their project management tool and adjust the tool to make it work for growth experiments. Others use a specialised tool which is built for documenting experiments, like GrowthHacker.com's 'Experiments tool' or Growth Tribe's 'G.R.O.W.S. tool'. We often actually prefer a simple Google Sheets overview or a simple tool like Airtable, especially when starting. Yes, it could be considered a bit old school, but it works, especially if your client is just starting with growth hacking. An extra tool will cost extra effort, onboarding and costs, when you can get 80% of the same benefits from an Excel spreadsheet or Google Sheets overview. Once you are a few steps further, a more advanced tool can take it to the next level.

For simplicity, we will refer to our solution as Google Sheets as that is where we set up a template for you which has been made explicitly for growth experiments. You can find that template available in the resources section: growinghappyclients.com/resources. This template allows you to document ongoing and completed experiments. It also provides two templates for prioritising tests. Feel free to change and adjust the prioritisation framework to a structure you prefer.

As we mentioned in the last chapter, it may vary how you prioritise per project, the same goes for documentation so set up a structure that works for your client and you.

> **Time for Action**
>
> This action point is only relevant if you don't document experiments. If you do, of course, still feel free to run through our template. You might adapt your way of working once you've tried it differently. It's based upon 100+ client projects, so hopefully, you can learn something from it.
>
> Walkthrough the template we have shared and copy it to your drive to adjust it according to your client. There is no need to add every single past experiment; this will only demotivate you, instead:
>
> 1. Add the running experiments to the overview.
> 2. Decide how you will document your experiments.
> 3. Add reminders to your calendar.

Finally, we would advise approaching documentation in one of two ways.

The first option is to be documenting continuously. So any time there is an update about an ongoing experiment or an experiment is completed, document it. Whilst this is less efficient, it is more accurate and keeps documentation at the top of your mind.

The alternative option is to have set times or moments when you update documentation. These moments might be before and after a sprint meeting, or after a standup. This second method is more efficient as you can check in one moment that everything is up to date and adjust accordingly. You will need to make sure those moments are frequent enough so that you stay on top of all running experiments.

There is another beneficial way to document an experiment, and that is through slides. We will share how to do that with you in the next chapter, Chapter 17: Presenting the Results.

16.3 How to leverage your documentation

We've already mentioned that documentation can be very beneficial in progress meetings. Next to that, there are a few other ways you can get more out of your documentation:

1. **Share insights during growth meetings.** If you have everything documented, it's effortless to share statistics frequently, such as the current number of running experiments, winners and losers of the last sprint, etc.
2. **Easy to follow up structurally on open experiments.** If you clearly document which experiments are running, you can check the status of each one in one overview. You can use this almost like a to-do list to see what the status is and what you still need to follow up on.
3. **Easier to onboard new team members onto a project or in the company.** When a new team member joins (whether on your side or the clients), they can look through all the previous experiments. They can understand what tests have and haven't run until now, and immediately learn from all your previous work and learnings.
4. **Smooth transfers of the project.** Sometimes you need to transfer the project. It could be that you have completed your part as a consultant or that you are going on holiday. Having an overview can save a lot of timing in explaining what has been done until now.

Now that you're a documenting machine let's move on to how you can present all those great results. It's one thing tracking it all in a Google Sheet, but your client will probably want a flashier presentation of it all.

> **Key Takeaway**
>
> You can love or hate documentation, but it will save you a lot of time further down the line. Find a way to remind yourself to update overviews regularly.

CHAPTER 17

Presenting the Results

Picture this; you're in a meeting with the management of a new client, and you're trying to convince them of the importance of improving their SEO. You feel yourself growing warm as you nervously stumble over your words. If they invest in SEO, there is so much potential given their current base of content. So you explain and push why you think it is essential.

"Fixing the SEO will improve our rankings driving far more traffic."

Nervously, you look around the room as the discussion begins. They aren't convinced, they have other priorities on their minds.

"If we do this, won't it get in the way of that new feature?" Someone calls out.

The room starts to agree with them, murmuring loudly. Your mind is frantically racing as you search for some way to convince them.

"We already have the content; it would mainly mean updating it."

No luck, the battle is lost. You feel yourself blushing as you consider moving on to the next part of your presentation. Finally, one of the team members comes to your rescue and pushes for the focus on SEO:

"You do all realise that our current content drives a huge amount of leads which results in consistent sales throughout the year. Even if we just increase the traffic by 10%, the revenue boost would be huge. We have no guarantee that the new feature will do the same."

Suddenly the other decision-maker listens and agrees. Five minutes ago you said it would increase traffic too! And now, they suddenly agree? So frustrating, right? You dwell on it that evening while grumbling furiously to your partner. You finally realise why they were successful, and you were not. That team member brought it from an alternative perspective, and that is what hit the mark.

Same message but radically different results, what's their secret? Packaging, how they told the story. They probably knew exactly what would trigger the other members and packaged it to drive the message home. It wasn't the increase in traffic that they cared about but the fact that it was a more certain increase than that shiny new alternative. The team member made the alternative look like a risk and less attractive. They translated the actions you wanted to take into the results that management wanted to hear.

Take how we opened this chapter. We could have just told you that your story and slides are essential, that you should tweak them for success. But that wouldn't have gotten the message across the way this scenario did. When we tell a story, slide in a few emotions that you may experience, and highlight the importance of packaging, it triggers far more. Telling a story is what you need to do with your slides too. There are a ton of practical tips we'll share on how to set up your slides, but first things first: it's all about storytelling.

17.1 The basic storyline

Us growth hackers are a bit geeky; we love our data and models. We get all excited about our experiment passing the robustness tests

- nailed it! Yet, sadly our clients don't share our excitement about our fancy statistical models or hundreds of ranking factors.

Can you sense their eyes slowly glazing over as you cover graph 10? Can you feel yourself racing through the slides because you're losing their attention? Your clients are busy, and they usually aren't data geeks. They want a story that tells them:

1. The pain that was involved
2. How you triumphed over it
3. If there was a happy ending

That is the basic storyline for most growth hacking romance bestsellers. What does this look like in practice? We'll base it on the topic of SEO as this is sometimes a tough one to turn it into the next 50 shades of grey. Each bullet point represents an individual slide:

1. **Pain:**
    a. We see that our competitors rank above us (bonus points for a visual from Google).
    b. We are only getting 10% of search volume on this critical keyword, among others (show the Click Through Rate).
    c. We're this close to outranking our competitors, but our backlinks need to be improved (graph comparing domain authority of competing search results).
2. **Potential Solution:**
    a. We improved our backlink profile during the last three months (show domain authority and number of backlinks increasing per month).
3. **Results:**
    a. We improved our ranking for significant keywords, on average by two positions (double bonus points for

> a visual from Google again but then with your client higher up in search results).
> b. This change resulted in a 12% increase in traffic for those keywords.
> c. It creates additional revenue of approximately €7,300 per month.

In the span of those few slides, you take them from the pain to the solution. This story is far more potent than "So the extra backlinks increased our traffic".

Now you could say this is easy to spin into a fun story; it is a win, what about a loss? Even a loss is a win and can tell a story: you stopped the implementation of something that would decrease purchases by 7%! You tested a channel in a small way before your client wasted thousands on it! Those too are powerful stories.

17.2 How to tell your story

Telling a story is vital, but how do you set up your slides so that they tell *your* story? Often your slides will get sent around internally by your client. How do you ensure that even if you aren't presenting them, they still tell a story? We've combined our best tips for setting your slides up for success by keeping in mind your target audience. We've even included our favourite slide hack at the end.

1. The titles should tell your story.

Busy people are scanners. How many times have you seen the same boring title used for five slides: SEO Analysis (1), SEO Analysis (2), SEO Analysis (3)... too many right?. Think about how you scan through articles: you zoom through the headings. The same happens with your slides so let your titles tell the story not your 12pt bullet point lists (slightly ironic saying that within a list, we get that!).

2. Clear and concise visuals.

Don't you get weirdly enthusiastic from graphs that go up? Clients do too. Upward trends (if they are real) make them excited. Don't try to show five things in one graph, instead have only one large visual that makes one point. The title should explain that point in turn. If you aren't sure, do a five-second test for your graph. If another person can figure it out in five seconds or less, you're probably onto a winner.

3. No cognitive overload, please.

Go back to our SEO example for a second. Note how each slide (the individual bullet points) covers just one topic. It is like a strong landing page. There is one clear call to action for you to focus on. People often worry about having too many slides and instead try to squeeze more stuff on fewer slides by filling them with bullet points. This is the worst thing you could do. It just leads to confusion and will take longer to get through it. Don't overload the audience as they try to figure out what the slide means or get distracted by minor details. Remember, one main message per slide.

4. Use your client's language, not yours.

Sometimes we play buzzword bingo with slides: stuffing as many technical phrases in as few slides as possible. We fill our slides with terms like "View-Through-Rate", "Statistical Power" and "Quality Scores". Your client may not ask you what any of that means, but they are probably thinking "Lions, and tigers and bears, oh my!" If you haven't scared them $hitless already, you can bet they are making a mental note to Google what you just said... Try using their language instead that includes killing the fancy statistical analyses we mentioned earlier. Talk about numbers that matter to them, like the end profit. So, whilst we agree that those analyses are cool, they do need to be delegated to the appendix.

5. Consider which slide deck you use.

Your client has a house style and so do you, so which is the right one? Sorry, it's *that* reply again: it depends. Using your deck can get your name known within the company. Your client may even prefer it if you have a beautiful house style. It is a great way to present the results as something shiny and new rather than the same old.

Whilst the same old style can be tedious; it is also comforting and familiar. It may give them the feeling that the results belong to them. Their house style, in turn, will make it more likely for them to send it around internally. How do we choose? We tend to ask our client what is essential for them. What are they trying to achieve by sending around the slides? Finally, we always asked which type of program they use: is it PowerPoint, Google Slides or Keynote? Sounds stupid, but trust us, after transferring 200 slides from Google Slides to PowerPoint... you never make the same mistake twice.

6. The devil is in the details.

Imagine you're wearing a fancy shirt, that blue one that makes your eyes twinkle. It's got a few creases in it because you haphazardly shoved it into the cupboard - your bad. You are about to grab some groceries, but as you check yourself out in the mirror before you leave you to notice the creases. Do you bother to iron it before you leave? If you hate ironing like we do you can probably live with a few wrinkles, right? Now imagine you are going to a client meeting instead, in that same fancy shirt. What now? Time to grab the iron? Picture those eight sets of eyes noticing all those creases. Suddenly ten minutes of ironing doesn't seem so bad after all. Our slides should be ironed out in the same way. All eight sets of eyes will be on the slides. Not only that, as we mentioned, your slides often get sent around internally. You wouldn't want everyone to see you in your creased shirt, but you do leave creases in their presentation: missing commas, inconsistent bullet point colours, five different font sizes, etc. Seems small, but when your client's eyes are on you, those creases seem huge - they may be so bad your client doesn't even bother sharing your slides with the wider team. If the content is fabulous, but the presentation is not, you've already lost. People always judge a book (or presentation) by its cover.

7. Management summary.

Few high-level managers have the time, or the patience, to run through fifty slides on the project. So it's important to have a few slides at the beginning called the management summary. When you send it to your contact person you can say "Hi Ellen, here are the slides we walked through earlier today. I can imagine your manager will want an update on the progress. I've added a few slides at the beginning that summarises it." All Ellen is thinking is "You're the best. My manager was asking me yesterday how the project was going. I still needed to create a short update." Additionally, this is another way that you help them in their ABC!

8. The slide hack

And it wouldn't be a growth hacking book without a slide hack. This will save you hours throughout your project. You've been making slides for all different meetings already, and in those slides, you highlight what's going on per experiment. How can you get so much more out of that with a little extra effort? The trick is to make sure that each time you follow that same structure. Just a few slides that explain: what the hypothesis is (the pain), what the experiment is (the solution) and what the outcome was (the results). Then adding that to a master slide deck which has all the experiments, organised per area. It has a double purpose:

1. You can use it as a learning document for new people joining the projects.
2. You can also use it for board/quarter meetings. Then you can choose a few experiments to highlight. If you have a

master slide deck and a structured overview of all the experiments, you can whip out quarterly slides in no time.

Now that you know more about improving your slides and presenting your results, it is time for action. It is time for you to do a teardown of your very own presentation.

Time for Action

Take the slide deck of your last client meeting and run it through the checklist:

- Did you tell the experiment as a story?
- Do your titles explain that story?
- Have you used clear and concise visuals?
- Does each slide only have a single focus point?
- Have you used their language, not yours?
- Have you considered which slide deck you should use?
- Have you included a management summary?
- Are you consistent in the layout?
- Have you double-checked there are no spelling/grammatical mistakes in the slides?

Bonus points, of course, for using the slide hack.

Now that was a bit of fun, spicing up how you present your results. Time for a bit of a tougher chapter, how do you get feedback? How do you continuously build evaluation into your process?

Key Takeaway

Tell a story through your slides. When skimming through your slides, the key takeaways and general message should be apparent immediately.

CHAPTER 18

ABEing - Always Be Evaluating

18.1 Failing to get feedback

"Do you have any feedback for the sprint, what went well, what could go better? Anything I could do differently?"

Seven pairs of eyes stare at you, all belonging to your client's team members. It's the review section of the sprint, the opportunity to gather feedback. You wait for someone, anyone, to say something. You urge yourself not to speak for the sake of it, to keep your cool and wait. But still, no one talks, the silence stretches on. Has it already been ten minutes? It feels like it, but the clock on your laptop reminds you that it has barely been two. You decide to try and guide the conversation, get the fire started.

"I felt that I could have indicated earlier the development capacity needed," you offer up.

A strained smile fills your face; you hope that by indicating your mistake, it would encourage them to be more open with their feedback. It doesn't. You look around the room one last time.

"Anyone? Well if you have any feedback, let me know."
You swiftly click the enter button to the next slide. You feel relieved that you won't have to do that again for another week.

Well, that was awkward. After experiences like this, you might grow hesitant to have any form of feedback in your client meetings, instead choosing to leave it to the account manager to deal with. The failure was not that you asked for feedback, but how you asked for it.

In that meeting, everyone was put on the spot by asking them for feedback directly in front of the group. They would consider it to be shaming you in front of everyone else, and they weren't that cruel, luckily. By not providing you with feedback, they believed that they were helping you to save face, rather than making the situation even more uncomfortable. It all lies in the questions asked. The questions tend to be phrased as follows:
"Do you have feedback?"
"What could I be doing better?"

You might like or be used to getting candid feedback. As Dutch people, we are renowned for being blunt and forthright, which means that we always give and receive feedback heartily. Yet, with a client, you have a different relationship, and they may not be used to giving or receiving such direct feedback. Try to get specific in the feedback and not too personally:
"How could we improve the process?"
"What should we do differently next sprint?"

18.2 Why is feedback crucial in consulting?

No matter how you feel about feedback (either giving or receiving), the undeniable truth is that feedback is crucial. Maybe, you don't have an account team, or the account team doesn't have the time to check infrequently. Even if you do, it could be that the account manager could call at the wrong time, and you get a rushed "all is fine". But is everything fine? And is fine enough? Then your client leaves you the next month, and you're sitting elbow deep into a tub of Ben & Jerry's wondering how it all went so wrong. Neither Ben nor Jerry seem to be able to give you the answer.

A successful relationship with a client is getting to know them, what does and doesn't work for them. Not too different from an actual relationship. As much as we try to give you the tools for your toolbox, you need to understand which tools to pull out with each client. One client likes a strict approach with constant reminders whilst the others may hate you for it. Finding the right process is challenging, which makes frequent feedback moments essential.

So how can you Always Be Evaluating? Or as we like to call it ABEing.

18.3 Plan in retrospectives

We have a saying in Dutch that goes "Beter goed gejat dan slecht verzonnen", which roughly translates to "It is better to steal something good then to invent something bad" (we promise it sounds better in Dutch). There is already a robust feedback system used in Scrum known as a Sprint Retrospective. Even if you don't use Scrum with your client, you can 'steal' the use of a Sprint Retrospective.

The idea of a Sprint Retrospective is that after running a sprint, you look at the following:

- What worked well?
- What could have gone better?
- What will we commit to during the next sprint?

It is about not only looking for improvement points but also being proud of what is working because you want to do more of that.

There are many different techniques for holding a Sprint Retrospective. Like with brainstorming techniques, we feel you are far better off Googling for ideas. Search for "sprint retrospective techniques", and you'll get a ton of inspiration, and just like brainstorming feel free to mix it up regularly. One of our favourite Scrum Masters we've worked with brought a new technique every retrospective; we had to admire her creativity. As a result, everyone is engaged in the sessions and curious to see what original method there would be this time.

We will share one of our favourite techniques here to give you an idea of what such a session looks like. You want to take about 30 - 45 minutes for a sprint retrospective - long enough that everyone can share their thoughts, but not too long that they lose interest. Here's how you could structure it:

1. Everyone has three different coloured post-its.
2. Each colour is for a different group of feedback. Sometimes they are known as the various houses like the story of the three pigs. This technique makes it less personal and more comfortable to indicate feedback:
    a. House of Straw: What did not go well. A house of straw can fall apart at any minute, so these are the things that didn't go well and need improving.
    b. House of Wood: What went so-so. A house of wood is a bit more robust but isn't flawless; it is the in-between issues. What went okay, but could have gone smoother.
    c. House of Bricks: What went great. A house of bricks is stable, no wind nor wolf will blow it away. Consider what went well. These are compliments to others and are also things to keep doing.
3. You create three columns on the table or wall. You want to organise the post-its into each of the columns: House of Straw, House of Wood and House of Bricks.

4. Everyone in the team (both you and your client) has five minutes to write down their feedback; it can reference any part of the process. There are no pointing fingers; rather, it is about taking a step back. It is about looking critically at the different parts of the process.
5. Each person, in turn, shares their feedback with the group and adds their post-its. Post-its about the same topic either doesn't need to be added or discussed to avoid repetition.
6. Then you choose one or two key points to improve on the coming sprint or period. You define what the key action points are to improve it.

The great thing about this is that everyone first takes a step back and gets to reflect in private. Like with brainstorming, this avoids groupthink or pressure to speak. Having frequent feedback sessions helps the team get comfortable with sharing feedback. Don't worry about it being awkward the first few times, just keep having these sessions at least once or twice a month. Over time they will go smoother. The above technique also works well with an online tool like Miro, where you can create virtual Post-Is.

Even though you do these sessions to gain feedback and insights from your client and your team, there is also an added benefit: it builds trust. Your clients will see you actively looking at how to achieve the goal, not just in terms of experiments, but through collaboration. Often you won't even need to point out where they could improve because their team brings it up.

There are many different techniques you could utilise. Some prefer the Sad Mad Glad method or labelling it under KALM (Keep, Add, Less, More). Others have a system that works with account management. Whichever you choose is up to you. What matters is the following:

- You have a structured and frequent method to gain feedback.

- You create a safe environment where everyone can give feedback.
- You listen with an open mind to that feedback and do your best to implement the key points.
- You vary the techniques to keep the sessions interesting and engaging.

Time for Action

If you don't have regular feedback loops with your client, choose a technique and try it out. Don't worry if it is a bit awkward at first; it takes getting used to.

If you do have regular feedback moments, try to mix it up with a different technique.

Key Takeaway

Build a system where people feel comfortable giving feedback, and you'll receive it regularly. This is especially important for Green clients who may struggle with giving feedback.

CHAPTER 19

Quarterly Zoom Out

19.1 Caught up in the day-to-day

It's so easy to get caught up in day to day business when you keep running forward without taking a break to reconsider where you are going. That is why we are a big fan of quarterly zoom outs.

The idea is that you take time to zoom out on the project, get a bird's eye view of it all and adjust course accordingly. We both like these meetings, as many new ideas come out of them. We realised that often issues start when you get too caught up in the day to day. Such issues include:

1. The client loses the overall vision

The client ends up feeling like you're doing the same old tasks, just a new day. This is a more significant risk when you are running sprints rather than working with specific projects. They also might miss progress made in particular areas that are less visible, e.g. measurement.

The individuals that join a quarterly zoom out meeting are usually one layer higher in the organisation. Their role means they miss a lot of the less visible progress, especially if results have been slower, so this is a perfect moment to discuss moving forward. Bear in mind, however, that you should never wait to indicate that results are slow until this meeting, we will talk about this more in Chapter 33: The Needle isn't Moving. Instead, you should treat this moment to look at how to turn things around.

2. Not enough time on brainstorming and implementing new channels

Of course, you'll have moments of brainstorming throughout the project, but these tend to focus on ongoing issues, not on the overall strategy and approach. If you are juggling multiple clients, it's easier to continue sticking to the same things. A zoom out forces you to to look at whether you should be doing something new or different. It forces you to get creative and do your best to impress your client.

3. Not enough alignment with the company's overarching strategy

As indicated, the top level of the organisation that is at a zoom out meeting is often not involved in the day to day of it all. These individuals are usually involved in the company's own quarterly planning meetings and strategy. As a result, it is good to have a quarterly zoom out around the same time to align the process and resources with the growth plans.

19.2 What does a quarterly zoom out look like?

The meeting should involve key stakeholders of the organisation. If you work for an agency, we recommend inviting other project members and your account manager (if you have one).

The meeting usually lasts around two hours and requires a fair amount of preparation (unless you've used the slide hack and have your experiments structured). Part of that preparation should involve checking the planned actions and focus points for the coming quarter with your contact person. This is a sanity check that what you believe should be the next step aligns with the company. Your contact person is probably not the one to decide that overall strategy, but they are close enough to the action to know what the planning is.

When you are just starting as a consultant, it can be tough to lead such a meeting. If you are an agency, we would suggest getting a senior team member to join and help run that meeting. You should still prepare and join it as you will learn so much from it. If you are a freelancer and that is not an option, you should try to have the meeting with a slightly lower level of the organisation. So one level above your contact person. This will limit your influence slightly but will be easier than sitting down with the highest level but will be an easier step. We say this to be honest with you; strategic experience and practice are key in being successful in quarterly zoom outs. So if you can find a way to make it easier, this is worth your while. We will walk through the quarterly zoom out as if you are leading it so that you know what to prepare and what to cover whether you lead the meeting or someone else.

During the meeting itself, we would suggest covering four parts.

Part 1: Reflection on the last quarter

Take a look back at the progress towards the NSM and OMTM(s):

- What were the goals?
- What is the current status?

It's also beneficial to highlight a few specific experiments that stand out either in terms of wins or learnings. We usually would also recommend a general overview of all tests:

- How many were run?
- How many won / inconclusive / lost?

Next to that, any significant changes made such as improved measurement systems, setting up any new channels, redesign of specific pages, etc. Keep it high-level, don't get too caught up in the details.

It is essential also to initiate a discussion for everyone to reflect and be honest. Reflecting might not come naturally (as you saw in the ABE chapter) but will help you adjust the project. One way to do this is to go around the room and ask everyone for:

- One area or experiment they were pleased with.
- One place where they would like to have seen more improvement.
- Then ask for the why.

This individual reflection is also an excellent way to understand what drives critical stakeholders. What do they look for and value?

Part 2: Where we are now

It is also good to look at what the current status is of certain areas relative to where you want to be. One technique is to show a status bar or timeline per area:

1. Where we were
2. Where we are now
3. Where we want to go

The timeline helps to give the feeling of progress. It's especially beneficial for areas that are tougher to measure the impact of such as measurement - ironic as that is!

You don't want only to show the OMTM but also the bigger picture. How does the whole funnel look now, and what is the current status? Usually, a OMTM is relevant for perhaps one or two quarters, so you want to use this opportunity to reevaluate the OMTM. Which area of the funnel needs the most focus right now?

Part 3: Recommendations for next quarter

Based on the above, the next natural step is to look ahead:

- What are the suggested focus points?
- Should the OMTM(s) stay the same or change? Are there new areas you want to pick up?
- Should we stay within current channels or test new channels?

It is a balance between avoiding "shiny object syndrome" — always fixating on the new thing — and giving the client a sense of innovation. Clients often look to growth consultants to also keep them fresh on what is the latest in the industry. It doesn't have to be a new channel, but innovations within channels will also interest them.

Part 4: Align approach with the company's focus, planning and resources

The final part is more of a discussion. Starting with:

- Is this what we want to focus on?
- Does it align with the company's goal?

Your check with your contact person should ensure that you avoid any major surprises here, but you never know. Be prepared that you may need to go back to the drawing board and rethink the approach. This usually occurs when the company is busy with significant company changes they couldn't share with you before; we have seen mergers and new internal startups completely throw off our planning. Don't try to solve it on the spot but instead seek to understand for now. Ask plenty of questions, and schedule a new meeting.

Let's assume that all goes well and you have aligned on what the next steps are. Now is the time to also align in terms of planning and resources:

- What is the high-level timeline?
- What resources do you need to be successful?

The timeline helps to break down large goals into smaller steps where possible to manage your client's expectations of what will be done and when. You might also need specific changes in resources, e.g. who is involved in the project, budget, development capacity. If so, indicate this here immediately. The goal is to attain commitment and buy-in during these meetings to get what you need to reach the goals.

19.3 When to have a quarterly zoom out at another time

If you have a shorter project, you might choose to do a similar form of this meeting in a different way. For example, if you have a four-month project, you might have a zoom out at the end. Then you end the meeting with 'what you'd recommend doing next' instead of 'what we do next'. You can also highlight how you feel you could work together to achieve this.

Another reason to have the meeting at a different time is when a significant change occurs. This change could be a substantial internal change:

- Merger or acquisition
- New product launch
- New round of funding
- CEO change
- Downscale
- Sales greatly decreasing
- Rebranding
- New website

It could also be an external change, e.g. an industry change, a financial crisis or pandemic. Rather than wait until the next meeting, it is often better to have a zoom out. You want to discuss the impact of the change and from there, determine how to proceed. As much as we like to plan for an upcoming quarter, changes can happen. Try to be ahead of them whenever possible.

Finally, if it's a (corporate) startup, you might choose to have zoom out meetings in a smaller, more frequent format, e.g. every one or two months. The tempo is high, and in some cases, the investors put pressure on the organisation, meaning it makes more sense to meet more frequently.

Now it's time to look at the various stakeholders involved in more depth. That way you can better work with the organisation as a whole.

Key Takeaway

This is probably the toughest meeting you will have with a client. When starting out try to take a senior team member along, even in just preparing the session you'll learn so much. From there, the meeting is a success if you are very aligned on how to move forward to drive further growth.

CHAPTER 20

Internal Fans

20.1 Goodbye my friend

Think about how much time you spend with your contact person; it might even feel like you spend more time with them than your best friends at times. Your project is like a building you create together; it continually grows and towers upwards into the sky. They are the ones with whom you discuss the strategy and individual experiments; you work day in and day out with them to create growth. Heck, you might even develop a friendly relationship with them. After all, on this project, you are practically colleagues.

Now imagine you suddenly hear that they are leaving the organisation (you may or may not have experienced this before). Shock fills you, everything you built up with them disappears with them. Your growth building is suddenly more like a Jenga tower; it is a fragile setup that could crash down without your contact person. Time to either stabilise it or build it up again from scratch.

All of a sudden other people are coming in to inspect the Jenga tower, judging the work and making the decisions. Maybe, they have a different freelancer or agency they prefer to work with. Perhaps, they don't see the need or importance for your project or work. That is not to say you haven't done a good job up until that point. They may not have seen the Jenga tower for the last few months or weren't closely involved in the building of it. But still, they get to make that decision.

Unfortunately, we have seen consultants get kicked out, not because of an issue, but simply because their primary contact person left for a new job or a new role within the company. It all comes down to this. If other people are not preaching your project, then the new contact person may be quick to dismiss it, especially in the beginning phase, where you might still be building the infrastructure.

But just how risky is it to have your contact person leave? The risk depends on the other relationships you have within the organisation. We dedicated a whole chapter to your contact person, yet, they aren't the only ones you need on your side, which is why we will talk about how and why you should build an internal fanbase within the organisation.

In the chapters that follow, we will cover many other key stakeholders:

1. The Board
2. Branding
3. Development
4. Sales
5. Customer Support
6. Legal

For each of them, we'll discuss how to work with them, what challenges to be aware of and how to tackle those, as well as how to get the most of their added value for you as a growth consultant. These next chapters will be a bit shorter due to the narrower range of topics, but they are still brimming with useful information.

First, though, let's start with internal fans.

20.2 What are internal fans?

Internal fans are individuals within the organisation who are enthusiastic about the work you do, and they can be in any department. They are likely to be involved in one way or another with the project and want it to continue and succeed. It's beneficial if at least one of your internal fans is a key stakeholder or decision-maker.

Internal fans see the value of your work and want to keep you involved. Often, if we're honest, you tend to also get along on a personal level. With a consultant-client relationship, there is always an individual element to it, an emotional connection.

That doesn't mean you have to be best friends and see each other on the weekends, but rather that you know more about them than just their job title and responsibilities. You have a chat at the beginning of meetings or during lunch about their interests. Do they love to fix up their house at the weekend? Are they crazy about their new dog (ahem, Daphne)? We have seen that a real personal connection is a common trend with raving internal fans.

How many internal fans are enough? It is not about trying to connect with everyone and have everyone be a fan, as that isn't realistic and will most likely be too time-consuming to achieve. Like with friends, a few great ones are worth far more, try to aim for at least two or three fans next to your contact person. Have at least one of those be a key stakeholder.

Think of it as Product-Market Fit. You would want them to be very disappointed if they had to stop working with you or if the project didn't continue.

Note: Building internal fans should be after you have grown a strong relationship with your contact person - that should be your priority.

20.3 How to create internal fans

Building internal fans come down to four parts:

1. The involvement in meetings.
2. Developing a connection.
3. Showing the bigger picture.
4. Figuring out both what frustrates and drives them.

Firstly, the building of internal fans begins in the meetings. During the growth meetings, you want to be consciously creating room for everyone's ideas. You want to be finding ways to put other people in the spotlight. If you know that someone is working on a relevant project, or a specific experiment, see if they fancy presenting it. Some people will not want to, and that is also okay, but others will enjoy the chance to be in the spotlight. They will feel more involved in the project. They will be appreciative of the opportunity to show the results of what they've done.

The second part was already hinted at in the explanation of what an internal fan is: the building of a personal relationship with individuals. It can be easy to continuously feel the pressure and try to put on a work face, but people want to work with real people. People want to connect. What we try to do is find common ground and talk about that. That comes far more naturally. Daphne is absolutely not a cat person. If she pretends to care about what her contact person's cat is up to, it will be disingenuous and only backfire. Talking about dogs; however, she can do that endlessly.

Start with asking questions, not prying, but taking the time to show interest. Sometimes simply showing that you are human is enough to encourage others to do the same. Try, if possible, to have lunch with the team regularly, as this is often where these conversations start.

The third part is involving more people in the bigger picture. You are always busy with the big picture, so it's easy to assume that others are too. However, they have fifty other responsibilities and may not piece together the bigger plan. Even if people are at the meetings and feel a connection with you, they need to see the end value of what you do. How can they sell your work internally if they do not know where you are working towards? Help key stakeholders, or individuals within the growth team, understand the roadmap of the project, frequently refer back to the overall plan. You can do this through:

1. Zooming out regularly in growth meetings.
2. Having quarterly zoom out meetings.
3. Talking about what your hopes are for the organisation and project.

That last one is key. Sharing your hopes shows your enthusiasm for growing the organisation. That enthusiasm helps to get others enthusiastic too.

The final part is knowing their frustrations. It's the same as with your contact person's ABCs: what keeps them up at night? What would they want to change about the organisation? Perhaps it's the speed at which everything goes, or maybe it's the lack of time to work on the projects. Knowing their pain points will help you work on improving them. If they feel everything goes too slow, but you show them that speed has increased through the project, they will be much more motivated to keep you involved.

20.4 Internal fans are not a magical solution

Even if you have internal fans, it's never a guarantee that your project will continue should your contact person change. Next to the fact that there are always political decisions, you still have to drive results. A connection will not replace the expectation that there should at least be some results.

We don't say this to pressure you, but rather to remind you of the balance of short vs long-term and that you ensure you are continuously going forward step-by-step. From there, having internal fans ensures that your impact is not underestimated, or even completely missed. Now it is time to look at how you get the board, well, onboard.

> **Key Takeaway**
>
> Once your contact person is a fan of you, it is time to start building other fans within the organisation. Unfortunately, your contact person could leave so if they do, it is critical to have other team members fighting for you to stay.

CHAPTER 21

Getting the Board on Board

21.1 Why is it your job to get the board on board?

Often your contact person is not the end decision-maker; they have a boss. That boss has a boss who, maybe, even has another boss. Don't you love the corporate ladder? No matter how much autonomy your contact person has in their day to day work, someone else is still pulling strings. So when we talk about the board, we only mean the ones making the decisions. The board isn't necessarily the highest level in the organisation, but it is near enough to the top of that ladder. They determine the overall business strategy and the growth strategy is a part of this. If you want to drive a more significant impact and lasting change, you need to be talking to them too. The marketing manager (a prevalent contact person) will not be able to decide alone that there needs to be more focus on product or brand. On their own, they can't ensure you get the development resources or budget required for you to do your thing.

First, we need to take a step back to when you joined that organisation as a consultant. This matters because it will determine how you approach getting the board on board. There are two possible ways you were brought in:

1. **Up-Down Entrance:** The board brought you in.

2. **Down-Up Entrance:** Your contact person or someone else brought you in.

Figuring out the answer to this is knowing to whom the project was sold and why. Who had the idea to work with a growth hacking agency or freelancer? If you didn't sell the project, ask the account manager or individual who did.

If the board was the one who brought you in, then this is an Up-Down Entrance. This is the ideal situation. The board may then have a confirmation bias: they want to prove they made the right decision by hiring you. The board will want to show the rest of the organisation that you will help them to reach the organisation's goals. This confirmation bias makes it easier to work with them as your success also reflects positively on them. They hired you so they can claim a part of your success. When you are brought in through the board, it will naturally be easier to get them to play along.

The second way is if someone else brought you in, a Down-Up Entrance. This person could be your contact person or someone else at a similar level in the organisation. They need to be 100% convinced that they made the right decision by bringing you in before they will start convincing others. In a Down-Up Entrance, you, together with them, will need to convince the board of the project. The board most likely approved the budget for hiring you or the agency you work for. So that is win number one, but they haven't seen the details of it. In such a setup, you need to be even more conscious of the relationship with the board and building it up. In either format, your contact person likely stands between you and the board communicating directly. They are the ones who will have the majority of the communication with the board. This means that they will play a vital role in building the relationship.

21.2 Step-by-step: how to get the board on board

It all begins right at the start of the project. You want to push for the following:

- That at least one or two individuals are at the growth meeting.
- That they are at the NSM session, we talked about in earlier chapters.
- That they sign off on the priorities of the growth program in the quarterly meetings.

They need to stand behind the focus points and believe that they are essential. When you meet them, it's a great time to ask them lots of questions to understand what drives them:

- What is their vision for the growth of the company?
- What do they see as current challenges in achieving that growth?
- What are the organisational changes they hope to see?
- When is the growth program/collaboration a success for them?

You want to figure out their why, what they want and the reasons behind that so that you can relate all your actions to that initial why. That is how you get them on board. As with the rest of the organisation, you need to Be Them. Try to get in their head regarding what drives them.

Are you unable to convince your contact person that the board should be at those first meetings? Don't panic. You don't want to push your luck. The board is jam-packed, and you want to show you understand this. Make it clear that it's not that you don't think your contact person can't approve it and instead call it a double-check. The first alternative is to have a quick follow up meeting (e.g.

30 minutes) with them to walk them through what was discussed. If that isn't possible, instead ask your contact person to check off the priorities with them. You can even offer to set up a few slides for them if that makes it more manageable. This is not ideal, but you gain that trust little by little as you start showing results and that the project is worth noting.

Your contact person is vital in this. If they are hesitant about putting you and the board in touch, it is usually because they are scared you will get the credit. Or that they don't want to receive the pressure of the results should the project fail. That is why we suggest not pushing it too hard in the beginning. Build that trust first. When you show your contact person that you will make them look good to the board, and the results are coming in, they will start demanding that time for you. That is far easier than you as an outsider pushing for it.

Now the slides are vital if you manage to get a meeting with them. We already talked a bit about this in Chapter 17: Presenting the Results. Your key stakeholders are often busy; they don't have time to read or scan long reports. We would advise instead to do as much as possible via slides. That way, they can flick through them quickly between meetings. Again, how you present is, of course, key, try to see when and how it is appropriate to keep them in the loop. It could be with your weekly update or that you agree on a quick meeting every month. If they don't have time to meet then see how your contact person usually reports to them and get involved with that. Even if this isn't the actual board and just one level up, that's also beneficial. Now another key point comes back here, which we want to dive deeper into. How are you communicating with them? How are you sharing results with them? For this and the following chapter, we will be sharing a few insights from Arnout Hellemans. You may remember him from the beginning of the book, he has 13+ years of consulting experience and has noticed the same issue as we have when growth consultants talk with the board.

> "We are using the wrong language. We talk about conversion rate, number of conversions. Have you ever heard of a retailer ask their employee how many items did they sell? Nobody cares; what they care about it is how much profit was made. Yet, we keep communicating wins like a 20% increase in conversion rate. Instead, if we say the average visitor was worth €1.00, then we have now made them worth €1.20. Money talks, percentages don't." - Arnout Hellemans

So if you want to work with the board successfully, you need to talk in terms of revenue and ideally profits. You need to measure it frequently. But the primary reason we don't do that is because it isn't measured automatically in our tools. If you manage to get a rough profit estimate, you can start integrating that into your tools and working from there.

Now another fun way to tackle this, especially in the kickoff, is adding a quiz to your presentation. The board will be quite confident that they know what is going on with the growth of the company but realising they might not know that much yet can build your authority with them.

> "I've done this [run a quiz] at plenty of places, using a tool like Kahoot. Say on the topic of SEO. I would generate these questions such as "What were our impressions last month?" and "How often did we appear on the first page of Google?". You just make a ridiculous number, average number and low number. You get people to guess the answer. By having that gamification, it plants a seed that they don't know that much and that they assume too much. I've had it that the guy who was the most vocal didn't even rank in the top three of his whole team. It creates a nice dynamic." - Arnout Hellemans

This helps position you better with the board as they realise they don't have all the answers. Not only that, but it gives you insights as to their level and helps you adjust your communication style to it. It doesn't have to be SEO specific; it can be more generalised or about an area that they undervalue, e.g. Analytics.

Then, of course, there is the quarterly zoom out meeting we mentioned earlier. See, you already have many of the tools to get them involved and now it is just about using those. Use this meeting not to dive into the details but rather show them on a higher level what was achieved and the following steps. Try to get them enthusiastic about what is happening by showing them the profit you are bringing in.

So you have some internal fans, and the board is raving, how about aligning with the brand?

Key Takeaway

Getting the board involved is crucial to growing the influence of your project. The best way to do this is by having them at key meetings and speaking their language: profit.

CHAPTER 22

Brand - Policing or Protecting?

22.1 Branding vs conversions

When people talk about growth, it is often too quickly equated to marketing. We talked about this before; it's the result of the way we've been explaining growth hacking and who hires us within the organisation. So we get lumped together with marketing, squeezed in between the brand team and awareness campaign. As they say, you need to work with what you have. You start focusing on growth which for you probably means bringing new customers and conversions. So why is all that budget going to branding? What is that bringing in? Before you start kicking and screaming about a waste of budget, let's turn to Arnout Hellemans for his advice:

> "It is our fault that we get lumped together with marketing. We started talking about traffic and eyeballs. So we are being brought in by the marketing part of the organisation and are being limited to that side when the bigger impact is in the rest of the funnel. Not only that, but we are lumping marketing altogether and start measuring brand awareness by our metrics of conversion." - Arnout Hellemans

> "What if we went so far as to split it up so that you have both branding and intent-based? Branding is everything around awareness, e.g. PR, branding, awareness, engagement etc. That stays by Marketing, and the success is measured based on awareness and brand KPI. Intent-based is everything around people actively searching for your product or solution. That is commonly placed with the marketing team but should actually go to the product team. That allows Marketing to be all creative and Product to focus on delivering the best possible experience to drive purchases. The minute you focus only on conversion branding you will always lose because they will never deliver the same cost per conversion as intent-based."
> - Arnout Hellemans

Let's say we do have a tantrum and push that budget to conversion campaigns. Now you are expecting people to convert immediately and investing less in branding. That means the company will undervalue building a brand and drive focus away from that.

22.2 The big brand versus growth fight

Brand and growth often end up in a tough battle. Growth asks the brand team to cough up the conversions they have, and they show you a small handful plus a long story of what that branding delivered in other ways. As if that wasn't bad enough, they also then get in the way of the running experiments. Experiments get blocked because they are not in line with the brand. Definitely not those cheeky quick and dirty experiments that are not entirely in line with the house style, oops. Don't think the brand manager is going to approve of that.

Growth hackers are all about the data. Branding can feel so fluffy in contrast. You can measure the result of an experiment, but how do you measure the impact of being off-brand? When you are testing the limits, it can be tempting to fear or be frustrated by the 'brand police'. They feel like the brakes yanking you back when you want to go go go. Sadly the brand is often equated to the house style; this does not do branding justice. It is far more than that.

You need a strong brand to help you stand out and build a relationship with your end customers. We have said it a few times and will repeat it: growth is more than marketing. It also comes down to the data, the strategy, the culture and yes, the brand. The brand is what helps customers to build a relationship and attachment to your company. Customers are often willing to pay more for your product or service when they feel strongly about the brand when they trust it. It is what humanises your company, making it more relatable and likeable. What if we listen to Arnout and stop holding the brand up to the wrong standards and give them a chance to shine too?

22.3 The best of both worlds

When brand and growth work together, then the brand can be seen less like an anchor. Instead, it can be an accelerator of growth. The brand will help to create an emotional connection throughout the customer journey. It also ensures we stay true to what triggers the customer in the right way.

Just like customer support, the brand team often knows the end customer well. They can show you how to build a long-term relationship with the end-user rather than just short-term. That will not only ensure retention but also drive word of mouth. Which, in our opinion, is one of the most potent traction channels out there. No matter what the challenges are on the micro-level, growing a company with a great brand is far more straightforward. Finding the best of both worlds is worthwhile.

So involve the brand managers in the growth project. Have someone representing the brand but show that sometimes minor compromises may be needed to drive growth. Agree on who does the branding check and how to make this efficient (e.g. combine with the person who checks design or copy).

Ask for the brand guidelines as well, and go through them to understand when something is and isn't in line with the brand. The brand guidelines will save you much hassle and going back and forth.

What should you do if you really can't get to an agreement with branding? Or when they are slowing you down, because they want to check everything, rewrite every word to the correct Tone of Voice and manually edit every visual? Well, you have a few options for such moments:

- Discuss the matter with your contact person or a higher stakeholder. You need to find out where the line is drawn in the sand and at what point you can step over it to bypass Brand, and just how bigger a step you can take. Higher-level stakeholders will most likely prefer to put more emphasis on commercial growth. They don't mind a 6/10 quality visual with results in two weeks, rather than let's say a 9/10 visual that takes eight weeks to return a result. Discuss where they'd place that line.
- You could also suggest that branding only needs to be taken into consideration when you'd be reaching more than X amount of people with a specific visual/copy. This might give you the possibility to test quicker, but be sure that your tests have a big enough audience for any sort of significance.
- Book enough design/copy hours from the brand team every week so that they can continuously work on the quality of your experiments.

Lastly (and this should really be your last resort!), you could learn from Ward's experience. He had a contact person who insisted on quick ongoing progress, but at the same time had a design/branding department would get crazy mad if the growth team would ignore them. It would take ages to get ads, and they were not allowed to make their ones. How could they keep up the speed and not create internal conflict? In accordance with the key stakeholders, he and the contact person came up with the idea of geographically excluding a radius of 50km around the company's headquarters. That way they were able to launch the experiment quickly without anyone from branding being able to see the self-made ad… Don't try this at home work, without the supervision of an adult stakeholder.

Hopefully, these ideas can help you to find the workarounds available in a collaboration.

22.4 Growing without a strong brand

Can you grow without a strong brand? There is always branding to some extent, right? We just reiterated the importance of not equating brand to house style, and so even with a house style present, branding may not be. Does the brand have a personality? With this, we mean a clear tone of voice, attributes and purpose. Is this in line with what triggers the customers?

We've discussed the benefits of having a strong brand, but what do you do if there isn't one? How do you convince your client of the value? Branding is one of those long-term actions that will not show results quickly. However, it is worth the discussion, but it's not something you want to suggest in a random growth meeting. Instead, discuss this with the board and your contact person. First, though, you need proof that branding is off.

There is no perfect way to measure this. The best solution we've found is using a Customer Loyalty Index (CLI). Figuring out the CLI is done by asking customers to rate three questions from 1-6. 1 stands for "Definitely Yes" and 6 stands for "Definitely No". The questions are as follows:

1. How likely are you to recommend us to your friends or contacts?
2. How likely are you to buy from us again in the future?
3. How likely are you to try out our other products/services?

You then score each of the three questions per individual response and calculate the average based on the figures below.

6 = 0
5 = 20
4 = 40
3 = 60
2 = 80
1 = 100

The idea is that it indicates a connection to the brand/company. So if you see that the average comes out at around 25, this suggests that there isn't a strong connection or attachment to the brand and that there is certainly work to be done.

That said, it could be that their lack of attachment is an issue with the product or service. That is why the biggest impact comes from combining this with asking about Product-Market Fit. Then you can double-check for any other significant issues that are causing a lack of attachment.

Doing this first will give you grounds for asking to invest in improving the branding. If you coordinate and discuss this with the brand manager first that will also help strengthen your position.

Now it is time to work on some trickier relationships. Hello busy developer, do you have a minute for growth?

> **Key Takeaway**
>
> When you start measuring brand purely on conversions, you kill any chance of brand being successful and investing in building a strong brand. You need that strong brand to grow so either fight for it by showing it lacks through measurement or if it is strong, allow them to focus on more brand awareness metrics.

CHAPTER 23

Development - Your Fleeting Friend

23.1 IT & growth hacking together

Does this sound familiar? You finally get to meet the development department of your client only to find out that they will not have much time to help. It's not that they don't want to; they are just super busy and have an endless list of to-dos. We've never seen a development department that is chilling or just lazing about waiting for your call. Nope, never seen that. They are incredibly hardworking and don't get any joy out of turning you down, but the pressure of major stakeholders gives them little to no choice.

But what are the alternatives? Either they say no, or they work themselves to the ground. Then we come along: "Hey... we just have a little extra request for this week" or "We are starting to A/B test the website and would like to involve development". You can almost hear the development team groan with "Oh another person wanting more to be done with the already limited resources, great!". Not exactly what they were waiting for. However, for most projects, you will need development resources at some point—that or at least knowing how to manage without them.

So let's take a look at how you can work without development if there are no resources available. If there is development, we will talk about how to improve the collaboration the best.

23.2 How to work around having no development resources.

It is not ideal, but you can get pretty far implementing tools without development. The following are examples of tools that don't require external assistance:

1. Building landing pages
2. Pop-ups
3. Browser notifications
4. Opt-ins
5. A/B testing tools to implement tests at 100% coverage, until development has the time ("has the time" does not mean for "infinity")

Where possible test through tools or workarounds first. We are not claiming that these tools are ideal or that development isn't needed, but just that you should live up to Be Bold. Sometimes you need to get creative in how you solve problems. Even if they are not ideal, the benefits can outweigh the costs of waiting.

There is a flip side to this which you need to consider. It's one of the main reason's developers are not a fan of growth hackers. Using these tools have several potential risks:

1. **Performance.** Certain tools can slow down performance. Heatmap tools like Hotjar often get blindly run on every single page even though they slow down performance significantly.
2. **Security risks.** Tools can introduce possible security risks, does it make the website or personal data easier to hack?
3. **Introduce bugs.** Tools can introduce bugs as it uses secondary codebases, which makes debugging extremely difficult.

So don't just choose a tool and implement it. Discuss this with the developer to figure out what the best solution is and especially keep them up to date about which tools you plan to use.

Next, we have to say it: don't underestimate the impact of copy changes. Sadly too many growth hackers go straight for the big fancy tests before improving the copy. We have seen crazy growth just from improving the copy.

Why are we preaching copy in a development chapter? Because most of the time, you don't need development resources to change the copy. Talk about a win-win. You get your lifts, and they don't need to do anything. Let's say you test copy, and it results in several winning tests. You have shown that optimisation drives results. Now, it is much easier to convince the critical stakeholder (the guardian of development hours) that you need development resources to continue the progress.

No matter what the situation is, don't let development challenges be an excuse. Show your client you are willing to be creative and work around it, that is why they hired you. Sometimes you will suggest workarounds, and they will not go for them. But having them see the workarounds will help them realise that they are not the best solution. They will start pushing for development resources themselves, and your problem gets solved either way.

23.3 Getting to know the developers

It can be tempting to push development or the organisation to provide the resources you need. Pushing rarely works positively with development. Instead, we will look at a few ways to collaborate better with them.

The first is, as always, getting to know them and getting them involved in the process. Take the time to have a one on one meeting with development. Ask development questions, such as:

1. What is their experience with the platform/app/website?
2. What would they change if they could?
3. What are their current frustrations?
4. Are there other ideas that they feel would be interesting to test?
5. What are areas of the platform/app/website that are unstable/difficult to make changes to?
6. What is the development process, e.g. two week sprints?
7. What process for working together is best for them?
8. Who determines the priorities for the development team?

Often development has a lot of ideas, but they are summoned afterwards rather than involved in the process from the outset. Instead, they hear what needs to be changed and miss the whole journey before that.

The first few questions are to get them involved in what you are doing and asking them to share what is on their mind. You want to have them at your growth meetings and involved in decisions. This involvement is a crucial but straightforward approach to get them feeling appreciated and in control.

The last three questions focus on their way of working. You want to be considerate of their planning and how they do things. From there, you can see how many hours are available for the project per week. Development tends to plan in sprints; this means there are a set number of hours available every week or two. So agreeing on fixed hours per week is an excellent solution that works for both sides. Nothing is worse than having a full schedule, and then you come along with 'one little request'.

You may not have much that needs to be done, or it may be challenging to get a set amount of hours. In that case, you can strive to fix the major issues in the coming period. Try to get the bulk out of the way.

23.4 Improving the collaboration with development

The key to this relationship is to change the way development sees you and the marketing team. You aren't there to add extra tasks to their to-do list. Instead, you want to reduce it by A/B testing first or finding other creative ways to test changes.

Too often, development has a backlog of features that stakeholders wish to have implemented. Yes, the organisation feels they are essential, but the changes are not always tested first. This means the changes may fail and end up getting removed. Or they keep making further changes.

If you can show developers that you can do small tests to trial new features they are unsure of; then you suddenly become a powerful ally. You save them wasting time building features that only end up being redone or removed, making it a win-win situation. Development can then use you to give pushback on large new solutions that have not even been proven to work.

The second is planning. Whilst agility is vital for growth hacking; sometimes it isn't possible with development. Their planning can often be full weeks in advance. By preparing as much as possible, you can show consideration for their time. Thinking ahead gives them more time to estimate issues and fix them. That means there is more chance that they will be implemented in the end.

Finally, the way you choose to brief development can make a big difference. All-day they hear "there is a bug" and "the website is broken". What's the bug? What's broken? You will make them so happy by merely being specific in your briefing. Not only in what the issue is but particulars. These include the browser version, device and what action causes the bug, such as does it only happen when you click a specific button? Specifying will save them so much time. We even send them screen recordings of bugs, so that they can understand what is going on.

So those are the three ways to improve your collaboration with development: test ideas first, be considerate with their time and create ready-to-develop briefings.

23.5 Inviting development to growth meetings

In most cases, it's relevant to have development at your growth meetings. However, this is not always possible. It may be that they don't have time or that an external agency carries out development. Your client won't want to pay for them to join every growth meeting, which is understandable.

Instead, we would suggest having a separate regular meeting with them to run through everything. Even if this is a standup of fifteen minutes per week or thirty minutes every two weeks it can save a lot of emailing back and forth.

Now let's move on to sales. We want the same thing right, new customers? Then why can it get so challenging...

> **Key Takeaway**
>
> Get Development on your side by running them through any decisions that could impact them and by getting to know them. For many high impact changes, you will need their help.

CHAPTER 24

Sales: Commission and Data

When it comes to B2B clients, the sales cycles are longer. It can take months before a lead closes. Your role is not the only one responsible for converting leads to clients, that is up to another department: sales. Only together can you measure and grow fast.

If you don't work with B2B clients or the sales department, then feel free to skip this chapter. If you do work with sales departments, we will walk through some of the frustrations of collaborating as well as techniques to improve the collaboration.

24.1 What drives sales?

Often the most significant difference in what drives the sales team is they tend to get paid commission (this is not always the case, but we will highlight the challenges if they are). Being paid through commission means that it is all about converting for the sales team; they need to bring clients in and have the sale attributed to them. The result is that they can end up very focused on the short-term and trying to convert clients no matter what. Now you are focused on retention, and it doesn't help retention if the sales team makes false promises.

Commission results in other issues too. Let's say you come up with a new email flow for leads that ensures that more potential clients end up converting. Great! But who brought that sale in? Does the sales team get the commission? You did half the work after all. See the risk? You as a growth hacker have got too involved in the aspect that leads to a sale, and their manager may decide the conversion is not attributed to the sales team. Meaning conversion percentages increase but not necessarily their sales bonuses.

Sales often work with account managers, and this is a smart principle; one main contact person for a lead. It ensures that there is an overview of the client and that communication is consistent. However, what if you want to do the previous idea of an email flow? Will they allow it? That means that two people are communicating with the client, not one. They may end up so protective of the client that they don't let you help to convert them.

What is even causing the client to convert? To answer that requires data and tracking, and as a growth hacker, you'll want to know:

- What contact is there with the client?
- Where did they come from?
- What caused them to purchase in the end?

Yes, the sales cycle is long, but there is so much data there, waiting to be analysed. Yet, there is only one way to do that: track the data. This tracking is where the next challenge comes in. Salespeople are usually talkers, smooth with their words and charms. They are rarely the documenting type, considering it too much effort to note everything down. For us, it ruins our attribution and data; for them, it is avoiding the hassle.

So what is the ideal situation? For experiments, it is to work closely together with Sales so that they help you gain the data and insights you need. That way, you know what the quality of leads is for various experiments. With such a long sales cycle, they will be the first to see the results of your experiment and know whether it was a winner or a loser. You want to share the insights frequently with each other.

Sounds great, but how do you get there? How do you get a win-win? One where you align your goals and ensure that you get the data without the hassle for them? That's what we will explore next.

24.2 The win-win of sales and growth

Aligning with sales starts with the metrics, as this lack of alignment often is what causes the issues. You'll need to discuss questions such as:

- Which metrics are the most important?
- How do we balance quality vs quantity?
- Do we count leads from the same company?

That last one sounds like a strange question, but it's where a lot of issues occur. Imagine, Sales have already had contact with a company's developer. Then you gain a new lead, the CTO: jackpot! The CTO ends up being the one to purchase, so did your campaign bring in the lead or did the salesperson? You need to agree on what attribution model to use. You will also need to decide on how to deal with an existing lead and avoid issues in calculating the impact of your experiments.

The next step is learning from them; they have a lot of contact with the end customer. They know them very well and are usually eager to share what they know. In particular, you want to understand the following:

- What characteristics do they look for to identify a high-quality lead?
- What do they currently measure around how a lead comes in?

- What is the biggest challenge to close leads right now?
- Is there anything else Marketing could do to better support Sales?

The sales team knows what kind of leads convert well, but they may struggle to put it into words. Digging deep into what they look for and how they spot signs of a low-quality lead can help you to bring in the right leads, allowing you to adjust your targeting accordingly.

Next step is seeing how you can bring in more sales and commission for them. You want them to feel like they get more commission with your help by ensuring that the last part of the journey gets attributed to Sales. Yes, it will cost the company more, but they will get more revenue in return too. Share new ideas with them based on what you learnt from them.

It is not just about looking together and bringing in new leads, but also automation. Automation is something not every Sales member knows how to do or is even willing to consider. Helping them set up automation with If This Then That tools (like Zapier) can save them a lot of time and enable them to handle more leads. It can also reduce repetition for them, which makes it less time consuming and more fun. See also where you could add attribution or relevant data—for example, linking their emails and phone with the CRM.

Once they see you want to work with them and save them time, they will also be more open to measure attribution manually where needed. You have the win-win of more leads and better tracking, every growth hacker's dream.

Now it is time for one of our favourite departments (yes, we are playing favourites): customer support!

Key Takeaway

The different targets make collaborating with Sales difficult. Start by winning their trust, and from there, you can make the whole funnel more measurable.

CHAPTER 25

Customer Support - The Fuel You Need

25.1 The role of Customer Support

We have so much respect for Customer Support, we really do. Often the customer support sees all the most challenging things:

1. The negative reviews
2. The complaints,
3. Things not working

You need to be one tough cookie to man the customer support phone line/chat/email. Sadly, most of the issues they see are also outside of their control. They deal with the crap and do their best to get problems solved pleasantly and quickly whilst having someone shouting at them about how terrible it all is.

What we've seen in several organisations is that they are not listened to systematically. They feel like they've been mentioning issues for ages, but no one does anything with it. This is very unfair, especially considering the above.

Yet, it also presents a potential opportunity for you: they are an untouched gold mine of insights silenced by years of neglect. Even if the organisation actively listens to customer support, you should take the time to meet with them. They are likely to be the individuals in the organisation that understand the end customers the most. It is a great way to dive into the end customer's head and uncover critical bottlenecks.

25.2 How to gain their insights in a frequent and systematic manner

Start by meeting with them early on in the project. Find out what the current system is for documenting and reporting insights. If there is one, that's great, make sure you can access it. If those insights get used for experiment ideas, see it as an additional source of information. If they aren't, then there is likely a gold mine of ideas and undiscovered potential experiments waiting for you, add this to your planning to help solve them and start listening.

From there on, try to understand what they get contacted about the most—time to plan in a meeting.

Time for Action

Plan in a meeting with Customer Support and consider asking them the following:

1. What are the top questions that potential and existing customers ask? How do you answer these questions?
2. What are the key concerns customers indicate before and after purchase?
3. What information is on the website but customers rarely find?
4. What do they indicate as valuable features or benefits of the product/service?
5. What are the biggest frustrations customers experience that you can and cannot solve?

> 6. If you could change just a few things, what would they be?
>
> Asking these questions will help you to understand the end customer better for the personas. It will also help you identify potential areas for further exploration. If you can get access to their conversation logs or documentation, please do as going through this data is an effective way to get into the head of the end customer.

We turned to Els Aerts, who co-founded and has run the conversion and usability agency AGConsult for the last twenty years. She is also an international speaker on user research. Hence, it only felt fitting to ask her about working together with Customer Support, as you can bet that she talks to them as part of the user research in every client collaboration. She highlights two additional points worth considering:

> "Talking to your client's customer service agents is extremely valuable. Getting your hands on the raw data even more so. Especially in a long-term client relationship, it pays to optimise the way customer service data from calls, chat and email is tagged and processed." - Els Aerts

The first is getting your hands on the raw data, this is literally what the customers say, and it can provide powerful insights. The second is making sure there is a robust tagging system. This allows you to spot trends far quicker:

> "Ten complaints about a certain issue from the same free trial user don't have the same value as ten complaints from ten different paying clients." - Els Aerts

25.3 Should customer support be a part of the growth meetings?

You should consider involving Customer Support for specific organisations. There are several projects where this could be interesting if:

1. There is no Product-Market Fit (PMF).
2. The focus is heavily on conversion optimisation.
3. It's a subscription or frequent purchase product/service.
4. It's a high-end product/service.

If you realise that you do not have PMF, it is worth involving Customer Support in the meetings. They will have valuable input on critical points of friction that may be preventing PMF or what the driving factors of PMF are. They also might be able to help you better understand which market to focus on to gain PMF.

Sometimes companies believe they have PMF and don't feel the need to test it. You can show them the retention data, of course, but that is subjective: what is good retention? But hearing about significant issues from their Customer Support team members is much harder to ignore.

Another project type where it might be interesting to involve Customer Support is conversion optimisation projects as they can provide valuable insights into understanding issues. With quantitative data, you can figure out where there might be issues and find insights into why. Are there specific questions they get asked a lot on that page? Is there an issue (e.g. a bug) they encounter on that page?

The third type is a subscription or frequent purchase product or service. In these cases, retention is even more crucial to the success of the business model. Customer Support may know why people are leaving and can ask questions about that.

The final type of project that we feel is hugely relevant to involve Customer Support is a high-value product or service. Higher-end products and services have less leeway for mistakes and issues. The expectations of customers are very high (no pun intended). Being sharp in resolving potential matters is crucial.

The reason why you might not want to involve Customer Support in your meetings is that they're very emotionally invested. They talk with customers day-in and day-out and are often doing their best to help those customers. This emotional investment makes it harder to look at the facts and data.

Their vision of the product could easily get blurred: maybe the same problem gets mentioned a lot, but always by the same loud customers. That can cause it to look like a frequent problem. In contrast, the data shows the opposite, or maybe they've heard vivid stories from people who were seriously impacted by a UX-mistake (e.g. a doc seemed to save, but then it wasn't), which makes it seem like a huge problem to be fixed when in reality it only happens a few times out of a thousand customers annually.

In those blurry situations, it might not be fun for them to hear that you involve them, but not taking on their input. At the same time, it won't be fun for you either if you have to dive deep every time to convince them that they are wrong. As we said from the beginning we are huge fans of Customer Service, but they must also realise you can't solve every tiny problem, you need to look at the quantitative and qualitative data.

> **Key Takeaway**
>
> The customer support team is a goldmine of insights. Make sure you sit with them as soon as you can and start asking them plenty of questions. Next to that, try to get access to the raw data and make sure they are tagging questions to spot trends.

CHAPTER 26

Legal - Your Essential Ally

26.1 Where Legal can block growth and why

Legal has a growing role in organisations, especially in larger corporations. This ever-increasing role is due to growing data protection regulations such as GDPR. GDPR is not a black and white policy; there is much room for interpretation. The lines are grey and Legal is responsible for ensuring the organisation plays within those lines. This means it can take time to look into and decide the best approach, so not checking off with them promptly can lead to considerable delays in the whole process. What should you be checking off with them?

1. Adding tools to the website/platform/app.
2. Data collection, e.g. sending out surveys, tracking specific data on the website.
3. Making significant copy/communication changes, especially around promotional messaging / finance options / payments mechanisms / delivery pricing & offers etc. Messing up on those small details can have enormous consequences.

Legal doesn't want to block ideas, but they also need to cover the assets of the organisation. They are also, like Development, very busy. If they have the feeling that you are taking too significant risks, they may be quicker to block you out of fear and the potential of fallout.

26.2 How to prevent them from impacting your speed or blocking your growth endeavours

If you are working for a larger organisation and you feel Legal will be a concern, plan a meeting with them early on. Try to get all the tools you want to use throughout the project on the table prematurely so that they can look into them.

Keep in mind that within Europe, tools from outside of Europe are not always GDPR proof. This makes them more likely to be turned down immediately, so save them and yourself some time by double-checking this first and have alternatives ready.

Also, discuss with your contact person and some higher placed stakeholders about how strict they'd want to be with Legal, instead of asking that to Legal. Legal probably want to minimise every risk there could be and thus will ask you to check in with every experiment, tool or promise that you put live. In reality, many stakeholders will tell you what you should and shouldn't check with Legal. Most of the time, if regular consumers wouldn't be scared by the things you're implementing, then it's not necessary to check it with Legal either. The key is to be respectful of the end consumer's data.

Next to that, ask them about their concerns. What are they worried about in terms of tooling and data collection right now? That way, you can keep that in mind when working on the project.

26.3 Cookie policy

Cookie policies are an area that we see growth consultants frequently being asked about. Sometimes it's because they don't have a legal department and other times they just assume it's a marketing thing. After all, we're the ones using the data. *Oh, this is about data, you must know the answer!*

What should you do when a client asks about tracking regulations? Our advice is simple: always indicate that you can't give legal advice and to check it with the legal team. If there is no legal team, they are usually smaller. Whilst the risks are lower, we play on the safe side when we're working for an agency, and usually, advise them to seek legal advice. Yes, it's a grey zone for many countries in how strict you want to interpret the law; for example, some companies choose for a simple accept or decline cookies option. Others will hide their whole website behind an impenetrable cookie wall. Still, it is not worth potentially making a mistake in how they should set it up or saying which cookies should be in the privacy policy. You don't want to risk being held liable for that mistake. So, in summary, cover your arse.

What you can do is be helpful; of course, we aren't trying to be difficult here. Ensure that the individuals responsible for the legal aspect have a full list of tools, preferably with links to the legal section of the relevant websites. Almost every tool will have one page or more explaining how they track and what cookies they use. Next to that, make sure the growth team is aware of the impact of a stricter setup. If you choose to have several types of cookies that visitors have to accept or decline, that will affect your opt-ins. You are adding friction, and this will impact your data, e.g. fewer users to retarget. We are not saying you should not do this but rather that it is your responsibility to make them aware of the impact on the data.

The next one is just a pet peeve we couldn't help but mention: double-check that the tracking of cookies is working correctly, please! Too often we have seen useless cookie statements, e.g. there is a cookie statement, but it fires cookies whether or not it is accepted. You might as well have not bothered; it's usually not compliant. So always double-check this. Legal will be happy with you for doing so, and you'll be pleased to know that there is a minimised risk of legal issues for the company.

26.4 Inviting Legal to growth meetings

We would say that it's optional to have a Legal team member present for your growth meetings, unless you have a product susceptible to legal risks, e.g. pharmaceuticals, gambling, etc. Then in many cases, you can also check off quicker. However, if that is not the case, we would suggest contacting them on a case by case basis. The exception is if a Legal team member is highly motivated and has a serious growth mindset. The reason for this is that you actually wouldn't want to discuss legal in brainstorming or progress meetings. It's easier and more effective to reach out when you have a legal topic to discuss.

26.4 Cheatsheet for Creating Internal Fans

We've gone through a lot of departments. To make it even easier for you, we summed up how to deal with all different departments in one overview.

	Cheatsheet for Creating Internal Fans
The Board	- Understand who initiated this project: Was it top-down or bottom-up?
- Get board members to join the growth meetings.
- Get the board involved in the NSM session.
- Involve them in priorities in the quarterly meetings.
- Understand their picture for long-term growth and relate your actions to those bigger targets.
- Create bite-sized alternatives for the board to stay up-to-date, like executive summaries or a video where you talk them through your presentation.
- Talk in profit (or alternatively revenue).
- Challenge their knowledge by creating a quiz, for example, to poke their growth mindset.
Brand	- Don't start talking about marketing, or you get limited to only top-of-the-funnel departments.
- A company with a great brand is much easier to grow due to better retention and word-of-mouth.
- Agree early on one person to do the brand-checks.
- Ask for the brand guidelines to save yourself several feedback rounds.
- Discuss with your contact person or a higher stakeholder, where they'd draw the line between perfect branding versus speed.

	- Discuss a threshold for how many people to be reached before Brand needs to be involved. - Book several hours of Brand per week to make sure that you don't have to wait for them. - Use the Customer Loyalty Index (CLI) to prove whether you need to work on branding.
Development	- Consider independent tactics where you don't need IT, e.g. adjusting copy, pop-ups, notifications, etc. - Mind the performance, security and bug risks that you might introduce before IT has to. - Understand their processes. If you know when they're prepping their planning, you know when to check-in to get hours for your agenda. - Get them involved. Sometimes you can help them by testing their ideas so that they get the extra budget to execute their wishes for the platform. - Be concise in your briefings to save them time. - Consider joining one of their standups instead of having them involved in growth meetings.
Sales	- Align for win-wins: When are they winning? - Agree on attribution models. - Understand when leads are valuable and when not. - Learn from their insights in the hopes/dreams/fears of customer personas.

	• Create time-wins by sharing your automation knowledge to make their work easier.
Customer Support	• Create a system for frequent input to your team. • Involve them in meetings when you want to understand the 'why', but only after you already know 'what' is going to be the priority.
Legal	• Meet with Legal early in the project, so that you have all tools approved when you want to start. • Prepare alternatives for tools from outside the EU. • Discuss with your contact person or a higher stakeholder, where they'd draw the line between taking risks versus speed of impact. • Understand what Legal is most afraid of so that you can emphasise those things when you ask them a question, to get an answer quicker. • Check if the cookie bar is actually holding back cookies until the user allows them.

Now it only makes sense to look a bit more at how they play or don't play together. I'm sure this word won't be new to you, Silos…

> **Key Takeaway**
>
> You usually don't need Legal in the growth team itself but do make sure they are on board with what you are tracking. Otherwise, it will just be a huge hassle down the line or a significant risk for you.

CHAPTER 27

Breaking Down Silos

27.1 Silos are still around

We hesitated with this chapter. Silos feel like something from the caveman era of growth hacking when organisations had departments, each focused on their target. You probably thought that no longer occurs nowadays, to have mid-tier targets outweighing the end goal, so outdated. Sadly, it is still happening all the time — especially in large corporates.

Departments have drifted apart, and everyone is busy focusing on their projects with far too little interdepartmental communication. Rather than working together to achieve the NSM and OMTM(s), they are focused on their own KPIs. That is why we felt it was worthwhile to end our advice on working together with different departments with a short piece of general advice for improving departmental collaboration.

Even within the Marketing department, there can be conflicting goals. Conversions may be the optimiser's target, but the social team reports on engagement. What can happen to post engagement when people click on the website? The engagement goes down; people are clicking and not commenting. So how can they hit their target? Easy, don't link to the website. Yes, these types of issues actually occur.

27.2 Breaking down Silos

Luckily, your growth project could be a great way to start breaking down the company silos. It comes down to the following four steps:

Step 1: Ensure that all departments are aligned and have a clear understanding of the NSM, OMTM and leading KPIs

Goal setting, in the beginning, is crucial in avoiding siloed metrics. Setting the OMTM is where a large part of the department alignment starts, are we focused on the same goal? Do we know where we are going? We talked about tiered metrics in Chapter 9: One Metric That Matters, these levels of metrics help departments understand their metrics relative to the primary goal. It's not that their metric doesn't matter, but that the main goal trumps it. With this, their managers have to be on board as often the departments feel that their managers judge their success based on the department's KPIs. Pressure from their manager can drive further misalignment.

Step 2: Bring people together in the growth meetings

Push for everyone to join the growth meetings. Getting everyone talking together in one room can make a world of difference. That is when the discussion and collaboration can begin. The teams will become more aware of what other departments are working on, and they can gain ideas from each other and start to feel the value of collaboration.

Step 3: Brainstorm with a mix of different departments

Brainstorming with various departments is a sneaky way to bring people together, as they are more informal than a sprint meeting.

This lack of formality makes it easier to start conversations and can also help team members see their ideas contribute to the end goal.

Step 4: Have cross-department responsibility for specific experiments

Usually, it is better to have one person have the end responsibility for a task, as this avoids responsibility dilution. The idea is that there is only one throat to choke (we didn't come up with this saying, but indeed we're guilty of using it). However, sometimes this isn't the case, and getting two people to work together to solve a problem is better. Doing this helps them get to know each other by working on the experiments and ensures they actively work towards the same goal. Hopefully, they will also see that execution is quicker through intense collaboration. Keep mixing up the combinations so that the team gets to know the different departments more. Be careful that the shared responsibility does not lead to any one individual feeling responsible. Keep a close eye on the tasks where there is a shared responsibility to prevent this from happening.

Luckily, Silos are appearing less and less, but they do occur, and as a growth consultant, you must always prepare for the worst. Thankfully, the growth program will naturally help align focus and start connections between departments.

Now it is time to keep diving into what we call the Ups and Downs. Your project is up and running; what are all the types of challenges you might face along the way? How do you best deal with them?

> **Key Takeaway**
>
> The best way to kill Silos is to get departments working together regularly. Make this a necessary aspect of your growth process.

SECTION 4

The Ups and Downs

CHAPTER 28

Fixed Mindsets Alert!

28.1 Spotting a fixed mindset

As a growth hacker, you are probably familiar with Carol Dweck's work on fixed vs growth mindset. If not, here is the super short version: people tend to have either a more fixed or growth mindset. A fixed mindset individual tends to:

1. Feel that things have to be a certain way.
2. Get frustrated with failures.
3. Not like being challenged.
4. Be cautious and scared of new things.

In contrast, someone with a growth mindset sees failures and challenges as a way to grow; they love trying out new things and expanding their horizons. No one has a complete fixed or growth mindset; it's more of a scale, and we all have areas where we might have a more fixed approach to something and other areas where we expand our growth mindset.

The risk is when someone has a fixed mindset about growth, especially if they are in the growth team. The individual with a fixed mindset maintains the above attributes towards experiments and how things work. You can recognise them by the fact that they often feel they know best as to how things should be, an audible sigh fills the room when you suggest ideas that are similar to previous tests, "We've tried that, it doesn't work for us".

Sometimes you notice a fixed mindset when the pace increases, fixed mindset individuals start to struggle with the changes. They will grip for control by asking lots of questions. Another telltale sign is that they often fixate on all the problems of a new idea. Time for another Dutch lesson! In Dutch, we say "beren op de weg zien" which translates to "seeing bears on the road" - and we don't even have bears in the Netherlands. As you can imagine, when you see lots of bears on a road, you don't get very far down that road. Whilst this is a good thing for a forest road inhabited by animals that could do serious damage, the same can't be said for the adventurous path to a project, and being stopped by imaginary bears. The worst part about the fixed mindset is that it can impact the motivation and energy of the rest of the team.

Luckily we have rarely experienced a contact person that has a fixed mindset, as they are usually the ones who helped to bring you in and are enthusiastic about the project. That said, it's still frustrating to have a fixed mindset within the team that can impact driving results. We will walk you through some options to deal with a fixed mindset. Starting with the most preferred solution and working from there.

28.2 Dealing with a fixed mindset

As always, we are a fan of starting with the Be Them principle to understand the other individual, try meeting with them one on one to get to know them better. Once we had an individual in a client team, who had such a fixed mindset, we often thought of him to be like a Dementor from Harry Potter, as he kept sucking the energy out of the room.

Over a drink that followed a team meeting, we got to know him better. We found that he had so many frustrations to get off his chest because he had a million and one things to do. He felt that working on solutions would often cost him a lot of time. The reason was that each experiment got discussed separately, rather than as a larger project.

Through discussing how we could better work together, we concluded that having two meetings of an hour would help. It would allow us to work out a whole roadmap for his area of expertise and will enable him to skip out on the general meetings. It solved their impact in meetings and saved time for both sides.

Often people who appear to have a fixed mindset have reasons for their attitude. For example, sometimes, individuals with a strong Blue personality appear to be fixed in their perspective when missing specific data or insights. Suppose they struggle to feel comfortable with new decisions, they aren't intentionally acting that way and continuously clashing with them will only escalate the situation. It may sound strange but aim to be grateful for the fact that they often bring potential risks to your attention. Their love for analysing helps them spot risks early on in the process. Ask them which data or approach would make them more comfortable. Indicate that you would like to work better together and open a dialogue about how you can improve the collaboration.

If this doesn't work, the next step is to have an open and honest conversation with your contact person about the situation. Hopefully, you are at a point in the project where trust has grown between you and your contact person. You could say something along the lines of: "I feel like there is a bit of resistance to the project from person X, what could be the possible reasons for this?". Try to start a dialogue about it and see if they can help with solving it.

In some cases the contact person is also aware of it, they've seen it themselves in the meetings. As a result, they may have advice on how to deal with the situation or they can talk to the individual and see what's possible. The fixed mindset individual may be more open talking to their team member or boss, than to you directly.

The final option is not ideal but sometimes the only way forward. Try to see if you can get them less involved in the project in a professional manner. You can try to focus more on other areas within the project or find other individuals that work in the same area as the fixed mindset individual. Then you can consult with them instead, to involve them more and only check off the bare minimum with the fixed mindset individual.

28.3 When you start seeing bears

You, as a consultant, also run the risk of starting to see bears on the road after a while (dare we call it a fixed mindset). We are not judging; we have had our moments too. After working on a project for a while, you start to get more and more frustrated by all that isn't possible. Maybe in the beginning, when starting up the project, you had a lot of setbacks. You feel like everything you suggest isn't possible, or has taken too long. Is growth even possible with such a company? This mindset can lead to a negative relationship with the client. Just like a fixed mindset team member, it can kill the energy in the room.

We said it from the very beginning; being a growth hacking consultant is tough. For many companies, a lot more is not possible than is possible, so you have to develop a thick skin to be okay with the challenges and to hear the dreaded word 'no'. Easier said than done; it will require a bit of a reset.

If you feel like you are getting a bit too caught up in what isn't possible rather than what is, take a step back. Plan either time alone or with your internal team to look at the situation from a bird's eye view. Push yourself not to get caught up in what is wrong but rather what is possible. If the issues are one of the red traffic lights we mentioned earlier on, that's a different story, but there are even ways around that. Try to brainstorm solutions and what is possible:

1. Are there proxies you can use if you have a measurement challenge?
2. Are there other areas that you do have influence over if you are struggling to improve the most significant bottleneck?
3. Are there creative workarounds you can use?
4. Can you do more of what has worked until now instead?

If possible, try to get a fresh pair of eyes on the project. Explain your current setbacks and ask how they would deal with it. Try to avoid going "Yeah, but" too quickly and instead try to see how their solution would be possible.

> **Key Takeaway**
>
> As a growth consultant, you'll spot fixed mindsets quickly, but more crucial is noticing when you start seeing bears. You can't grow a client in that state of mind so really push yourself to take a fresh perspective.

CHAPTER 29

Too Many Focus Points, Too Much Choice

Does this sound familiar to you?
"Can we have A to J done, and also by tomorrow?"
"Could you do this one little extra task before the end of the week?"
Only for it to turn out to be a pretty complicated adjustment, to say the least. Well, if you haven't heard this before, we certainly have. Queen said it best with the lyrics: "I want it all, I want it now". They struggle with what the priority is and what they want to focus on. They may say "but we only have three focus points". But what if those focus points are broad, to say the least?

Don't get us wrong; we know they aren't doing this on purpose. Most likely, when you have this problem, it's because your poor contact person also gets pulled in a hundred directions. Or they could just be super excited. But even so, having a scattered focus is risky. We talked a bit about that in the principle Be Focused and would like to cover some more of the risks of a scattered focus. Then we will walk you through some potential solutions for them.

For this chapter and the one that follows, we will be calling in another amazing consultant to help explain the reality of it all. Abi Hough has experience both on the agency side and freelance side, which provides her with the full 360 on being a consultant. Not only that, she worked as a developer and UX designer for ten years before becoming a consultant for another eleven years. Needless to say, she knows her shit and has seen a fair amount of organisational challenges along the way. We will be quoting her experiences and advice throughout the coming two chapters. We were initially only going to choose one or two quotes, as with most of the other experts who contributed. Yet, her advice and humorous analogies were too brilliant to shorten. We will say it in the acknowledgements again, but we want to say it here too, thank you Abi.

29.1 The risks of scattered focus

Remember our throwing-darts-blindfolded example in the Be Focused principle? It took so much longer to shoot all five targets at the same time instead of shooting them one-by-one. Switching or scattered focus impacts speed. We always say a little movement on everything is the same as no movement at all. In the Scrum process, it's even said that work in progress is not work until it is completed, and we couldn't agree more. When you start a lot of things and have plenty in progress, but nothing finished, then you don't have many deliverables to show for your work. Not only because our client wants multiple focus points, but sometimes we get overwhelmed by all the choices ourselves and struggle to choose despite knowing that we need to focus.

> "The problem is that any programme of improvement, by its very nature, will provide a gazillion possible things to look at. And those initial gazillion things multiply like gremlins leading to more and more options to choose from. It's no wonder that making the right choice can be difficult. As humans, we react like a deer in the headlights of an oncoming car and freeze. The more choices we have, the less likely we are to choose any one of them, as the more choices we have the likelihood of making a poor decision is higher. It has a name; it's called choice paralysis." - Abi Hough

Even if you manage to choose, by selecting several different areas, you can also make less impact/learnings around one area in particular. You are doing loose tests here and there, but not structurally building it up in a targeted way. You are not learning from what works there, and as a result, it will be harder to drive impact. Whilst being too focused on one small area will not necessarily create effect either; it's about finding the balance. Often the different focus areas tend to be lots of little side projects, your clients come to you and say "We are also working on this, I'd love to get your input". You warm up inside; it feels great that they want to know what you think. Then it happens again and again. You are not making a significant impact on those projects as you are only looking at them for an hour or two each time. At the same time, it is stealing attention away from the rest.

The risks accompanying a lack of progress are why it's your job to keep your client-focused. You need to keep guiding them back to what matters and what isn't possible, but how do you do this?

29.2 Dealing with multiple focus points

There are four methods we'd recommend for keeping a client-focused and realistic in what is possible:

1. Take the time to define the North Star Metric (NSM) and One Metric that Matters (OMTM)

It all comes down to the kickoff and bringing focus through a clear high-level goal, the NSM, as well as your key bottlenecks to improve upon, OMTM(s). By taking the time to set and agree upon a NSM and OMTM(s), it makes it easier to give push back; you can agree to challenge each other to stick to this. So when a client gets sidetracked, you challenge them by relating things to the OMTM(s), "Will this help us reach X?".

2. Prioritise together

Prioritising together can help your client understand the impact of various experiments as they will see that their additional requests are less beneficial than other opportunities. If that's not the case, when their additional requests rank high, then it's time to reprioritise and check that you're focusing on the right area. Did you prioritise well enough before you chose the next experiments?

Another part of prioritising is working with tradeoffs; if we add the new request, what can't we do instead? Especially when it comes to additional last-minute requests on different areas, don't be afraid to ask your client what has more priority. Feel free also to suggest what you feel has more importance.

Yet, all these are just plasters on a wound as you're solving a lack of priorities on the micro-level. If you want to solve the problem as a whole, it comes down to prioritising the focus points overall. Once you do that it is far easier to give push back on the day to day. However, if you have hit this point, it may mean the focus points are not clear anymore or that they were never right, to begin with. We set priorities all the way at the beginning, based on the data we had then. There is a chance that it changes or that our client can see things that are making them question the priorities that we may have missed. The easiest solution is just to stay fixated on those original focus points, whether they were the right ones or not. But this would make us ignorant to one of the biggest consulting risks:

> "To prioritise well, we need to overcome another bottleneck in the human psyche— and that's confirmation bias. This is where us mere mortals fall flat, and will interpret evidence to fit our existing belief or theory about something. We'll go so far as ignoring other evidence if it doesn't favour our belief, or combining irrelevant facts to present something more

favourably. We are all guilty of manipulating the world to fit our preferred reality." - Abi Hough

We are so eager to be right, and to know what is right, that we may adjust the priorities to suit our beliefs. This is crucial to mention here as you may be so concentrated with bringing focus that you choose what you feel is right and resist alternative suggestions. To put it less politely but in the most precise terms:

"Ask yourself and those you're working with if you are blowing smoke up your own as$ holes." - Michael Aagaard

Michael is a CRO Consultant who presents at conferences internationally on the risks of the confirmation bias. He demonstrates how we, too, often feed our ego by choosing what to focus on. So how do you avoid this? How do you bring focus without being pulled in twenty directions? Simply, it's by using a prioritisation framework (feel free to check out Chapter 15 Prioritising - More or Better Tests for a refresher) and from there double-checking what you believe the priority is. Force others to choose what they think the priority to be and justify why. Stay open-minded to their perspective and be aware of your own confirmation bias:

"Get perspective, someone else's perspective. You might be amazed at what you discover. Finally, realise and accept that you're predisposed to believe your bull$hit. You know what they say…The first step to overcoming any problem is admitting it exists in the first place." - Abi Hough

Being aware of your own and other's Confirmation Biases means that you now also know that seeking clarity, agreement and where necessary redefinition about what the focus should be amongst yourselves is something you should actively be pursuing. Sense check each other and call out BS (nicely!) when you spot it. By doing this, you have a safety net to catch prioritisation disasters before they strike - and this in itself will save you a whole heap of heartache further down the line.

3. Take a step back together

Sometimes it gets too much, not just the number of focus points but the pure mismatch in expectations of what your client thinks can fit in the project versus what is actually possible. They want so much, and you are thinking "How the hell am I going to fit this into 16 hours per week?". Deep breath, let's take a step back together.

> **Time for Action**
>
> First list the key bottlenecks you want to solve in either Google Sheets or Excel. What would you recommend doing in the coming period? How many hours does each area take? If it's more than the hours available (as it often is), don't worry. Prioritise. Keep in mind the pesky confirmation bias and see which of that list you would suggest doing within the hours you have.
>
> Next, start with a fresh sheet and make a list of all the different areas. Write down all the other areas they want to have done. Then for each item indicate the hours needed to complete the given task. Don't forget to keep hours over for communication and meetings as this often gets overlooked. How many hours do you need for that? Then add this up

> and see how it differs from the project hours. Now you know what they would like done.
>
> Time to compare the two. It is easy to end up doing what your client wants you to do. That is why we suggested first looking at the bottlenecks. Then you may have focus, but is it the right focus? Hopefully, you have worked this out in the last step, starting with the actual bottlenecks and critical actions.

Once you've walked through the two sheets by yourself, it's time to sit with your client and explain that you feel that the focus has broadened too much. That you want to make sure you are focusing on the right actions. Often quantifying and listing it can help as clients don't always realise how much time tasks take in reality. They may also not realise what other people within the organisation are asking of you. Going through the whole list helps to clarify this, and from there, you can decide the focus to ensure you work together to determine the key action points.

4. Saying no without actually saying no

The final tip is one we have talked about before in Chapter 10: How to set the Right Expectations and Priorities. It's worth mentioning again since it's a tough one.

Often consultants struggle with saying no. It feels like the client is the king/queen, and you have to say yes, however, your client will respect you more for giving push back rather than leaving work half-finished and not driving results. Remember there are always alternatives to saying no, especially if they come with last-minute requests. For example:

- "I think it would be better to do XYZ instead."

- "I can take a look at this, but it would be next sprint/week."
- "If we pick up X, we'll need to remove Y from the planning."

It all comes back to weighing the options, what has more priority? What will drive more impact?

Keeping focus is like maintaining a garden. If you take your eye off your garden for too long, weeds start to creep in and take over. Continue to leave it, and it becomes a big mess that will take ages to fix. Instead, always be on the lookout for weeds, or in this case distraction. Nip them in the bud (pun intended) early and your garden will be far more pleasant as a result. It will also flourish far quicker.

> **Key Takeaway**
>
> Your client won't bring focus to your project; you are the one who needs to do that. Throughout the project, be aware when focus slips and what will drive long-lasting results.

CHAPTER 30

Too Many Stakeholders, Too Many Opinions

30.1 Trying to get a browser notification live

You've finally got your client so far: ready to test browser notifications. You've been gathering opt-ins for the last few weeks, and now it's time to run a test, the first automated notification to reduce checkout drop-off. Now all you need is approval to go live.

So you send it over to your contact person, Ashley, for a quick check, optimistic that you can put it live later that day. Only Ashley emails back the next day that she also wants Dan, the Brand Manager, to have a look. You should have known better, of course, the brand manager would like to see it too. Not to worry, you wait for Dan to email back that the notification is approved. I mean their designer made the image after all so how off-brand could it be? Just a simple yes and you can go live. Come on Dan… You send him a reminder the following day and then finally two days later Dan gets back to you.

"Could the image be a bit lighter? Right now, it doesn't meet brand guidelines."

Okay, Dan, no problem. You lighten the image yourself and ask Dan if that's what he had in mind?

"Yes, but has Mary-Ann checked the copy?"

Um no. It's 150 characters in total, follows the tone of voice guidelines and crafted to convert. Well, apparently Mary-Ann has to check every single bit of copy that goes live. You sigh, it's Friday afternoon already, you'll have to wait until next week to get it live. You are going to miss all the individuals who will drop off in the checkout over the weekend which, as luck would have it, is when the most sales occur.

At least your Monday starts well, kind of. Mary-Ann has emailed back that the copy looks good, only could you change two words. You think her new copy makes it fluffier and vaguer, but okay, you are past arguing. You change it and immediately email Ashley:

"Dan and Mary-Ann have approved the browser notification, can I set it live?"

But Ashley is a fickle one. Whilst she's enthusiastic about the experiment, she wants to make sure everyone is on board about it. So she forwards it to her boss, John, and her CRM colleague, Winston. Ah great, again, you are waiting for approval. Finally, on Thursday, they email back that they are happy with the experiment and are looking forward to seeing the results. Yes, you are too… You are about to go-live when you get an email from Patrice:

"Hi, Winston forwarded me the experiment we are running. I was thinking, shouldn't the image be a bit darker?"

All you can think is about Robin from How I Met Your Mother, "NOBODY ASKED YOU, PATRICE!". With gritted teeth, you explain that the image was made lighter, as per the request of Dan, so no you can't change it.

You're almost two weeks down the line because of two minor tweaks, but you can finally go live.

Wasn't that exhausting? Now imagine this happens for every single one of your experiments that you'll need five people to approve each experiment, sometimes even more. The bigger the organisation grows, the more opinions there are. The more you have learnt the risk of not getting approval, and the organisation can get slow and scared to move.

> "There is a saying in the UK, too many cooks spoil the broth. The same can be said when you're faced with too many stakeholders and opinions – it spoils progress, productivity and can lead to procrastination. It cooks up a pretty stodgy soup of indecision and disgruntlement, simmering away with discontent and sprinkled with croutons of misery." - Abi Hough

There you have it, said in every way possible, too many stakeholders kill results and speed. Now it is time to narrow it down and get rid of some of those cooks. But how on earth do you subtly kick a few individuals out of the kitchen?

30.2 Techniques to reduce stakeholder overload

Too often we see our clients behave in the way described above and how our colleagues have to struggle with it. Luckily, there are a few simple techniques that can help:

1. The Approval Matrix
2. Mass Approval
3. Thinking Ahead

We'll walk through each one in turn, in far less time than it took Ashley to approve the browser notification.

1. The Approval Matrix

You need to understand how approval works within the company to work with the process rather than against it:

> "The biggest piece of advice I can give here really surrounds how well you understand the company makeup and processes of approval from the outset. There is no point just diving in head-first and expecting everyone to follow you into the murky depths of growth and testing with wild abandon, throwing all caution to the wind." - Abi Hough

To build upon that frame of approval, it all comes down to trust within the organisation. Who do people trust in to check something and ensure it meets the organisation's standards? Or the more pertinent question is who *should* they trust? When the branding manager says it's okay, why would anybody else need to look at the design? You leverage the trust to reduce the number of required approvals through an Approval Matrix. The Approval Matrix is a simple table with the following:

Area	Who can approve it?	Back-up	Maximum Response Time
Email			
CRO			
Facebook Advertising			

For each area, you have someone who can approve the experiments. Sometimes this can be the same person for several areas, but it always has to be a maximum of one per area. You often also need to double-check with the brand manager and the copywriter as well. That already brings it up to three individuals which is more than enough.

Most of the time, your contact person will love to help you with this, since they also prefer to get results quicker and get more 'bang for their buck' instead of having every experiment delayed.

You can agree with the client regarding who is the right contact person per area and what would be a suitable response time. The back-up field is alternative individuals you can contact if the primary contact is on holiday or sick. It's crucial to agree on the response time collectively. Focus on highlighting the importance of speed in experimenting but also agree on something fair, e.g. two days. If your contact person wants to check off with ten other people within those two days, that's up to them as long as they get back to you in time.

We like to set this up at the beginning of the collaboration, especially when we notice that there is a high number of stakeholders involved. It's never too late to set this up though, and we've found clients to be very open and supportive of the matrix as it gives them peace of mind. They know that quality and speed will be upheld. That way, you can use the trust existing within the organisation before building up the trust they have for you.

> "You need to build trust with each person who may be involved, expand their understanding of what you are doing and why, and then preempt any possible feedback by covering all of your bases. By doing this, you build trust, and trust is the single most valuable asset you can obtain when it comes to working efficiently. If people trust you to do your job, and they believe and understand the logic behind your decisions, then the easier it will be to bypass the

> nitpickers, jobsworth and pixel perfectionists." - Abi Hough

The next two techniques are focused more on how you plan things. They sound simple, but we don't see them in practice enough.

2. Mass approval

Some tasks take more time to be approved. That's why, when possible, we send a few smaller items for approval in one go, such as when the items are similar and need the same stakeholders to check them, e.g. different copy, several images. We do state they can get back to you one-by-one if that's quicker and sometimes they do. The goal is to build a deck of approved material to be able to act quickly when needed. If you check three browser notifications one-by-one, it takes far more time than getting three checked in one go.

Another form of Mass Approval is checking off experiments or ideas in a planning meeting as that's a moment when everyone is there and involved. We often walk through several experiment ideas at once with the whole group. Discussing this in the planning meeting often results in additional ideas on how to improve the experiments. Be strict, though, such as setting a maximum of five minutes of discussion per experiment; otherwise, you risk an endless debate about one experiment alone.

3. Planning ahead

Some areas will almost always take more time, such as development and legal. We have covered a few techniques already for working together with those departments. The fact remains that, at times, it's best to plan. Whilst we love agility in growth hacking, it isn't always possible. Getting a pixel on the website can be tricky, or if there is not enough design capacity, that can be a blocker. That is why we would challenge you to start preparing specific experiments 2 - 3 sprints ahead of time. Try to get in place what you need to make them happen. The quarterly zoom out meetings are also a great time to think about precisely what you'll require. This will allow you, in the end, to move far quicker when you run the experiment.

> **Time for Action**
>
> Choose a client that tends to have too many approval rounds, the one that you immediately thought of in our example at the start of this chapter. Then set up an Approval Matrix for them.
>
> Fill it in with your client and be strict, no, they can't add three names per area. Challenge them to consider who they trust to make that end call if no one else would be available.

> **Key Takeaway**
>
> Stakeholder overload kills the momentum, which in turn kills growth. The Approval Matrix can be a big lifesaver in decreasing the number of stakeholder rounds. Create one and use it regularly to keep things moving forward.

CHAPTER 31

Experiments are on the Side

As a growth hacker, if anyone were to ask you "Is growth really that important?" you would just give them the 'glare'. What kind of a stupid question is that? Duh, growth is life; life is growth. When you live and breath growth hacking, it is hard to believe that it isn't everyone's number one priority. Sadly, this isn't always the case. Sometimes experiments and, in turn, growth are seen as a side project. Yup, it's true, we were just as shocked to discover this.

You realise this is happening when slowly, more and more tasks don't get finished. You notice the number of team members at the meetings starts to decrease. At first, you excuse it, "must be a busy week" or "lots of people were on holiday". Then it sinks in; you realise you've lost their attention. Experiments and growth are now a side project; how did that happen?

31.1 Causes of experiments becoming a side track

There are multiple reasons for growth getting pushed aside, knowing the cause is crucial as the solution is dependent on it.

We will get the saddest reason out the way first: the enthusiasm is gone. When people hear about growth hacking, they often think of silver bullets and fancy hacks. It makes growth sound easy and fun. Growth is fun, but it is also challenging and is by no means a magical formula. It is, however, a lot of elbow grease and persistence. There may be a few low hanging fruits at the beginning, and the ease at which they were picked gave the wrong impression. So now that you are down to the nitty-gritty part, it may feel like it's just mundane tasks left. Other new exciting projects steal their attention, and you'll know this is the case when you struggle to get any input, and people no longer have that same active involvement as they did in the beginning. We will get to solutions in a second, but first, there is another reason we want to look at.

The second reason this happens is a sickness that we all have been subject to the lack of time. Corporates may have a whole army of employees, but that army is extremely busy. They may have more people power than a startup, but they need it as things take far longer than with a startup, so team members look at what they can skip and what isn't urgent. When you are at the stage of your growth project where you are running experiments, it's easier to miss meetings. Experiments feel like the extra and not the main course to growth. "We don't have time to experiment right now" is how they justify this. They may say this directly or just try to answer their emails on their laptop during the sprint meetings.

31.2 Moving growth back from a side track to THE project

So how do you get growth back into the limelight? How do you convince them that whilst you may not have any silver bullets, there is still gold buried deep if you all are willing to dig? There are a few ways to do this.

First, it's time to zoom out. Yes, we say that a lot and we do that for a reason: it is easy to get caught up in details. Take the time to zoom out with the team if you're not doing that already. This zoom out can be a part of the sprint meetings where you show them where you are going and what steps have already been made. Remind them of the why, the North Star Metric. It's no coincidence that very mission-driven companies tend to be more successful; that mission is what pulls them through the ruts.

The next part is making it fun again. Making it fun is especially important if a lack of enthusiasm is the reason that growth got shoved to one side. How do you do this? Firstly, celebrate wins. Make a party out of hitting milestones and big successes. Put the people whose win it was in the spotlight. Not only that, remind everyone of how their input contributed to the mission. Focusing on the mission helps team members connect to the project again.

Now if you believe that enthusiasm is not the issue, but time is, then it's time to start talking. Sit down with the contact person and discuss the struggles as you see them and what the most significant bottlenecks are right now, and in this instance, it's time and resources. Find out if it's possible to get dedicated time back onto the project, and how you can rekindle enthusiasm for the project.

It is, after all, in both your interests that this project gets back on track. It's not fun to have these kinds of conversations, but it is better that you're the one bringing bad news to the client than the other way around. Whether it's signalling problems to be solved or problems that are already way out of hand, you need to be the one starting the conversation.

If you need more people power in the team, then remind them of why growth hacking is so efficient in the first place: for the first time one person or one team has the sole responsibility to improve growth. It's the lack of distractions and multitasking that allow growth hackers to be so efficient. It doesn't work if your partners in growth hacking are part-timers or are not able to devote some

298 Experiments are on the Side

serious effort to do this. If growth hacking is viewed as a sideline, then your project will be side tracked and any growth will be stalled.

Talk to them about it: remind them of why this principle is so important and why they started this project in the first place. Was it to stay ahead of a specific competitor or to break free from a downward growth-trend. Maybe everybody on the team decided that things could be done differently. Show them where it went wrong: discuss with them which other things got priority over the growth project. Discuss whether this was that much more important, because honestly… there's (almost) nothing more important than the company's growth, particularly when you look a few years ahead. If you're not growing, you're losing: because either you're shrimping or you're stalling. Either way, you're giving your competitors the perfect reason to catch you up and take over.

The most likely reason for shifting attention are urgent problems… they're everywhere; company events, time-sensitive campaigns or newly launching features. They are important for now perhaps, but not in a few years. This is a conversation you need to have with your client, so that they realise that they need to give growth the top priority and other things need to make space, instead of the other way around.

Now you might be thinking "What if they say that they had no other choice but to work on those urgent matters?". Well, that's precisely the answer we'd be hoping for! Because if they agree that there are too many tasks for the team to actually handle (and thus choices that had to be made), then that means that they've grown and now need to grow their team as well. This either presents the urgency for them to get new team members on board, or it shows an opportunity for you and your consultancy-team to upsell extra opportunities.

Then the next problem arises: how to justify the expense of hiring an extra team member for the sake of the growth project? Well, that's something that you should already have proven with the potential of your experiments. You could calculate what specific experiments would bring in financial return if they'd be successful. Don't be scared to calculate the ROI of an experiment across the upcoming years. For example, if you'd identify a new tagline that improves the overall conversion rate, then that's something that most likely will be used for many years to come! We personally wouldn't calculate for more than three years ahead, because the whole world could be different by then (hello 2020!) and thus your ROI might also have changed entirely. Most experiments, if successful, can justify the invested hours in the upcoming three years. You have nothing to lose, so give it a try and do some calculations. These steps will most certainly help you to get more priority for your project.

> **Key Takeaway**
>
> After a while, it is easy for growth to become a side project. Keep bringing people back to the reason you are there (NSM) and making growth a priority. If the current team refuses to make, time don't be afraid to push for extra resources.

CHAPTER 32

Any Slower and We'd Be Going Backwards

32.1 Six months and 1,260 coffees later...

Some organisations are painfully slow; it feels like they are running through jelly. They have the feeling that they are always rushing, but barely getting anywhere, making one big sticky mess. It never starts this way, the jelly sets as a result of the years passing. As they grow, the following begins to occur:

1. **Bureaucracy.** Or as we like to call it 'arse-covering'. Mistakes are not welcomed with open arms, and they need to avoid them at all costs having learnt from bitter experience. So they created processes and checks, forms and approval that must be in place to get just one tool on the website. All these additional steps make the most straightforward tasks time-consuming.
2. **Size.** Growth of the company is matched by an increase of layers and teams. Everything is connected (unless you have silos) meaning everyone wants to get involved in all decisions. Now lots of individuals and lots of decisions don't mix well together; big meetings and a multitude of opinions kill momentum.
3. **Standards.** With brand awareness and recognition comes expectations. When you are small no one will notice your spelling mistakes or that your landing page broke. The traffic isn't high enough, and that is part of growth. Now,

however, when something similar happens, people notice, or at least your client feels like they do. Their well-known brand gives them the feeling they need perfection, meaning they spend a lot of time on the 80% that drives only 20%.
4. **Legacy.** Ah, the joys of legacy. Past decisions are coming back to bite you in the arse. If only they had the same type of standards then that they have now. Well, they didn't, and so things are fixed the way they are, or at least they feel like it. They struggle with changing certain things because they think it can't be done, or that this is simply the way they do things. We often see this coming back not only in the way of working but in two main areas. The first is the app/website/platform, code gets built on top of code, and the base is shaky, which makes the smallest changes time-consuming. Another one is measurement. It ends up a big mess of old and new tracking with everything patched together so it 'kind of' works.

Now, these are the reasons it's slow, and the risks of this are apparent. How the hell are you going to deliver all those results if it takes so long? How do you hit the gas or at least cut through the jelly?

32.2 Time to start moving forward, fast

As a good growth hacker, you know that it's essential to understand a problem properly before jumping to solutions. You now understand why it can be slow and based on the above; you realise that it is rarely intentional. Your client may not even realise how slow they are, as we said, the jelly thickened slowly over time. That is why awareness is critical.

Start with showing them the implications of the slowness. We always measure our wins, but how about calculating the opportunity cost of not implementing these wins? If the slowness is causing you to have to wait with experiments, show your client the impact. You can do this by calculating the average win per week multiplied by the number of weeks delay.

If slowness means you can only run half the experiments, what would the growth potential be if you could run twice the amount of experiments? For these calculations, your documentation comes in handy. If you've been noting the results of all experiments this should be easy enough to calculate.

Now you can open up the conversation further; this is a crucial aspect of changing things if perfection is the cause. Indicate that you have noticed experiments are taking longer because it has to be just right. However, this is impacting speed now. Is there a way to find a balance between the two? Ask your clients if they have ideas on how to balance it out.

We are not pretending that this is an easy conversation. It's possible for a client to feel attacked or offended by the suggestion that they are slow. You also don't want your client to feel like you want to rush or deliver imperfect work either, that you're skipping the dotting of the i's and the crossing of the t's. It's about finding the balance by keeping the discussion focused on your common ground, e.g. more results, reduced costs, organisational change.

Now let's start implementing techniques to get the speed up from Jell-oh to Jell-Go!. You've shown them the costs, you've opened the conversation, now to find a solution. You don't want to be all talk and no game, so rev your engines with the following:

1. Get your contact person's input

Your contact person will want results too. They also know their organisation best and will know the ideal ways to deal with the slowness. We recommend having a brainstorm with them regarding what you can change. Ask again "What can I do to speed things up?". That will help them see that you are willing to actively work to increase the speed and take ownership of it.

2. Approval Matrix

We talked about this in Chapter 30: Too Many Stakeholders, Too Many Opinions. Feel free to go back and remind yourself of the Approval Matrix again. The primary goal is to reduce the number of approval rounds when slowness is caused by too many checks.

3. Agree clearly on standards

High standards usually come down to a few crucial factors that should be accounted for. Once you know and understand those factors, you can look for a way to balance high quality and speed. You also gain more trust to just get on with it.

Is it that they find it crucial for the copy to be entirely on-brand? Then don't write the copy yourself, find the individual in the organisation that they would trust with the copy. Is it that they are worried about making a legal mistake? Then get a Legal team member at the growth meeting. It all comes back to Be Them through understanding what drives them: what do they see as a risk?

4. Break significant changes down into smaller steps

There is a wise saying that goes "How do you eat an elephant? One bite at a time". Too often as growth hackers, we see and want the whole elephant but are your clients ready for the entire elephant? Sometimes slowness and a focus on perfection is the result of fear, the fear of a change that is too big for what they are comfortable with. By breaking the change down into smaller experiments or steps, you can make eating the elephant far easier to digest.

5. Challenge legacy

Legacy is an easy excuse to accept as the truth. Yes, specific changes to the website might be challenging, but are they impossible? Is there no solution or workaround? Experiments held back through legacy are potential goldmines that everyone decided not to do because, well, it is legacy. If you are the one to Be Bold and make it happen, then you also get the credit for the results. When legacy truly makes change a no go, then it still doesn't mean there aren't workarounds. Can you use a tool to make the change? Can you use another platform to build a landing page? Remember the ideas we talked about in the development chapter, and apply them to this situation, time to get creative.

We are not saying that speed is everything. There is a lot to be said for taking your time and ensuring quality is high too. However, most organisations don't struggle with that; they struggle with speed. A great example of this is how well businesses dealt with the Coronavirus pandemic. Corona turned the world upside down in ways that few companies could have predicted or had even prepared for. So which companies survived and thrived? Those that reacted and acted. Those that changed for the new world and kept the end customer in mind. The companies that rewrote their whole website overnight to match what people were looking for, not the ones that released one article about it on their blog a month later. It is almost always time to speed up because if you don't; your competitors will.

Key Takeaway

There is no one cause for slowness, but that doesn't mean you have to accept it as the way it is. Always ask yourself how you can increase the speed to drive more impact - whilst maintaining the quality, of course.

CHAPTER 33

The Needle Isn't Moving

33.1 Is it a blip?

Imagine this; you've been working on a project for a few months; at first, it was terrific. You were in the honeymoon period, and there was so much love (aka growth). During this time, flaws (losing experiments) were easy to ignore; life was bliss. In your happiness high, you set more stringent targets to hit, you feel on top of the world, invincible.

But then, as the months go by and the shine wears off, you realise you've missed your target for a week. This dip in results has to be a blip… you prefer to be optimistically daydreaming of those sweet honeymoon memories.

One week becomes two weeks, and two becomes three weeks. Okay, that is too long, you try to bring the love back with an extra ad, a new campaign, you adjust the landing page. You and your client need to talk and figure out together what's going on. You procrastinate planning this in, don't you? What if bringing it up makes it worse?

Suddenly, three weeks becomes four weeks; four quickly becomes five, six and then seven. You are freaking out and then the phone rings. Spoiler: it's your client with "We need to talk about the results."

It happens, growth stalls at times. It could be because of internal factors: a channel is milked to its max, you don't have enough products or variation, etc. Or an external factor: you have a new competitor, market desires are changing, advertising platforms are getting more expensive, etc. It doesn't matter what the cause is; you're smart enough to look into that and figure it out. What matters is that you stop. Yes, stop. But, what usually happens when results start to lag is the situation we described above. We become an optimist hoping it's just a blip. The alternative is that we race around like a headless chicken… Neither reaction works.

33.2 What should you do when growth slows down?

Scrambling to improve the situation and trying to get more done, won't solve the situation. When you get stuck, the worst thing to do is more of the same again. Doing more of the same will not solve the situation, it will only get you more stuck.

Don't worry, there is an alternative, but it is the opposite of what feels natural to most. Take a deep breath and take a quiet step back. We would suggest notifying your client as soon as possible; nothing kills trust more than a client having to come to you with the dreaded phrase "We have a problem". By that point, yes, you do.

Rebuilding trust from that situation would be painful and slow, so let's not take that risk. Instead indicate it to your client (calmly and relaxed) and tell them what you've found so far, focusing on:

- Potential causes
- Potential tests to improve

Ask for their opinion, what do they think is happening? And then work together to create an action plan. Suddenly this bad, shitty news you were dreading to share becomes a way to work together.

Not only does it soften the blow, but it can also even strengthen your collaboration. The two of you will face a hurdle together and overcome it, building more trust than if everything had gone perfectly in the first place.

If you have an account manager for your client, inform them as well. Account managers hate getting a call out of the blue that the client isn't happy. The bad news is always better received from the consultant themselves.

33.3 Turning it around

As we mentioned, turning things around is all about figuring out what happened in the first place. Maybe, you have already analysed internal and external factors but can't find anything crazy. Often this is a case of hitting a growth ceiling, as hinted at earlier in the examples of internal factors. It might just be that you've gotten everything you can out of the current setup, we've seen this happen on several occasions.

You get comfortable with a channel mix, say Facebook Advertising, Google Ads and email, a pretty standard combination. At first, it was setting everything up for your clients and making significant improvements, nailing it. Now you've gotten into a comfortable pattern: optimising each week with a few tweaks here and there. You've hit a point of diminishing returns, the same amount of time and effort brings back fewer results. No wonder growth has stalled, time to mix things up.

Go back to your North Star Metric. From there do a full-funnel analysis again, look at the whole setup. Look not just at the funnel but other elements that may be holding you back. Could it be due to the branding or the product/service itself? Take it back to the basics; the significant impact also comes from simple improvements. Act as if you're a new agency hired by your client to beat the current agency and that you need to show how it's supposed to be done. Now double-check:

- Do you have all the essentials in place that we listed in Chapter 8: Getting the Crucial Basics in Place?
- Have you checked all your messaging and websites against psychological principles such as Cialdini, LIFT model and 5-second tests?
- Are you sure that they *still* have Product-Market Fit? Remember that this can change over time.

We have seen growth stalls for a client who had a killer channel mix, but they still had no form of social proof on their website - just a smattering of reviews for a high-end product. Improving the social proof drove results for all products. So what is holding us back now? Perhaps:

- You need a whole different approach to retention.
- The website needs significant improvements to hit the next level.
- You need a new channel to bring in the volume required to keep acquisition up.
- You have hit the limits with the current market and need to consider looking into alternative markets.

Dare to think big, but test small. Don't forget to adjust your OMTM according to the new focus area.

If possible, get someone else in to take a look with you, it's easy to be blinded by working on a project for too long - you suddenly can't see the wood for the trees. The best ideas come from such discussions, looking together at new approaches and perspectives. Even if you work as a freelancer take the time to find a fellow growth hacker to discuss it with. Maybe there are senior growth hackers in your area or search online to see if you can find a growth hacking mentor who can challenge and inspire you.

Key Takeaway

The worst thing you can do is just carry on when results are slow. Take a step back and talk to your client as soon as possible to start solving it.

By taking a step back, communicating with your client and testing out new focus areas, you can get through a rough patch. There is always a way to grow further; it is about figuring out *how*. Stay calm and take the time to do precisely that.

SECTION 5

What Comes Next?

CHAPTER 34

Should You Continue?

No project runs forever. Yes, there are retainer-based projects which technically run until stopped. Even then you should be asking yourself regularly, do you even want to continue? Or do you just blindly continue until your client decides to stop the collaboration?

Of course, looking at the finances on a short-term basis, it almost always makes sense to continue. However, we feel that financial motivation is not good enough as the ONLY reason. Yes, on the short-term you or your agency will make some extra bucks, but that will happen at the cost of the relationship. In the long-term, it means you ended on a low when your client decided it wasn't worth it and stopped the collaboration. They may remember how it ended (recency bias) far more than all the growth that happened along the way.

We feel that the consultant easily gets caught up in the day to day of the project meaning the question of "Should we continue?" is not asked often enough. We are not saying that it isn't possible to drive long-term value and have a long collaboration, rather that you should always stay sharp and critical as to whether you are still adding value. Like a civilised break up, you should not let the issues exacerbate, but instead, conclude to end things amicably.

Doing this, in turn, increases the chance of future collaboration, referrals or at least a positive testimonial. Whilst there may not be an ROI now, this could change in the future with a new growth challenge or product. Even if there is no future project from them, it is still a positive word of mouth, they may refer other potential clients to you in the future. You can also ask them for a testimonial and/or if you can write a case study about them. Now let's start with situations where you should continue. From there, we will move on to reasons where it makes sense not to continue.

34.1 Let's keep working together

The most obvious reason: is there a positive ROI? Is your client getting a high enough ROI to justify the continuous investment in your collaboration?

Working with a consultant results in a higher cost than working on a project inhouse, which means that you need to make it worth their time. Not only in terms of ROI but also what you are working on. You may manage a channel for them as a growth hacker and generate a high ROI via that channel, but much of your work is maintaining ongoing elements with maybe a few tests here and there. At a certain point, your client will think "Maybe it is cheaper to hire someone for that or have someone internally take that over". You're then just costing them money.

Therefore, it will make more sense for your client to continue if you not only offer ROI but remain innovative and add value. Often, you do this on a strategic level, by continuously identifying and solving bottlenecks. Maybe you are implementing personalisation or improving the marketing tech stack so that they can finally measure end to end. You are building the organisation to keep it ahead of the curve. When you have this type of collaboration, there are far fewer questions about continuing.

It could be that you have brought that part of the organisation to high performance but that your client has other products, services, different markets or even separate brands to consider. By highlighting the opportunities there, you may take on a more guiding role in the original project and switch your focus to a new one. You may not even need to find these opportunities yourself, we've often had clients be the one to present them, "We've had such good results for the Dutch market, perhaps we can spend some time looking at the Belgium market".

34.2 Time to say goodbye

Even if there is still some ROI, there may be reasons to say goodbye. We talked about this briefly in Chapter 4: Watching out for Risks and Pitfalls. There we also mentioned that you should not be afraid to end a collaboration. Whilst we can't comment on any personal financial impact this may have, you still shouldn't treat this as a failure. Like relationships and friendships, some were just not meant to be or were right for a certain period of your life but not for now.

There are a few situations where you should choose to stop the collaboration:

1. Your client treats you badly

Remember what we said about the client being King or Queen and that you should treat your client well? Let us reiterate that it is in fact, a two-way street; you also should expect the same thing in return. A client who mistreats you is not worth the risk. Whether you're a freelancer or an agency, you should not accept that type of behaviour. You are only enabling it by doing so and as Craig said, let them drive your competition crazy instead.

2. A red traffic light you can't solve

Sometimes a client is blocking their growth, e.g. a fixed mindset, measurement setup, a lack of Product-Market Fit. There is something in the foundations that is not correct. You've tried to fix it, but no matter what you do, it remains a giant bottleneck for growth. There is a simple question to ask yourself honestly in such a situation: have I done everything in my power to change this? If you can say yes to that then maybe it is time to say goodbye.

An example is a client without Product-Market Fit (PMF). You've shown them they don't have PMF through the traditional PMF survey. Yet, they refuse to change the product. The product is perfect as it is, they argue. You look at the results, only 5% said they would be very disappointed if they could no longer use the product, the conversion and retention rates are screaming out the same issue.

You've tried to find a market where they do have good rates but still no luck. So you show them the impact of the lack of PMF through other ways:
- You walk them through the retention curves.
- You show them how the Cost of Acquisition would drop if you had PMF.
- You compare the Lifetime Value of clients with PMF vs those without PMF.
- You've tried talking to different stakeholders within the organisation about it.

At a certain point, you've exhausted your options. Either you keep taking their money and know you can't bring a reasonable ROI in that setup, or you say goodbye.

3. Your style isn't a match for the company

Consulting is a very personal relationship. You work closely together and need to be a match on an individual level. At an agency, you can switch your contact person if it is not a match on a personal level. Yet, for both agencies and freelancers, there remain scenarios where for whatever reason, it's simply not a match.

For example, say you like a very informal relationship with high trust, but you work for a very hierarchical client that it is all about proving yourself first. Definitely still give it a go and work together, as you'll learn a lot from it. You'll learn how to adjust your approach according to their style and from dealing with the differences.

But also don't be afraid to say goodbye if it feels like endless friction, that's no fun for you or the client. If you have to become someone you are not, ultimately, you are straying further and further from the principles Be Real and Be Open.

Next to that, working with a client that isn't a match will cost you energy that you could spend growing other clients and actually enjoying it. Use that energy to bring success to others or grow your freelancer/personal brand. Don't waste this energy where it isn't appreciated.

We honestly believe that by taking this approach and remaining critical on if you should continue is the best way forward for the long-term. In the short-term, you may lose a few clients, and that's okay, they've come to the end of their project cycle. Whether that was naturally (there is no ROI) or unnaturally (you've chosen to say goodbye), in the long-term, using that energy for other existing clients or new clients will bring more revenue.

Now let's move on to a more favourable situation. You've been working with a client for six months, and it is going great, the only thing decreasing the ROI is that you don't have time to do more. How do you convince a client of an upsell? Follow us to the next page to find out.

Key Takeaway

Stay critical of whether you should continue forces you to focus on driving value and to have a positive relationship continually. Never hang on to a client for short-term gains.

CHAPTER 35

How to Upsell and Cross-sell

So you're cruising along just fine. You can't help but share the results with your friends; you are just so proud. It's going so well that you can't help but wish for more hours. Your hands are itching to grasp the opportunities you see before you. Maybe, it isn't even more hours for you specifically, but you know you'd go so much faster if you got a designer or copywriter on the team. How do you go about this? How do you upsell or cross-sell?

35.1 Don't worry about it

The first step is not worrying about the selling aspect. If you are super comfortable selling to your clients, feel free to skip this chapter and move on to the next. Don't overthink this if you don't have to.

But if you aren't comfortable yet, no worries - read on. Being uncomfortable handling, a new "thing" is natural - we were nervous in the beginning too. We worried that it wasn't our role or place to sell to our clients. How can we be their trusted advisor yet be like a McDonald's drive-through "Do you want fries with that? How about something to drink?". They'll end up just like you are at the drive-through, doubting yourself, "Well I didn't, but the way you say it, maybe I should get fries with that…" What if that puts pressure on them and breaks the trust? There is also the fear of coming across as a sleazy salesman or pushy McDonald's employee. Daphne even chose not to freelance after RockBoost because she didn't like the sales part of it, that just wasn't for her. We may love to sell our client's product or service to their end customer, but that doesn't mean we feel comfortable selling ourselves to them. It doesn't have to become your primary skill, but it is valuable to be able to:

1. Spot opportunities.
2. Help your client to go for opportunities if they make sense.

If you are selling to your client, it can help to look at it from a different perspective. To remind yourself that you are not selling to earn more money for your company or yourself, but because you see the potential value and you want to help your client to grab that opportunity. You are not a door-to-door salesperson trying to sell them something they don't want or need. You know a way for them to grow faster and you're sharing the knowledge that you were hired for.

Now imagine not mentioning that opportunity? Wouldn't that be a greater disservice? Their bottleneck is now the lack of extra time rather than something out of your control. There is value to be added and potential ROI, so how could you not offer them that growth opportunity? Not mentioning it takes away potential growth opportunities from them, and that is the last thing you should be doing as a growth consultant. We believe that you should only upsell or cross-sell based on added value.

It works better when you sell something than when your sales agent has to (assuming you are in an agency) because you are the one who's built that trust and relationship with the client. You can spot value-adding opportunities, while sales agents are only stepping in when more cash is needed. Let's get into what the usual opportunities look like and from there some tips on how to upsell.

35.2 Value adding opportunities

The first step is understanding what potential opportunities look like. Where do you see the chance for you or someone else to add value? We will walk through a few typical cases to help increase your awareness of potential opportunities.

1. Additional or new channels

Sometimes you spot a new channel that has potential, and you want to test out. It can be tempting to squeeze this into the same hours when it is just a small test. However, the minute it starts growing as a channel, it's a struggle to do the same work in less time. You either need to be very clear that you'll only do this test within the budget or you'll need to ask for more budget to experiment with a channel. The only exception, when it does work in the current setup, is when other channels have been taken over or are more automated. In that case, hours often free up, and you can use them to provide additional value.

What if it doesn't work? What if you sell them this new channel and it flops terribly? That is where the calculation comes in that we talked about in Chapter 10: How to set the Right Expectations and Priorities. Your analyses should have shown what you can expect if it all goes to plan. Explain that to them and that if you see it isn't working earlier than that, you will indicate this too, as we never know for sure whether experiments will win. By starting a healthy dialogue about it, you can Be Open with your client and help them to realise that too.

2. Potential to increase velocity

Let's say you have an experiment program running, and all is going well. The wins pour in; the results are fantastic. Everyone wants to do more; they want to run more experiments and test new areas. However, all you can think about is the lack of time. That is when it is worthwhile to sit down and discuss the potential to increase growth and speed to explain that time is the current bottleneck. Would they be open to extra hours? You could always test the increased velocity for two months, and from there, depending on the results, you can see if they want to continue at that pace.

Remember, it's critical when increasing velocity to be extremely specific on what exactly you'd like to do extra. With a new channel, it is obvious what the extra work is. With velocity, it can be vague, and that causes the client to say no even though they want to increase speed. Define what exactly they'll get extra, e.g. one additional experiment per sprint, or even better the outcome you hope to achieve. How will the growth goal adjust according to the increased resources? Can you set a higher OMTM or solve an extra bottleneck that will result in a lift?

3. Specific skills are missing in-house

Maybe, you spot another area that they do not pick up at all or at least not very well. You see that this is because the client doesn't have the knowledge or skills in-house. You want to pick this up because you see that if this improves it will hugely drive results, e.g. CRO on the website. When they don't have the resources in-house, it is worth seeing how you can help in solving that.

For example, they are missing design resources, and that is impacting the social campaigns you are running. The CTR is very low, and you've already tested different audiences and copy. Yes, as a freelance growth hacker, it won't benefit you directly to get them to hire a designer. However, indirectly it will. Your ads will do better, the results improve, and your client attributes part of that success to you.

4. Teaching the client how to take something over

Let's say you currently handle a particular area, e.g. SEO. SEO is very time-consuming, and you want your client to take it over. However, there is no time to teach them how to take it over. You could suggest increasing the hours for a short period so that you can hand over that area. Show your client that this would cost more hours in the short-term, but in the long-term, they can then handle a whole area. It also means the skills on their team are growing, which is very valuable. Additionally, it renders you free to find new opportunities and new wins.

35.3 How to upsell and cross-sell

We have four main points of advice for upselling and cross-selling. These techniques will hopefully make you more comfortable with selling. It isn't about bringing out your inner salesperson, but instead using the growth hacker you already recognise within.

1. Build a business case

Once more, we find ourselves back to the managing expectations part. Let the data talk and convince your client to upsell by creating a business case of what it could bring and why it would be worth investing. They, in turn, will need this case to convince their boss. The ideal way to set this up is through a few slides that talk through the story. You should cover the following:

- What is the issue right now?
- What are we missing out on if we don't do this?
- What are the potential results?
- How do we plan to test it?

2. Run a small test first within the hours (if possible)

Sometimes running a small test is what you need to build excitement; it could be a single A/B test or a few ads. This strategy is a risky one; we admit that. Firstly, be careful with what tests you choose as whilst your client may understand that losing tests is a part of the process, this is their first experience of that area (another bias, this time anchoring). The result is that if it doesn't work, then they may no longer believe in that area. So you want to opt for high certainty tests and be ready to run a few extra if the first results are not favourable. Again, be careful to manage expectations beforehand. Indicate that you are not able to pick up the whole area within the hours available but that this is just a small test to get a feel for it.

3. Give your client options

Too often we come to a client with one proposal in hand, like in a casino, either you are all in, or you fold. Try to give your clients three options and indicate which you would recommend. This way, you provide them with the power of choice and to see how much they want to do.

Let's shuffle back to our SEO example. For large clients, you could easily spend your whole week improving their SEO. If you suggest that, even if you know you can bring value, it's a considerable investment. If you start a bit smaller and show them the initial results, you can then build it up from there. Providing them with options opens their eyes to different possibilities. This allows them to choose what they are comfortable with and remain in control whilst you still get additional hours to start exploring that area.

4. What is in it for your client?

This point keeps coming back throughout the book, primarily because it is so commonly forgotten. Let's continue with our SEO example: when consultants sell SEO, they talk about doing keyword research, building backlinks, etc. They provide a whole list of tasks of what they want to do. The focus is on the task rather than the outcome. What do you hope to achieve by doing this? By focusing more on the outcome, you can get them excited and only show them the tasks if they want concrete action points.

Upselling is a bit like jumping into cold water; it will be scary up until the jump. The first plunge will feel freezing and a bit nerve-racking, but almost always it turns out not to be too bad. You imagined it to be far worse in your head. Don't be afraid to suggest an upsell; your role is to grow them. Having the time and resources to do that is part of it.

So you now know how to look critically at whether you should continue with a client. You've learnt about convincing them of upselling and typical opportunities to upsell for. How do you handle a downscale? What do you need to change when a client chooses to decrease their number of hours?

> **Key Takeaway**
>
> For most growth hackers, the biggest challenge is daring to sell, to push for an upsell or cross-sell. Remember you are only doing this when it delivers value so you would be doing your client a disservice not to encourage the upsell if it will help them grow faster.

CHAPTER 36

Dealing With a Downscale

36.1 Downscales happen

Sometimes a client will want to continue working together but with fewer hours because the project has shrunk in size. Now, this can happen for a multitude of reasons, some are within you and your client's control, others are not. Common causes are:

1. **Less budget is available.** This could be due to bad results or other projects needing an additional budget. It could even be external factors such as a financial crisis. Sadly Coronavirus is the perfect example of this happening; as we saw freelance and agency budgets reduced on all sides.
2. **Reduced focus.** They want to reduce the focus to just a few areas. It could be that the other areas are already set up correctly or that they no longer see the return on investment there.
3. **Pick up more themselves.** It is not unusual for a client to want to pick up areas themselves, especially if you are doing a lot of hands-on work. It could be that they've hired or are training someone to take it over.
4. **Not enough ROI.** Though clients will not always say this directly, they may not see a worthwhile ROI for the hours/budget of the project. They'll give a reason such as

wanting to pick the project up themselves or no longer seeing the need for the project.

There is another reason for a downscale; which is that you suggested it. As we've mentioned before, this does not happen often enough, you should recommend a downscale when you see there is not enough ROI or that it would benefit the client to pick up tasks themselves.

Usually, you start a project with a lot of hours/tasks because there is a lot to setup. Are the same amount of hours necessary one year down the road? Can you still drive a similar ROI for those hours? Of course, there are always new possibilities or areas you could explore or expand on. The question is, are they within your field of control? Sometimes you have pushed everything to the limits, but the next step is a major one, for example, when they need to release a new product or website change.

Either way, we see it as our obligation as a consultant to honestly discuss the option with the client. To indicate whether, in the current setup, it makes sense to continue with the current amount of hours.

Now that you know more about why downscales occur, how do you deal with it? The funny thing about downscales is that it is easy to continue with business as usual. The client is still there; there are just fewer hours for the project. You may feel like exclaiming "It's fine! Really, fine!" and trying to pick up the project the same way as before the downscale. Understand now that your previous way of working just isn't possible, downscales change the scope and dynamics. We will walk through what to watch out for so that the downscale does not cause the project to fall apart.

36.2 Dealing with a downscale

Coping with a downscale comes down to three simple steps:

Step 1: Figure out what needs to change

We've had clients who halved the number of hours but still wanted all the same tasks and attention as before. It's a bit like always flying business class and being surprised that you don't get the same comfort, attention, food and legroom in economy class. This is the most significant risk, that your client thinks the same is possible as before in fewer hours. Spoiler alert: No one gets to have their cake AND eat it. Your project scope has changed, and in turn, expectations need to change too:

- What will the focus be now?
- What will the new OMTM be?
- What is and isn't possible within the hours?
- How will the meeting structure change?

That last one often gets forgotten, it doesn't make sense to have the same meeting structure as before. Just imagine that you scaled down from 20 hours per week to 10 hours per week. With 20 hours per week, you had 16 hours focused on growth (actual work) and 4 hours of meetings and organisation (overhead work). If you keep 4 hours of meeting, you have only 6 hours focused on hands-on growth. The hours have decreased by 50% but your impact time by 62.5! You have even less time to drive impact than if you had reduced the number of meetings.

Step 2: Make a new action plan together

Clients don't realise that how you handle a project of 4 hours vs 16 hours per week is not the same. It changes in terms of how many different things you can pick up but also other ways of working, such as frequency of contact. Once you have figured out how you would like to change the setup, it is time to walk them through it all and to make new agreements for the project.

Also, communicate clearly to them how many of the weekly hours are to be filled with actual work and how many hours will need to be reserved for overhead work. Think back to the calculation we did in Step 1. It's not fun to say that some hours are 'wasted' (in the eyes of the client) on overhead, but you need to re-set the expectations to show them how much you can do in the newly adjusted budget.

Step 3: Stand your ground on what is and isn't possible

Even if you do the above your client is going to push the limits at times. It's going to take time for them to get used to the fact that you can't do the same amount as before. Remind your client in a firm but a friendly manner that the same isn't possible. Have an exact list of priorities and of what is and is not possible. When they want other priorities go back to your OMTM and your list to see what makes the most sense. You can also offer to spend some time delegating tasks to their team members so that you can pick up more in the same amount of hours. That way they feel like you are not just giving pushback but proactively trying to solve it.

Once your client starts to see that results are still driven but less in the same hours, you can begin to help show them the correlation between the budget and results. Of course, you still want to do everything possible within those hours (and within reason), but if you only start getting strict on what is possible after a few weeks, it can damage the relationship. It can then come across as sour feelings regarding the downscale or slacking off rather than recognising the new limits. That's why the new boundaries need to be clarified and noted to avoid such miscommunication.

By handling it the minute the downscale occurs, you can maintain the relationship and increase the chance of an upscale later on.

> **Key Takeaway**
>
> Never continue as prior after a downscale. The dynamic has changed, so see how you need to adjust your approach accordingly. Imagine how you would structure this project if it would be a new project with the new circumstances.

CHAPTER 37

Project Reflection

We're here, we're finally here, the end of a project! Rather than going full steam ahead to the next project, take a moment to reflect. Let's look at what project reflection entails and some ideas on how to approach it.

37.1 What is project reflection?

A project reflection is taking the time to zoom out on the whole process and assess how it went as well as identify process improvements for your business. It is also a chance to look at what to improve in terms of your skills. As we like to say, Captain Hindsight is a genius. Captain Hindsight always knows what could have gone differently, now use Captain Hindsight's smartarse insights for good. Never make this a blame game of who did what wrong, instead it is more productive to focus on learning and understanding.

To start the process of reflection, analyse with the team that worked on the client. Do this without the client though, because there are some things you just can't say in front of them - there need to be no filters applied in this meeting with the team. So how do you do this as a freelancer without a team? If you are a freelancer, we would suggest the opposite, have the meeting with your client (and some filters applied perhaps), so you have someone to discuss it with. Take some time besides that meeting to also do it alone, writing down your answers to each question we suggest covering. It's ideal for most solo entrepreneurs or freelancers to get out of your regular working environment to give yourself the time and space to reflect, and set new goals.

37.2 What to cover

It's useful to cover the following four areas in such a session. With each area, we've added some guiding questions to get the ball rolling. First, though, consider how to approach the meeting setup. Similar to Chapter 18: ABEing - Always Be Evaluating, your team may choose first to write down the answers to the first two questions, only from there, you can discuss everyone's responses. Writing down answers first helps to avoid groupthink and encourages you to share what you think of how it went.

We like to cover the following four areas. You don't have to answer each question of every section; they aim to get you thinking.

1. **What went well**
    a. What are the things that were picked up well?
    b. What are the things that helped to grow the client?
    c. What are other factors that made this project successful?
    d. What are things to be proud of?
    e. What should be continued for future projects as well?
2. **What could have gone better**
    a. What did not go as smoothly as hoped for?
    b. What areas could have been handled differently?
    c. What slowed down the growth of the client?
    d. What did not go as planned, and why?
    e. What was underestimated?
3. **Learnings**
    a. What are the new things that were tested with this project?

    b. If I/we were to start this whole project again, what would I/we do the same and what would I/we do differently based on the above?
    c. What can ensure these are done for future projects too?
    d. What do I personally want to work on improving?
4. **Action points**
    a. Are there any concrete action points that stem from this, for example, adjusting processes, discussing specific challenges with the broader organisation (if in an agency), etc.

We would suggest documenting project reflections in one place. That way, every few projects you can walk through them again and ensure you are implementing the learnings. This overview can help you avoid making the same mistakes over and over again.

Now don't rush the first area too much, it is easy to get critical and caught up in what did not go well. Let yourself also consider what did go well. Take time for this; acknowledge how you or your team members have grown over the process. If you struggle with this, make an achievements list and add to that after every project. Whenever you doubt yourself, you can go back to that list and run through it.

> **Key Takeaway**
>
> After every project, take the time to reflect. That reflection time will teach you so much about the project and spot trends between projects you might have otherwise missed.

Where to go from here

First of all, let's just say you're incredible! It's incredible that you took the time to learn more about how to be a better growth hacking consultant and that you are so focused on driving value and action for your client. Congratulations on completing this book and becoming a better growth consultant. Thank you for allowing us to play a role in that. Now it is up to you to keep the ball rolling. Don't worry; we won't leave you hanging. We have many resources for you that we have put in the resources section that can be found at growinghappyclients.com/resources. The reason we put them there and not here is that we frequently update them.

Action drives results

Now it is *Time for Action*. Just thinking about what to do differently or better will not help you the most out of this book. Get yourself into an actionable mood. If you didn't do any of the Time for Actions throughout the book, then try to implement one every week or month for the coming period. Or refer back to the chapters when that topic comes up to see how to deal with it.

Next to the resources and action point, there is another powerful method to use: role play. Together with team members in your agency or other freelancers, do practice runs of tough conversations. Some great subjects to do this for are.

- Setting the NSM
- Trying to get the right OMTM in place
- Talking about issues with focus and trying to bring the focus back in the project
- Having a feedback session
- Leading a kickoff
- Suggesting an upsell to your client

One of you can play the client and the other the consultant. The most challenging conversations don't happen very often, so taking time to practice those will go a long way.

A final farewell to that lack of confidence

In the very beginning we talked about how it can be tough to be confident, we hope we managed to kill some of that self-doubt and build you into a confident growth hacker. It takes time; it takes (and now we are getting cheesy) self-love and kindness too. Focusing on what you did well, the results you drove, and the lessons you've learnt — concentrate on what is in your control. Don't get too caught up on what didn't go well but instead learn from that. Self-doubt reared its ugly head in writing this book. So all we could do is remind ourselves throughout the process to:

- Be Real, in how things will go in reality with your client.
- Be Open about what we struggled with and how to solve challenging situations.
- Be Bold and not just give you conventional wisdom.
- Be Focused on what will help you the most and not the rest.
- Be Them, in this case, you, and focus on the questions you asked.

Now reread those five points but this time about you and your client. Isn't that the best you can do too? Isn't that the best way you can help your client? It is time to focus on what is in your control and accept that mistakes are a part of it. You are on your way to becoming an exceptional growth hacking consultant. Aim for progress, not perfection.

All the best and always feel free to reach out with questions,

Daphne Tideman and Ward van Gasteren

Acknowledgements

Firstly, Fleurine Tideman, who edited the whole book and pushed us to improve the writing continuously. She is an extremely talented writer herself (this is not sisterly bias, we swear) and we are looking forward to seeing her books in stores having had the privilege of a peek preview of several of her novels. Not only was her editing spot on, but she provided so much encouragement and support when the deadline loomed near, and the pressure started to kick in.

The contributors of this book, whom we have quoted throughout, added an extra dimension that we feel had added character to the book. Thank you, Abi, Arnout, Chris, Craig, Els and Ethan.

Abi Hough has been a fantastic support in general to Daphne over the last year. She not only contributed funny and real quotes of how it goes but also read the book front to back to help us with editing.

Arnout Hellemans, for an entertaining and insightful interview. He is never afraid to go against the norm and develop his views.

Chris Out, who contributed to this book so much through all he has taught both of us. He is the one who introduced growth hacking to Daphne and mentored her throughout her five years at RockBoost. He also took the time to go through much of the content and give feedback.

Craig Sullivan was vital not only in getting the kickoff chapter right but also in bringing the flow into the book.

Els Aerts, for her advice and insights about working together with customer support and always focusing on the end customer.

Ethan Garr, a new connection since this book, helped with ensuring we did the use of the North Star Metric and Product-Market Fit justice in this book.

Though this book is not based on the processes or ideas of RockBoost, we do want to take the time to thank the growth team there. Working with such a talented group of individuals has taught us both so much. Nothing drives personal growth more than being surrounded by individuals who push you forward. Thank you specifically to Justyna Ciecierska-Goceryan, Natalie Jamieson and Fay Lodder for reading through several chapters and giving feedback.

It is not only time in the book that makes the difference but the support behind it all. It can be scary to admit that you dare to tackle a project as big as writing a book and costs many extra hours of work on top of your day job. Both Jill Schok (Ward's girlfriend) and Martijn Hoogerland (Daphne's boyfriend) have been unbelievably supportive throughout the process.

Daphne's dad was a tremendous support and driver for her. Writing her other book (not yet published) two years ago helped her process some of her grief after his passing. He always supported her dreams and writing. He even made printed copies of her first book when she was twelve (Double Trouble and the Hidden Room). Not her best piece of writing.

There are countless individuals who showed their support throughout the process. Thank you, those words of encouragement mean more than you can imagine when you are wrestling a book to shape into what you've envisioned it to be.

Now in fear of being cheesy, okay, we will just go for it. Thank you, the reader, for choosing to spend your time reading our book. We really appreciate it. We hope you enjoy reading it and learn from it. Feel free to reach out to either of us via Linkedin or email: questions@growinghappyclients.com. All feedback and questions are welcome.

Happy growing clients,
Daphne and Ward

About the Authors

Daphne Tideman was the former Head of Growth Consultancy at RockBoost. Daphne joined RockBoost as their very first employee. From there, she grew RockBoost to an organisation of twenty-five individuals and worked for large clients such as Cisco, Fox Network Group, ING and Parkmobile along the way. She ran the three consultancy teams at RockBoost as well as the operations. After RockBoost she joined Heights as their Head of Growth, an innovative venture-backed startup focused on brain care.

Ward van Gasteren has been active as a freelance growth hacking consultant for fast-growing startups (e.g. Catawiki, TikTok, Planto), Fortune 500 corporates (e.g. KPMG, Rabobank, NN), and innovation & growth agencies (e.g. StartupBootcamp, Aimforthemoon, Spark Optimus). Ward has an entrepreneurial background and was one of the first twenty certified growth hackers in Europe through Growth Tribe's first class. Next to that, he has a blog on growth hacking and gives talks about growth hacking to share the knowledge.

In 2019, RockBoost brought in Ward to strengthen their consultancy team. He and Daphne collaborated for over a year while he worked with multiple growth agencies in that time. Out of a shared enthusiasm and one too many debates fuelled by beers, this book was born.

Printed in Great Britain
by Amazon